PRAISE FOR *FOR BETTER OR FOR WORK*

"In *For Better or For Work*, Meg Cadoux Hirshberg has given us one of the best descriptions of the entrepreneurial experience that I have ever read. It is quite simply a marvelous book—beautifully written, unflinchingly honest, profoundly true."

—Bo Burlingham, author, *Small Giants: Companies That Choose to Be Great Instead of Big*

"I loved this book! I wish I'd had it when I was trying to start a business and raise my kids. It's a must-read for anyone trying to build a balanced, passionate life."

—Eileen Fisher, Founder and Chief Creative Officer, Eileen Fisher

"Meg Cadoux Hirshberg knows from whence she speaks. Using her own experiences and those of other real families, she brings to life those crazy start-up years, those crazy entrepreneurial personalities, and the crazy effects of both on families trying to live with it all. Meg offers excellent advice for surviving the madness."

—Ben Cohen, Cofounder, Ben & Jerry's Ice Cream

"Meg Cadoux Hirshberg hits the sweet spot where remorse and laughter meet. I grew up around the kind of entrepreneurial energy she describes, and now I'm living it, so I know how exhilarating and frustrating the experience can be. While it is important to celebrate the accomplishments of those who turn dreams into brands, we must also recognize the hidden costs to their families and relationships. This book is a therapy session for founders' families and for entrepreneurs themselves (assuming they can make time in their superhuman schedules to read it). As for me, I absolutely loved it!"

—Nell Newman, President, Newman's Own Organics

"As a third-generation entrepreneur, I had a deep, emotional response to Meg Cadoux Hirshberg's *For Better or For Work*. Meg has been first mate on an entrepreneurial voyage for most of her adult life. Having lived the adventure, body and soul, she distills her experiences and the gentle wisdom gained from them to readers on their own entrepreneurial journeys, which are the hope of America's economic and social future."

—Jeff Swartz, former President and CEO, Timberland

"Meg Cadoux Hirshberg presents an eminently practical guide to living with an entrepreneur without going insane. Written with authority and uncommon good sense, *For Better or For Work* champions entrepreneurial drive while helping protect the families who are the beneficiaries of that drive and—at times—its victims."

—Danny Meyer, CEO, Union Square Hospitality Group, and author,
Setting the Table: The Transforming Power of Hospitality in Business

"I found Meg Cadoux Hirshberg's story deeply moving. Her willingness to share the unvarnished, intimate details of living with a driven entrepreneur and his ever-struggling start-up is generous and heroic. Through her own story and others, she provides much-needed transparency into the complicated experience of company building and advice for achieving love and satisfaction in both the business and personal realms. *For Better or For Work* is a gift and an inspiration."

—Paulette Cole, Cofounder, CEO, and Creative Director, ABC Home

"Meg Hirshberg's book will become the *What to Expect When You're Expecting* for entrepreneurs and their life partners. If my wife and I had had a copy before we launched Honest Tea, we would have been better prepared to cope with the trials and occasional absurdities of developing a struggling beverage enterprise, a family, and a marriage all at the same time."

—Seth Goldman, President, TeaEO, and Cofounder, Honest Tea

"*For Better or For Work* is a must-read for anyone engaged in or thinking about beginning the entrepreneurial journey. Funny and accessible, Meg Cadoux Hirshberg chronicles the trials, tribulations, and triumphs of building a business while building a family. The stories of her own experience in the entrepreneurial trenches and of other families chasing their dreams are unforgettable, and the lessons she draws are powerful. Bravo to Hirshberg for her candor and courage in mapping such vital, treacherous territory!"

—Nancy F. Koehn, James E. Robison Professor of Business Administration,
Harvard Business School

"The business is as much a part of an entrepreneur's family as any human member. That is a fact my own family has come to understand and accept in the course of my career. My wife, Nancy, and I highly recommend that all entrepreneurial families read *For Better or For Work*. Knowing the reality upfront, you can prepare for it with eyes wide open."

—**Ron Shaich, Founder and Executive Chairman, Panera Bread**

"Starting Nantucket Nectars was among the most intoxicating, fulfilling experiences of my life. For my wife, it was a long, isolating period in which she didn't see enough of me. *For Better or For Work* brilliantly captured so many truths— when I read quotes aloud to my wife, she shook her head in recognition. All entrepreneurs can recall times when we've stared at our spouses without seeing them, absorbed, as we are, in the latest problems, challenges, or ideas. When we tell our stories before crowds we thank our teams, but rarely the people who suffered with us in our personal foxholes. Without our loved ones, who bear the brunt of our dreams and passions, entrepreneurs would be the loneliest people in the world. Hirshberg's book is a powerful reminder."

—**Tom First, Cofounder and former CEO, Nantucket Nectars, and Founder, OWATER**

"*For Better or For Work* should be required reading for the spouses and families of potential entrepreneurs as well as for entrepreneurs themselves, who rarely (if ever) appreciate the toll that entrepreneurship takes on their loved ones. Meg Hirshberg not only paints a concrete road map through many of the most important, but often-neglected, twists and turns on the entrepreneurial journey (every chapter has at least one "punch in the gut" realization), but also provides concrete recommendations for how to avoid the potholes in the road. Reading this book will help entrepreneurs and their families deal with the toughest parts of the journey, rather than being blindsided by them."

—**Noam Wasserman, Professor, Harvard Business School, and author, *The Founder's Dilemmas: Anticipating and Avoiding the Pitfalls That Can Sink a Startup***

"We celebrate entrepreneurs as the life blood of our economy, but Meg Hirshberg strips away the myths and misconceptions and paints a vivid picture of entrepreneurialism as it really is—the dreams and the sacrifices, the setbacks and the triumphs. As someone who started her own business years ago, I can attest to hard truths that are deftly embedded in *For Better or For Work*. This book is a gold mine of perspective and advice. It is a terrific investment for entrepreneurs or anyone living a mission-driven life."

—Kelly Close, President, Close Concerns

"This is a *must-read* for every would-be or current entrepreneur. Meg Hirshberg has lifted the veil on a little-discussed or noticed subject—what life is like for the loved ones of the entrepreneur building a company. The wild ride of entrepreneurship often translates into stomach-churning anxiety and confusion for the spouse and children. The challenge is that building a company and caring for a family are *both* intensely emotional, time-consuming, thrilling, and exhausting. Combining them well requires the insightful compass and map that Hirshberg provides. Her courageously honest, and deeply loving, book is an essential guide for those who want their families to not only survive, but to thrive, alongside their professional dreams."

—Linda A. Mason, Chair and Cofounder, Bright Horizons Family Solutions

"As an educator of aspiring entrepreneurs, I have just discovered the missing shadow curriculum! With this book, Meg Cadoux Hirshberg describes with candor the largely undiscussed challenges of building an enterprise and a family at the same time. Business schools teach future leaders about managing risk, but not about the risk incurred by families who have embarked on exhausting, unpredictable ventures. Hirshberg warns families what to expect and offers practical advice on dealing with the inevitable strains and setbacks. All will identify with her stories and benefit from her insights."

—Len Schlesinger, President, Babson College

"A thoughtful, witty, and humane look at the complicated connection between entrepreneurs and the people who love them. There are plenty of books about how to improve your company. With its wealth of memorable stories and sage advice, *For Better or For Work* is a must-read for improving the relationships that matter to you most."

—Dorie Clark, President, Clark Strategic Communications, and author,
What's Next?: The Art of Reinventing Your Personal Brand

"In my Wharton course on leadership and in my work with organizations, I try to teach people how to create harmony among the different parts of their lives. Meg Cadoux Hirshberg's warm, witty, and insightful book provides powerful ideas with vibrant illustrations of entrepreneurs in pursuit of this goal. Her engaging stories and commentary are filled with practical wisdom that will be of great use to all budding entrepreneurs as well as those intrepid souls, and their loved ones, who are already running a business."

—Stew Friedman, Practice Professor of Management,
The Wharton School, and author, *Total Leadership*

"When people start businesses, they rarely consider how much the business will take over their lives and sap their time and energy, much less that of their families. Hirshberg shares her story and others', speaking powerfully and emotionally about the trials and tribulations of an entrepreneur marriage...Along the way, she suggests marriage-saving rules and offers cool-headed advice, making the book an indispensable tool for those living—enthusiastically or reluctantly—for a spouse's dream."

—*Publishers Weekly*

FOR
BETTER
OR FOR
WORK

A Survival Guide for
Entrepreneurs and Their Families

MEG CADOUX HIRSHBERG

COLUMNIST FOR *INC.* MAGAZINE

AN INC.
ORIGINAL

AN INC. ORIGINAL
New York, NY
www.inc.com

This book is based on columns originally published in *Inc.* magazine. *Inc.* and the *Inc.* logo are registered trademarks of Mansueto Ventures, LLC.

Distributed by Greenleaf Book Group LLC

For ordering information or special discounts for bulk purchases, please contact Greenleaf Book Group LLC at PO Box 91869, Austin, TX 78709, 512.891.6100.

Design and composition by Greenleaf Book Group LLC
Cover design by Greenleaf Book Group LLC

Publisher's Cataloging-In-Publication Data
(Prepared by The Donohue Group, Inc.)
Hirshberg, Meg Cadoux, 1956-
  For better or for work : a survival guide for entrepreneurs and their families / Meg Cadoux Hirshberg. — 1st ed.
    p. : ill. ; cm.
  "This book is based on columns originally published in Inc. magazine."—Copyright page.
  ISBN: 978-0-9839340-0-4

  1. Businesspeople—Family relationships. 2. Family-owned business enterprises—Social aspects. 3. Work and family. 4. Hirshberg, Meg Cadoux, 1956—Family. 5. Stonyfield Farm (Firm)—History. I. Title. II. Title: Inc. (Boston, Mass.)
HB615 .H57 2012
338/.04   2011938694

Part of the Tree Neutral® program, which offsets the number of trees consumed in the production and printing of this book by taking proactive steps, such as planting trees in direct proportion to the number of trees used: www.treeneutral.com

Printed in the United States of America on acid-free paper
12 13 14 15   10 9 8 7 6 5 4 3 2 1

First Edition

For my beautiful family—Gary, Alex, Ethan, and Danielle

CONTENTS

Foreword

One thing I love about *Inc.* magazine is the raw humanity that marches across our pages. We not only teach aspiring and experienced entrepreneurs how to build successful companies; we also reveal to them—and to the curious world at large—what it feels like to do so. We write frequently of joy and triumph, the exaltation of realizing a dream and disproving the naysayers in one fell swoop. But our founder-subjects also love to talk about the "blood, sweat, and tears" they pour into their businesses.

In the summer of 2008, then-Executive Editor Mike Hofman handed me a proposal from Meg Hirshberg for a story about the early days of her husband's business, Stonyfield Yogurt. Stonyfield is among the iconic companies *Inc.* started writing about more than 20 years ago, long before it became a household name. Its Cofounder, Gary Hirshberg, is one of those visionary, creative, energetic-beyond-belief entrepreneurs who charms the socks off us regular folk while leaving us vaguely regretful that we haven't done more with our lives. Meg's

story sounded dramatic, even gothic. Mike and I figured it would reso-
nate with our readers.

She delivered the first draft, and I started reading. One paragraph
in and I was hooked. The pain of uncertainty that Meg endured, the
years in which she feared for her family's survival, the almost total
sublimation of her own wishes to the company's ceaseless demands,
felt both singular to her and revelatory of an unspoken truth about
entrepreneurial marriage. This was warts-and-all storytelling.

On one level, Meg's tale of Stonyfield's start-up was a great business story about calculated risk and uncalculated consequences. On a
more profound level, it was a love story. We were proud and excited to
publish it.

"Hitched to Someone Else's Dream" appeared in the September
2008 issue of *Inc.* Then came the letters. *So* many letters. Most were
from the spouses of entrepreneurs, who as far as we knew didn't even
read the magazine. They shared their own intimate stories of suffering
and sacrifice. They suggested coping strategies or asked for guidance.
They described the corrosive friction that results when loyalty rubs up
against flagging confidence. Mostly they thanked Meg for reminding
them that they were not alone.

We also heard from entrepreneurs. Meg and Gary's story had
inspired many of our readers to reflect on their own marriages and
to consider—often for the first time—what they were putting their
families through. Some resolved to be more considerate in the future.
Others didn't promise to reform but said the article had instigated
conversations in their households about fairness and feelings. They,
too, were grateful.

Over the years, *Inc.* has written much about work-life balance. But
Meg had struck a deeper, richer vein. Our readers didn't want admoni-
tions to make time for their kids' soccer games. They wanted to know
how to pursue two of the most absorbing, draining, fulfilling activities
imaginable—building a company and building a family—at the same
time without shortchanging either or dying of exhaustion. In May

2009 we launched Meg's column, "Balancing Acts," to address that quandary in all its nuance and complexity. "Balancing Acts" has proven enormously and gratifyingly popular. It is the inspiration for this book.

Great books, business books included, introduce readers to memorable characters. The people you will encounter in these pages are a wonderfully varied lot: frazzled and frightened and funny and full of hope—all of them doing the best they can. And while Meg's strong and lovely voice is this volume's heart, I come away from it with renewed admiration and affection for Gary. Not only for his business-building skills but also for his willingness to be open and vulnerable so that his family's stories can be told. Entrepreneurs are egotists, sure. But they usually are willing to bare their souls if they believe it will help someone else.

That candor is part of what makes working with entrepreneurs so rewarding. My appreciation goes out to Meg, to Gary, and to the other brave people in these pages who have laid out their lives so you and I can learn from them.

Jane Berentson
Editor-in-Chief, *Inc.* magazine

Notes on the Text

For simplicity's sake, I've used words like "spouse," "marriage," "husband," and "wife" throughout. However, this material is relevant to anyone in a committed relationship.

Likewise, the word "spouse" refers to anyone who is not an entrepreneur and is in a committed relationship with an entrepreneur. Sometimes I refer to the entrepreneur and her spouse as "spouses."

Gender pronouns in hypothetical examples are tricky. Roughly three times as many men as women start companies, but the number of female entrepreneurs is growing, and most of their challenges are identical to those of their male counterparts. Strictly alternating male and female pronouns felt artificial, however, so I've tried to mix them up as much as possible.

Some of my sources, not surprisingly, requested anonymity. In those instances, I created fictional first names that appear in quotes.

Introduction

In the mid-1990s, my husband, Gary Hirshberg, led a business seminar at the Omega Institute in Rhinebeck, New York. Gary is the Cofounder and CEO of Stonyfield Yogurt, and he came to the session primed with dramatic war stories about what I refer to, not fondly, as "the bad old days." As he spoke about the struggle and privation of Stonyfield's early years, the entrepreneurs in the audience redirected their attention to me, sitting among them. Many had tears in their eyes. "How did you survive as a couple?" they wanted to know. Soon the tales of woe came spilling out. "My husband left me." "My wife divorced me." "My mother's not speaking to me." "My kids barely know who I am." "She's risk-averse; I'm a gambler." "He thinks I care more about the company than I do about him. Sometimes I worry that he's right."

Our stories had tapped into a gusher.

When people start companies, they research the competition, market data, SBA loans, and the cost of office space. But they generally give little thought to how a business will affect their personal lives. The entrepreneur and his spouse assume they'll muddle through for the "year or two" it takes the company to gain traction. Sure, they know a start-up requires lots of work. But they reassure themselves that at least the entrepreneur will be able to dictate his own schedule, which should make life easier. And they imagine that most of the burden will fall on the company founder—not on the family.

In short order, these early assumptions reveal themselves to be myths, particularly the idea that business ownership gives entrepreneurs more control over their lives (a rationale many cite for leaving their jobs). The reality is that businesses are like babies: they need you when they need you. And they *always* need you—your time, your attention, and your energy. Maybe that new freedom arrives at some point, when the business is financially stable and the entrepreneur has hired and trained a competent management team. But until that happens (*if* it happens, and often even *after* it happens) founders are first responders to an endless series of crises. Or they're chasing after shiny opportunities that must be seized now—this minute—or lost forever.

The catch is, entrepreneurs' families need them too. Neglect is a ubiquitous theme when the spouses and children of company founders talk about their lives. It's a pervasive problem because so many people try to build their businesses at the same time they're starting families. And because the financial survival of the latter depends on the success of the former, the entrepreneur feels justified—perhaps morally compelled—to prioritize the needs of the company.

Of course, long hours are not the exclusive bane of entrepreneurs. What makes marriage to an entrepreneur distinctively challenging is the uncertainty. Gary and I like to compare the experience to riding shotgun on a curvy stretch of road. Usually the driver—the one in control—is just fine. It's the passenger who feels sick.

I've met very few couples in which entrepreneur and spouse are equally comfortable with the high-wire financial risk that company founding requires. Both are aware that the odds are against them: most start-ups fail. But in his heart, the entrepreneur believes he will be the exception, the lucky one who thrives by dint of persistence and smarts. The spouse is not so sure. She torments herself: what if the company goes down and drags with it the money our family and friends invested because they trust us? What if we lose our home, our children's college funds, our retirement savings? We've invested years of our lives in this venture. That's time we'll never get back. What if, in the end, it was all for nothing?

Yet if the spouse hesitates to refinance the house to fund the fledgling business or asks the entrepreneur to reconsider signing a personal guarantee on a piece of equipment, then she runs a different risk: namely, the risk of seeming unsupportive and disloyal. And not just disloyal to the business but also to the business's founder—the person she loves most—whose identity is inextricably tied up with his creation.

So the reality is that entrepreneurial business sucks the entire family into its vortex. But while the challenges are often consuming, entrepreneurship can also be a boon to families, for reasons beyond the possibility of significant financial reward. A business can produce unexpected and delightful experiences for spouses, children, and even parents and siblings of entrepreneurs. For relatives who work together in a company—even just stocking shelves on the weekend—the business provides ample opportunity to bond over a common purpose. Family members form memories and learn to appreciate each other in different ways. And as the company grows, so does the sense that they are all involved in something important.

Norman Cousins could have been referring to business builders when he wrote, "We discover ourselves as human beings when we move in the direction of our dreams." That is what entrepreneurs do: they pair imagination with action and move boldly and often joyfully in the direction of a vision only they can see. In so doing, they model for their children and their communities the values of determination, individualism, and passion. And they make people like me fall in love with them.

* * *

Today, Stonyfield Yogurt is thriving. With $370 million in annual sales, it is the fourth-largest yogurt company in the United States and the largest producer of organic yogurt in the world. In 2001, when sales were $94 million, Gary arranged for the sale of 40 percent of the company to Groupe Danone, which owns Dannon yogurt. (They bought an additional 40 percent in 2003.) The unusual deal gave our 297 shareholders a highly profitable exit, while allowing Gary to retain control of Stonyfield. It also provided us with financial security. Our children, all young adults now, are proud of their father and of the business, though none has chosen to work in it. The company has remained true to its mission of environmental activism and helping family-run organic farms.

So while there was nothing romantic about the early days of Stony-field, we did manage to eke out something close to a fairy-tale ending. Still, we'd have been better off doing so with fewer headaches and heartaches. That's why I've written this book. It's the book I wish we'd had when we were starting out.

Over the last several years, I have talked to and corresponded with hundreds of entrepreneurs and their spouses. Some are old friends or people I met through Gary. But the vast majority reached out to me in response to my writing. In September 2008, I published in *Inc.* maga-zine an article about Stonyfield's prolonged, harrowing start-up and its effect on me and my still-young marriage to Gary. That story knocked loose such an avalanche of emotional—and occasionally intimate—letters that *Inc.* asked me to address the subject of entrepreneurs and family in a regular column called "Balancing Acts." Most of the men and women featured in the following pages wrote to me after reading the original article or the columns, or they introduced themselves at conferences and other events where I now speak.

I'm grateful that these people—some happy, some hopeless, all carrying scar tissue—were willing and even eager to share their experiences. Over the years, I've heard countless variations on our personal story and on the stories told at the business seminar that day in Rhinebeck. While these tales were not always easy for people to recount, or for me to hear, there was yet some comfort in the telling. We were all reminded that none of us trudges this hard trail alone.

Practically, this is a guide to navigating the emotional and logistical terrain of business building while simultaneously enjoying a fulfilling family life. I have tried to examine every major area where entrepreneurship and domestic life intersect, including the trials of cohabiting with a home-based business; the queasy necessity of borrowing money from family and friends; the power struggles of couples who run companies together; and the challenge of maintaining a cheerful front for the children during dark times.

I've also drawn examples from all stages of company development, from the wobbly start-up years to that grand and gratifying moment of intergenerational succession. Whether your business is just learning to crawl or has already hit its stride, you'll find relevant advice. For those unsure about whether or not to start a company, this is your chance to take a good hard look before leaping.

Finally, although my subject is entrepreneurs and their families, much of this material is relevant to anyone pursuing a mission-driven life. The families of political candidates and nonprofit directors, for example, will face similar concerns about financial insecurity and loneliness, and discover similar joys that come from being hitched to a dream.

This book is a collection of voices: those of entrepreneurs, their spouses, and their children. You will read the words of wise veterans sharing their hard-won wisdom and of nervous beginners expressing alarm while staring pop-eyed into oncoming headlights. Chances are you don't know any of these people personally. But unless you are sur- rounded by other entrepreneurs and their families, you may find you have more in common with these strangers than you do with many of your closest friends and relations.

Particularly in the opening chapter, I draw upon our experiences at Stonyfield. I don't expect the story of our start-up years to inspire you, exactly. But I hope that as you read it you'll take some comfort from the realization that you are (almost assuredly) not as badly off as we were back then.

Gary and I wish you the very best of luck.

Chapter 1

In or Out?

*Entrepreneurs are easy to love, but the trials of a start-up
may test a spouse's loyalty.*

'm writing this while bathed in sunshine on the dock of our beautiful vacation home by a pristine New Hampshire lake. I am still astonished that we were able to afford this place, our good fortune due to the highly unlikely ... no, that's too mild a description ... to the *wildly improbable* success of our business, Stonyfield Yogurt.

To an aspiring entrepreneur, the story of our company is an inviting fairy tale. Driven by a mission to make a difference, Gary and his business partner, Samuel Kaymen, started churning out delicious cream-topped yogurt at their New Hampshire hilltop farm in the early 1980s. Our business is now successful beyond anything we could have imagined. With $370 million in annual sales, Stonyfield is the fourth-largest yogurt company in the United States and the largest producer of organic yogurt in the world. Today, company literature romanticizes the early years as "seven cows and a dream." But Stonyfield was more a place than a brand back then, and not quite the pastoral utopia those curated photos on our website suggest.

I came into the picture when I met Gary at an organic-farming conference, about a year after he and Samuel had started their enterprise.
I was an agriculture-school graduate who'd taken a job managing an
organic vegetable operation in New Jersey. Knee-deep in milk and muck, Gary and I fell in love.

Stonyfield Farm. A Jersey cow
ambles back to the barn.

Entrepreneurs are easy to fall in love with. They are charismatic, interesting, creative, and energetic. They dream big and with resolution—not "I'd like to do this someday" but rather "I'm going to do this soon." Before meeting Gary, I had a vague desire to heal the world by organically cultivating one small piece of it. That instinct was trumped by Gary's concrete, bold, and much grander vision for achieving the same end. Seeing the future through his eyes was like watching my own aspirations unfold on an IMAX screen. So I hitched my life to his dream and allowed myself to be drawn along on a Big Adventure.

With little exposure to the trials of entrepreneurship, I had no conception of the endurance it would require. If you've never owned a company or lived with someone who owns one, you cannot imagine the emotional whiplash it can induce. Smitten and naive, I had not thought through the personal implications of living with a business: how it would affect our lives, and those of the children we planned on having. Turns out, neither had Gary.

In January 1986, we moved my things into a rambling, dilapidated 18th-century Federal-style farmhouse on 134 acres. The large building was divided into four sections: an apartment for us; another for Samuel, his wife, Louisa, and five daughters (their adult son lived elsewhere); the offices of the business; and the tiny yogurt factory. Our honeymoon was short. With no locks on any of the doors, we had zero privacy. A stream of employees, many of whom I barely knew, flowed constantly through the house. Our woodstove could not compete with the farmhouse's leaky windows; my hair would ruffle in the winter wind, *indoors*. Unidentified furry creatures skittered across my slippered feet as I loaded laundry in our dirt-floor basement.

> Smitten and naive, I had not thought through the personal implications of living with a business. Turns out, neither had Gary.

One winter when my brother Bob was visiting, the Dumpster caught fire and nearly incinerated our barn, which held all of our non-perishable inventory. After Gary dealt with the fire, Bob—on the way back up to his freezing bedroom—remarked that Stonyfield was "a hard place to crash." The moniker stuck.

Even the coming of spring heralded problems. The effluent from the yogurt plant was piped into the leach field adjacent to our bedroom. As soon as the weather warmed, the sickening odor of fermenting curds and whey wafted through our windows as we tried to sleep. I didn't want the stench to be drawn in with our newborn's first breath, so when I was nine months pregnant with our first child, Gary and I laid polyethylene tubing through an overgrown field to direct the leachate away. But the field turned out to be overrun with poison ivy. I went into labor a couple of days later, my skin itchy and red.

Our first two children were born at the farm, in 1988 and 1990. Who knows what the employees were thinking as they vicariously endured my labor pains, which were audible through the house's thin walls. I was grateful, at least, for the roaring refrigeration compressor that regularly lulled our colicky babies to sleep. We considered recording the sound and selling tapes to other desperate parents. At the time, Gary suggested it might become our only profitable product line.

In those early years at Stonyfield, our life was the business and the business was an endless parade of catastrophes: spoiled product,

broken filling machines, delivery trucks futilely spinning mud-spattered wheels as they groaned up our mile-long dirt driveway. From my first day there, it was all hands on deck. Donning a hairnet and factory whites, I went to work in the hot, noisy dairy. Although back in New Jersey I had routinely shoveled manure, being a yogurt maker remains the hardest job I've ever had. Sweating from heat and panic, I labored to keep raw milk separate from pasteurized; to avoid overcooking the yogurt in the incubator; to feed the machine cups and lids of the right flavor; and generally to not screw up the produc-

Our newborn son, Alex, speaking for us all.

tion on which we all depended. I soon traded that job for sales, which I thought would be easier. Driving around to New Hampshire supermarkets, I felt my heart sink as I repeatedly saw our yogurt cups damaged, out of stock, or past the "sell by" date.

Draining and dispiriting as the work could be, it was our precarious financial situation that tied my stomach in knots. There was no escaping scowling creditors, mountains of debt, and looming bankruptcy. At times it seemed Gary and Samuel were working as hard as they possibly could in order to lose as much money as they possibly could. The only consolation for having no real income

Gary digs out a milk delivery truck.

was that, living as we did, we had nothing to spend it on. "It was the land of the cup and the lid," as Gary put it. "We did a lot of coping."

It's hard to say which was our darkest hour. We had so many of them. One incident that still raises a shudder occurred in April 1988. At that point, Stonyfield was burning through $20,000 in cash each week. In our just-completed fiscal year, we'd lost $500,000 on sales of about $2.3 million. Then, suddenly, light broke through the clouds. A large dairy agreed to partner with us and retire our debt. Gary worked with them for months on a detailed agreement.

Gary and Samuel drove to Vermont to sign the papers. But the meeting did not go as planned. The dairy executives and their lawyers knew we were in trouble and had changed the terms of the deal. The new offer amounted to dropping a few coins in our shabby hat and running off with the business. Gary and Samuel refused. Worried and dejected, they got back in their car for the long, dreary trip home—during a freak spring blizzard, no less. But as they hashed over what seemed like a calamitous setback, my husband and his partner emerged from their funk. Gary asked Samuel what he thought the minimum cost would be to build a bona fide manufacturing facility. Samuel confessed he'd been wondering the same thing. He pulled out a scrap of paper, turned on the car's dome light, and began scribbling numbers. As they drove, the two concocted a bold plan to raise money for their latest scheme.

When they arrived back late that night, I excitedly greeted Gary at the door, eager for confirmation of the newly minted deal. "Oh, no, that didn't work out," he told me. "But for just over half a million, we can build our own plant!"

I wept that night, pressing the damp pillowcase against my nose and mouth to filter out the stench from the yogurt waste still souring in our backyard.

EVEN THOUGH YOUR HEART IS BREAKING
Keeping a brave face through the fear

It was typical of us that in such a situation I saw only disaster, while Gary saw a way forward. Only later did I discover that our interpretations weren't so far apart—just our responses to them. I recently asked my husband what he was thinking during those years, a question that, strangely, had never before arisen between us. It turns out Gary had been as realistic as I had been, but far more philosophical. He told me:

> The devolution of our business into a tar pit happened slowly. But that's how it works. You don't wake up one morning and say, "This is awful." It's a series of lots of little things that happen each day. As the business grew, the weaknesses began to be magnified. We were like those frogs in the slowly heating water. I had a certain amount of denial, but mainly a lot of innocence. I had never done this before, and couldn't see the warning signs. I do think a certain amount of naïveté is essential. Without it, I probably wouldn't have gone forward.

The rural isolation and primitive accommodations of Stonyfield made our experience worse. If Gary had launched a software start-up in Palo Alto, we would have at least enjoyed ordinary physical comforts while losing our shirts. As it was, I envied our old college friends, most of them traditionally employed. Nose pressed against the glass, I gazed hungrily at their seductive "normal" lives and tried to figure out where Gary and I had gone so wrong. I didn't expect the white picket fence. But I had to wonder: wasn't there a less harrowing way to save the world?

No matter where it is or what it does, a business forces its founders to endure, in varying degrees, exhaustion, privation, and most debilitating of all, uncertainty. The entrepreneur—sure of himself, abuzz with excitement—sees those hardships as just paying dues. He may even welcome obstacles for the challenge and satisfaction of overcoming them. Gary likes to quote Winston Churchill's famous observation that "success is the ability to go from one failure to another with no loss of enthusiasm." Churchill would have applauded my husband, who remained calm, determined, and focused while ricocheting from crisis to catastrophe. "Eventually I became numb to the crises," Gary admitted to me. "I didn't really notice the privation of our personal lives, and even if I had I couldn't have afforded the luxury of thinking about that. Solving our endless problems required complete concentration. I felt bad that you were always freezing and that the circumstances were not of your choosing. But I had to keep moving."

Repeated failures are a lot easier to swallow when, after each one, you get to return to doing the thing you love. Gary certainly didn't love the disasters, but he was stimulated by the work. "I considered it a great adventure," he told me. "The setbacks were the price I paid for learning. How a cash flow statement worked, and spreadsheets. I learned what a private placement was, and how to manage dairy cows. I loved the marketing and sales, the creativity involved in package design, coming up with print and radio ads, giving out yogurt at events."

As for me, I was undeniably proud of what Gary and Samuel were trying to accomplish. But I wasn't doing what I loved. And in addition to accepting my own sacrifices, I worried about the adverse effects of the struggle on my husband and on us as a couple. Was he so obsessed with the company that its demise would crush him? Would the long hours and stress affect his physical and mental health, or take a toll on our relationship? Would we ever be able to buy a house or put our children through college? Would we be able to afford to retire someday?

Such concerns chew at the mind of an entrepreneur's spouse like termites in a wall. And at some point, she must ask herself a question. *Am I in?* In for as long as it takes this business to succeed? In for what is potentially a lifetime of financial risk? In for years of simmering on the back burner while the entrepreneur tends a pot that is always threatening to boil over? *Or am I out?* Out of patience? Out of hope? Out of my mind with stress and the bitterness of dreams deferred?

At some point, the spouse must ask herself a question. *Am I in? Or am I out?*

That's a hard question to answer. The entrepreneur's identity is so closely entwined with his creation that the spouse's rejection of the latter is implicitly a rejection of the former. Or if not a rejection, then at least a vote of no confidence. If the spouse pronounces "I cannot do this anymore," the entrepreneur may interpret that as, "I don't believe in your idea." Or "I don't believe in your ability to execute on your idea." Or "I don't trust you to make decisions that are in the best interests of our family." It's not a message conducive to an affectionate relationship.

The entrepreneur rarely poses the question—Are you in or out?—to the spouse. ("I assumed, more than I should have," Gary later said, "that you were there for the adventure too.") Yet the spouse does answer it, by giving or withholding support, encouragement, warmth, and reassurance—the manifestations of love.

Hate the sin, love the sinner is not viable in this situation. Consequently, many spouses stay "in" for the sake of the marriage. I spoke to one woman whose husband recently started a condiments company. She is not living the life she signed on for, but she can't bring herself to deflate her husband's grand plans or to pile on his already straining back the additional weight of her unhappiness. As she put it:

> Sometimes I feel like saying, "Can't we just stop and do real things? Things that aren't so hard and grueling for our family?" I'm sick of doing demos on weekends. I'm not that interested in it. I'm interested in how our family is going to survive. It's great that he's created something he's excited about. But I'm in the background wondering, how are we going to pay the bills?

My attitude toward Gary and Stonyfield was similar. I was "out," but I acted "in." More precisely, I *gave* in. There is a difference between acquiescence and agreement. I was *out* the night Gary was called into the factory for a machine breakdown at 2:00 AM, and the acid in the boot wash ate a hole in the top of his foot. I was *out* when he built a new factory with money we didn't have and personally guaranteed the loans for several expensive pieces of equipment. I was *out* when, as a result of errors in inventory counts, Samuel had to lecture the warehouse and production staffs on the difference between writing 4s and 9s. (Fours are open at the top!)

I was *out*, but I couldn't let other people know it. Even on my most miserable days, I was careful to conceal the tiniest sign of doubt for fear of scaring off investors, employees, suppliers, or other stakeholders. The smell of an ailing business is strong and carries far, so a certain amount of bravado is necessary. We might have lost a morning's worth of product because of a problem in the yogurt works and had the fouled curds trucked away to feed some farmer's pigs. But if an investor or friend called that evening and asked how things were going, I cheerfully assured them, "Great! Couldn't be better!"

I was *out*, but I never told Gary that. Skeptical as I was, I refused to stand openly with Stonyfield's doubters. Gary had enough to worry about with creditors nipping at his heels, potential investors laughing in his face, and employees writing 9s where 4s should be. Instead of criticisms, I offered my husband halfhearted congratulations for new accounts secured, batches unspoiled, sales slightly increased. Most of our victories were merely disasters averted. Still, I raised my arm feebly and stuttered out "Rah!" so Gary wouldn't know that mentally and emotionally I had left the stadium.

Though he didn't—couldn't—tell me at the time, Gary suffered his own dark nights of the soul. But he always rallied. He had to. As he put it:

Most of the time the business felt immensely fragile. But I had to keep believing that we could make it. If I stopped believing, we would have lost the business, and that would mean all our friends and family would lose their money. It would mean that I had failed. I didn't want you to know me as a failure. So I kept writing business plans. For a long time, the company was held together on the strength of my promises—to investors, lenders, and suppliers. As we got deeper into the hole, I felt that instead of staring up at the big blue sky of possibility, I had fallen into a well and saw only a narrow slit of salvation. My goals weren't grand anymore. All I wanted was a ladder to climb out.

OPPORTUNITY KNOCKS (ME OVER)
The strain of disparate risk profiles

The jury remains out on whether entrepreneurs are really more risk tolerant than other people. I would speculate that they simply find risk easier to live with because they have—or think they have—some degree of control. Most entrepreneurs, after all, are intensely hands-on with their companies. In the early years, they personally manage almost everything, from sales to accounts payable. Consequently, they think they know the difference between things that kill and things that make them stronger. That confidence in their own abilities translates into confidence that they can survive most anything.

Spouses, by contrast, have little power beyond the right to advise and—occasionally—consent in business decisions. Their lack of intimate knowledge of the business, combined with their impotence, increases their fear. Although launching a company is a risk couples assume together, unless they are equal business partners, only the entrepreneur can take the true measure of every hurricane and hiccup. The CEO comes home to a spouse whose interest is mixed with anxiety. Sometimes beneath the query "How was your day?" lurks the plea: "Reassure me, or at least don't say something that will leave me cowering in the coat closet clutching a vodka tonic."

Such disparate assessments of and attitudes toward risk can't help but tug at a relationship's seams. The pressure starts when the aspiring entrepreneur first floats the idea of quitting her job. Maybe she describes the venture as an experiment, a chance to get the start-up bug out of her system before returning to workaday stability. The couple makes a budget and the entrepreneur vows not to exceed it. But you'd be amazed how quickly a "lifestyle" company takes on a life of its own. When I married Gary, Stonyfield was producing a few hundred cups of yogurt per day. Then came a call from a large supermarket's dairy buyer, who demanded we supply his stores. When Samuel told him we couldn't make

Gary and me, on the right, with Louisa and Samuel Kaymen.

any more product with our (by then) 19 cows, the buyer responded, "Then get some more damn cows!" The rest? History.

So the spouse's concern rises with the stakes. The tipping point arrives when the spouse stops thinking of the entrepreneur as brave and starts thinking of her as crazy. He worries that her desperation to make the business successful is clouding her ability to make good decisions. His trust in her judgment erodes.

I believe my own comfort level with risk is pretty normal. Admittedly, when it comes to making decisions, I'm more deliberate and, as Gary put it, "evidence based" than he is. At first I was merely puzzled by my husband's willingness to go deeply in hock to investors and banks in order to build some elusive value later on. It was only later—notably as we brought three children into the world—that I became alarmed. I remember yearning nostalgically for my old job with its predictable rhythms and regular paychecks. Stock? No thanks. I'll take the cash.

And so while Gary was forever catching fleeting glimpses of progress, I drew the obvious conclusions from the facts around me. It was plain that our farm factory was grossly inefficient: we lost vast amounts of product to spoilage. Sales calls were depressing. Most supermarket buyers treated our low-volume brand as a hassle. Board meetings reminded us that our cost of goods was too high and our cash burn would continue for another quarter—always another quarter. We lost money on each cup sold. So why on earth were we trying to sell *more* yogurt? (When I recently asked him this, Gary was persuasively pragmatic. "Think about our options," he said. "We couldn't try to make no yogurt, or less yogurt, or the same amount of yogurt. We had to make more to cover our cash burn while we looked for a long-term solution.")

We came perilously close to losing the business dozens of times. Frankly, I often wanted to lose the business—anything to get us out of our plight. As I surveyed the wreckage of our personal balance sheet and the company's P&L, I couldn't help but wonder: did Gary and I live on different planets? What he saw as necessary investments I considered wild gambles. Yet I probably argued more with myself than with him.

Many spouses I spoke to described similar struggles with weighing loyalty against prudence as each new expense tested their priorities anew. As one explained:

> I'm straining to support yet another venture, another expense, another trip, when I have little faith that it will result in the financial provision we desperately need to support our growing family. Racked with guilt, I, in turn, lash out or lavish praise, feeling squirmily selfish and yet alone in my frustration.

Another spouse, who had recently put her name on a $2 million line of credit, was more upfront with her discomfort. "I love you and I'm here for you," she told her husband, "but *what are you doing?*"

Gary and I needed a way to live with our differences, particularly after we both learned how poorly I responded to disturbing business news. The solution we came up with probably wasn't the best long-term strategy. Essentially, we started acting like the three wise monkeys. When it came to the company's finances, I covered my eyes and ears so as to see and hear no evil. Gary went along by covering his mouth, and told me almost nothing about what was going on.

I embraced ignorance (or innocence, as I prefer to call it) for emotional survival. As the company chronically hovered near bankruptcy, I couldn't bear to learn the gory details portending its demise. I knew I *should* know what was going on. Our entire future was on the line. But I wanted to listen to a financial report the way I watched the movie *The Shining*: running out of the room during particularly terrifying scenes.

I wish I could have been the supportive spouse who listens sympathetically, then calmly puts everything into perspective. As it was, Gary accepted our pact because it prevented my fear from making him crazy. He avoided what he calls the "double penalty"—intense stress at work compounded by intense stress at home. After a day spent putting out fires, he didn't need my alarm ringing in his ears. Practically speaking, this tacit agreement may have been the only way to survive those difficult years. But it forced us to shoulder our respective burdens alone.

YOU CAN COUNT ON ME
The ultimate test of loyalty

Although a few companies are instant hits, most entrepreneurs and their families are in for a long slog. Even given that fact, Stonyfield's path to profitability did not obey the laws of normal distribution. We were on the very far end of the bell curve.

From 1983 to 1991, Gary raised more than $5 million for Stonyfield. All of it came from individual investors, none from venture capitalists. In 1989 alone, he raised $1 million to build the plant that he and Samuel had cost out on that car trip the previous spring, plus $1.1 million to cover Stonyfield's losses. We eventually had 297 shareholders even though we had never closed a quarter with a profit. We didn't see our first profits until 1992, when the company's revenue reached $10.2 million. You can do the math: it took us nine years to break even. I was never so happy to be wrong as when Gary and Samuel's wager on the new facility paid off. In fact, it became our turning point.

Frankly, I was amazed that Gary was able to persuade so many investors to write checks, given the bleak history of our little company. I'm grateful none of them ever asked me about my own confidence in our enterprise. I assume they were investing in Gary—in his smarts, his determination, his commitment, and his confidence. They were also persuaded by the quality of our product. (Although my mother, the third-largest shareholder at the time, didn't eat the stuff.)

Despite my opposition to our company's swelling debt—much of it owed to people we knew and cared about—Gary and I didn't quarrel much. We were too busy trying to keep the babies fed and the business alive. But after a while we noticed a pattern. When we did fight, it was about stupid things, unrelated to the business. And the arguments always took place in the car on the way back from my mother's house in New York. My mother possessed what were to us dazzling luxuries—a bathtub and thermostats. We dreaded returning to our primitive, punishing life at the farm, and that dread would convert to bickering on the ride home.

One day, after a couple of years of suppressing my most anxious feelings and gingerly stepping over the third rail in our marriage, the moment of truth arrived. I had to choose—really, truly, and finally—between allegiance to Gary and my own most fundamental need for security. Between his dream of what the future could be and my nightmare of what it would be.

When we married, I had asked Gary for just one financial commitment: that he never touch the $30,000 that was my father's legacy to me. It was meant to be my nest egg, a down payment on a home in the (likely) event that the business failed and we lost everything else.

> The moment of truth arrived. I had to choose—really, truly, and finally—between allegiance to Gary and my own most fundamental need for security.

In 1987, we moved production off our farm and began co-packing at a factory in Massachusetts. One day, without warning, our co-packer went bankrupt. We had three days to clean and relight the boilers at Stonyfield; hire new employees; and buy fruit, milk, and culture. There was no money readily available for any of that, of course. Except for my $30,000.

Gary came to me and said, "I need the cash." He had dreaded the prospect of asking me. "You were the last resort," he told me later. "I needed to buy fruit. I wouldn't have made the request if I didn't think the business would one day pay it back."

There we were. Stonyfield's continued existence depended in part on me. I couldn't straddle anymore. No weeping or wailing or gnashing of teeth would provide relief this time. So, Meg, *are you in or are you out?* Gary never put it that way, and he told me that's not how he thought of the decision. But that's what it came down to.

Well, Gary, I'm in, I guess. I'm in because you're in, and we're married, and my loyalty lies with you. I'm in because we have employees and shareholders and customers who expect us to climb out of bed every day and do the entire scary and difficult thing all over again. I'm in because I believe in your vision of a saner planet. I'm in even though I suspect we're going to go down and take other people's money with us. I'm in because your passion, your courage, and your willingness to have a dream and run with it are a large part of what attracted me to you in the first place.

So good-bye fantasy bathtub. Good-bye thermostat mirage. As I wrote the check for $30K, the door of my dream home shut with a thud. In my heart, I made a plea to my father. "Dear Dad, wherever you are: please don't think your only daughter is a fool."

Our family: Alex, Gary, Danielle, Ethan, and me.

Things to Talk About

- What is the best outcome you can imagine for the business? What is the worst? How will either one affect your marriage?

- If you want children down the road, how will the business influence that timetable? What impact might it have on their quality of life?

- How informed does the spouse wish to be about the business? Will the entrepreneur share bad news (there will likely be plenty along the way), or will he try, as much as possible, to preserve her peace of mind?

- What steps will you take to rope off your private life from an entity that tries to shoulder its way into everything?

Things to Do

- The spouse should independently research what starting a company entails and compile a thorough list of questions. The entrepreneur may not be able to answer all of them. But at least the spouse will be forewarned of the difficulties and can air his concerns upfront.

- When planning the venture, try establishing a "stage-gate" process in which you both review your progress at designated points and decide together whether to proceed.

- There are scores of biographies and memoirs of entrepreneurs. Choose a few and study the chapters about the subjects' difficult early years building their companies. Before going on to read about their successes, imagine what might have happened if they had failed.

- The spouse will always have reservations about plans for the business. But, ideally, he will give the entrepreneur the benefit of the doubt and trust her to make the best decisions possible with the limited information available.

Chapter 2

Brother, Can You Spare a Dime (or Twenty Grand)?

Relatives who invest in your business are making a profound
gesture of love and faith. Then along come doubt, fear, and the
complicated family gathering.

During the '80s, our first years in business, I felt great relief each
November as we left behind the ruts of our New Hampshire
dirt road, glided onto the interstate, and headed south to Mom's
New York home for Thanksgiving. But around Hartford, my anxiety meter would start ticking up. My mother and three brothers had
invested heavily in our company, and I knew that soon after our arrival,
the conversation would turn to the fate of their cash. Their questions
were sheathed in a kindness that barely covered a sharp blade of concern. *Profits?* Not even close. *Margins?* Come on. *Cash burn?* Lots of
that. I would sympathize with the turkey as slivers of explanations
and excuses were sliced from our tender hides. In those early days, our
carcass of a business felt cooked too.

Fortunately, those discussions were supportive. My brothers (two
physicians and a lawyer) were entertained and challenged by entrepreneurial problem solving. They enjoyed offering advice. Gary profited

from talking things out and getting some fresh thinking. At the very least, it was a break from making yogurt. But there was a lack of ease in the air as our Thanksgiving reunion morphed into a literal kitchen-cabinet meeting. At times, I wished we could just hold a shareholders' Q and A beforehand and enjoy the pumpkin pie in peace.

In building Stonyfield, Gary was driven by a lofty vision. He dreamed of each little cup of yogurt serving as a billboard to educate consumers about the benefits of organic agriculture and the power of voting with our food dollars for a saner world. Starting with Gary's mother, Louise, many friends and family members bought into that dream. Most of them stepped forward on their own, without Gary's solicitation. They wanted to help but were also excited to get in on the ground floor of a new business they believed had potential. Gary toiled around the clock to make sure their money wasn't lost—a possibility that I found deeply chilling.

In those early discussions with my family, Gary painted Stonyfield's prospects in rosier hues than I felt were warranted. He wasn't misrepresenting, but I couldn't follow his logic through my own maze of doubts. If Gary didn't make sense to *me*, how was he making sense to all these people I respected and loved? I was torn by their eagerness to saddle up for this potentially quixotic quest. I feared for their cash. But as our financial situation grew increasingly perilous, I realized Gary and I had nowhere else to turn.

My mother, Doris Cadoux, and me.

As the company continued to rack up losses, Gary turned more frequently to my mother, Doris, our largest outside investor. We joke about it now, but it's true: on several occasions, Gary would tiptoe to his office on a Wednesday night, before Thursday payroll, to call Doris and discuss whether she could afford one more loan, one more invest-ment. Wise to his late-night missions, I would dial her on another line and implore her to say no. In my view, this was money my mother could ill afford to lose. "It's good money after bad," I'd say to her. "The more yogurt we make, the more money we lose," I'd add, sensibly. But she would always say yes.

I became so distressed about the extent of my mother's risk with Stonyfield that, for years, Gary and I couldn't discuss the subject at all. As I mentioned in the previous chapter, Gary and I adopted—by mutual agreement—a "don't ask, don't tell" policy. Recently I asked Gary to reflect on the bargain we made. "It became a debt against our intimacy," he said. "It meant there were things we couldn't share. It was an unbearable load, and I couldn't talk with anyone about it. I couldn't turn to you for help and support." I do regret not sharing this burden with Gary. But that is a luxury of hindsight—safe to feel now that the company is successful. The truth is that even in retrospect, I think my mother gambled too much on Stonyfield.

Whenever I would try to convince my mother to *stop* giving us money, she would reply, "Meggie, I'm a big girl. Win or lose, I've made a choice." *They're both insane*, I'd think. *The two people I love the most are nuts.* I saw my family as financial innocents whom Gary and I were leading to slaughter. From my perspective, they may as well have been shoving quarters into a slot machine.

> I saw my family as financial innocents whom Gary and I were leading to slaughter.

Still, begging my mother not to trust Gary with more money seemed a betrayal of him, a public profession of my doubt. It came down to this: I had been a Cadoux for 30 years, a Hirshberg for only a few. Concern for my mother was bred deep in my bones. If I hadn't brought Gary into her life, her money would have been safe. Suddenly, the roles of supportive spouse and protective daughter had become mutually exclusive. How could I be loyal to both of them?

TRUE BELIEVERS
The vulnerability of investors who care

When it comes to raising money, family and friends are the entrepreneur's low-hanging fruit. But the people who love and believe in us are also those whose fortunes we least want to imperil, and whose positive regard it hurts most to squander. Venture capitalists understand this, which is why they often prefer that the entrepreneur's friends and family invest before they consider a deal. As one CEO said to me, "Venture people know you don't care about them, but that you'll work hard to make sure not to lose the money of loved ones."

The decision to invest is about the business, but it's personal too. After all, businesses reflect the passion, dreams, energy, and vision of their founders. What could be more personal than that? Entrepreneurs strive to keep people *believing* in them. Indeed, my mother now says that she continued pouring money into Stonyfield because, more than believing in Gary's endlessly evolving business plans, she believed in Gary.

But when things go wrong, losing the confidence of professional investors is far less painful than losing the faith of one's family. As Gary put it, you're carrying not just their assets but also the burden of living up to their belief in you. "Every day is a test of your integrity," he said. "Are you up to it? Are you reliable? The darker side of this is that you're not. And if you fail, you're not only the shit who lost their money, but you are unworthy of their respect. It's high stakes poker—and there's a lot more at play than the money itself."

The situation becomes even riskier if family members invest alongside professional investors; it's akin to the lamb lying down with the lion and being devoured. When entrepreneurs are forced to raise money from multiple sources, relatives command their affection and loyalty. But the professionals command the fate of their businesses. The entrepreneur wants to do right by her loved ones, but she often loses the power to do. That is because professionals typically install controls that protect their interests, such as vetoes, voting rights, and the right to force the entrepreneur to buy back their shares at a premium if certain conditions are not met.

Richard Simtob was 24 when he started Talking Book World, a company that rented out books and CDs to consumers. Family and friends invested. Three years later the company was profitable, and a few years after that it was approaching 40 locations nationwide. At that point, Richard decided he needed another $5 million to open yet more stores. He raised $1.5 million from the friends and relatives who had invested earlier; $2 million from a bank; and $750,000 each from two different venture financiers. "That's when things started to go bad," he said. One of the VCs became chairman and soon clashed with Richard over finances. Eighteen months later, by mutual agreement, Richard was out. "All my friends and family had invested in *me*, but now they found themselves invested in this venture group," Richard said. "These venture guys ended up losing all the investors' money. But thankfully, none of my investors blamed me."

Sometimes when outside investors start turning the thumbscrews, entrepreneurs will turn to family for rescue, deepening their financial and emotional debt. In 1988, one of Stonyfield's large investors lost confidence in the business and agitated to replace Gary with a "professional" CEO. She demanded her $250K loan be paid back within five days. If Gary couldn't pay it (he couldn't), she would have had the right to transfer it to stock, making her a significant enough shareholder that she could have forced Gary out.

> When outside investors start turning the thumbscrews, entrepreneurs will turn to family for rescue, deepening their financial and emotional debt.

My mother decided to buy this shareholder out, which brought her investment to well over a million dollars. This time Gary, who acknowledged things were not going well in the company, actually urged her not to do it. "In the end, she was persuasive and said she understood the consequences," he recalled. "But if I'd had any other option, I would have taken it." Doris saved the company—and Gary and me. As per my agreement with Gary, I didn't know about this while it was happening, and for that I'm grateful. It was only a couple of years ago that I learned exactly how much my mother put into Stonyfield.

STRAINED RELATIONS
Money places conditions on unconditional love

Building a business requires sacrifices. When relatives help fund the business, those sacrifices may include the relaxed family gathering, the casual lunch with a sibling, and the lighthearted phone chat with Mom and Dad. Anxious and exhausted, entrepreneurs yearn for the solace and support usually provided by families: a sheltered place to lay their weary heads. But relationships change whenever money enters the picture. After all, the adjectives traditionally paired with cash are *cold* and *hard*. If business problems also endanger the family treasure, the entrepreneur may find her weary head resting on cold, hard stone.

Sometimes the stress fractures are so severe that even close relationships can collapse. Around the same time we were building Stony-field, a friend of mine, "Sally," and her husband started what became a hugely successful consumer goods company. They were desperate for money and too risky for a bank loan, so early on her parents bought 20 percent of the business at a reasonable valuation (any outsiders would have demanded a bigger chunk of the company for what they invested). Sally tried persuading her parents to sign a minority share-holder agreement, but they were offended at the mere suggestion. She was grateful, never imagining that they would eventually seek an enormous return.

But a few years later, Sally's parents tried to force a sale or an IPO. Her voice still shakes when she tells the tale:

> At one point they threatened to sell the shares to a third
> party, and we couldn't have stopped them. The strange

thing is, we were doing *well* when they demanded their money back. The whole experience was probably the most painful thing I've been through.

You look at it as a child being supported by loving parents. They look at it as a calculation. What—money is more important than *me*?

Sally, who had been close to her parents, eventually saw them only in the presence of both sides' attorneys. She didn't speak to them directly for years. "It was horrible for me. Resentment is like swallowing poison and expecting the other person to die," she said. "The bottom line is that this was my *life,* and to them, the business was nothing more than an asset."

Sally's rift with her parents occurred over a *successful* venture. More common are strains imposed by failure. Between 2005 and 2007, Lisa Stahr took investment money (around $150,000) from friends, coworkers, and her mother to start Scout's House, a Menlo Park, California–based company that offers physical rehabilitation therapy for pets. The company flirted with profitability until the recession of 2008. Then, as Scout's House struggled, Lisa agonized over whether to sell it, go nonprofit, or find some other way to keep it alive. The first two options guaranteed her investors would lose their money, an outcome she dreaded. Lisa recalled:

Lisa Stahr with her dog, Cairo.

> I spent many sleepless nights trying to cope with the guilt of that. They all said they didn't need the money. Most of them told me they didn't mind, but a couple made comments that it would be nice to get their money back. I felt so responsible for those people who believed in my dream.

Uncomfortable conversations with professional investors are generally limited to business meetings. When people whom the entrepreneur sees everyday realize that their faith has been misplaced, their anxiety and disappointment—and the entrepreneur's guilt—taint even the most casual interactions. Lisa said:

> I became very conscious that they were not just friends. They were investors. In the back of my mind, I was always wondering: what and how much should I say? I didn't want to upset them. It affected my thought processes and feelings when I was with them. During the worst days I actually avoided a few of them a bit. I avoided the phone. Email was easier. With email they couldn't hear the anxiety and anguish in my voice.

Lisa did receive an offer for Scout's House, but at a price so low her investors would have lost everything. In the end, she couldn't stomach that. Instead, with the blessing of the majority of her shareholders, she struck a deal with a young veterinary surgeon, which should allow the business to ride out the downturn. "Almost every decision I made was influenced not only by how it could affect the future of the business but also how it would affect my shareholders," said Lisa.

DIDN'T SEE THAT COMING

What if your investors need it back?

Sometimes it's not the entrepreneur's circumstances that deteriorate, but his investors'. While founders dutifully calculate their own risk—usually underestimating it, in my experience—they rarely inquire too deeply about their investors' ability to withstand a financial hit. Nor should they, necessarily. Their investors are adults, after all. As my mother gently reminded me, she is capable of making her own decisions. Still, guilt is exacerbated when the people who could once afford to assist you fall on hard times and need that money back—and you are in no position to return it. It's as though you've accepted a blood relation's kidney and must now watch helplessly as his remaining one fails.

In 2003, David Issa launched a software company called XenLogic in Atlanta. Three years later he found himself in a tough place with cash flow. David's grandfather spontaneously offered him a loan of $15,000. Assuming that all would be well as long as David could make the minimum payments, the grandfather took an equity line of credit in his house.

Then, in 2009, the grandfather's health deteriorated suddenly and significantly. He had to sell his home and move into an assisted-living facility. The equity line of credit was deducted from the sale of his home. David explained:

> Neither of us had considered that this might happen. I have consistently been making the payments, but there is a possibility I may never be able to pay my grandfather back in his lifetime. This is a big burden to come crashing down on him this late in life. To the extent that I'm partially responsible for that, I feel guilty. To this day, I haven't been able to have an open discussion about this with my grandfather. These might be my last moments with him. Do I really want to be discussing the terms of our deal?

David's experience didn't teach him to refuse investment money from friends and family, just to consider the hidden costs to that money—emotional costs that may only become apparent with time. He reflected:

> In the beginning, everyone is excited about the possibilities. But what about a couple of years later when things haven't worked out as planned? The stress wears you thin, and wears thin some of those bonds of love and friendship.

The truth is, I needed that money. It was a lifesaver. The best advice I have is to make sure friendly investors understand that they should expect to lose that money. The problem with that, of course, is that they invest on the premise that you're going to succeed, and the money is their vote of confidence.

David echoes many entrepreneurs who regret mixing business and family. "I probably would have been better off negotiating this as a bank

David Issa, center, with his grandparents, Francis and Charles Schiedel.

loan," he said. "How much do I really care about the bank? I care about my credit score. But at least it wouldn't be a livelihood in my hands." Gary makes a similar case for venture capitalists. "They are big enough and smart enough to know better," he said. "There's no emotional burden that comes with them."

GUILT BY PROXY

Friendly money comes in; the spouse's chagrin

The entrepreneur is not the only person whose relationship with intimates becomes more complicated when they invest. Inevitably, the spouse feels the strain as well. A woman who works with her husband in a home-fitness start-up told me she became "furious" with him after finding out that he had borrowed money from his sister to keep the business afloat. "I didn't want her looking at me funny because we owed her money," she said. "Debt erodes healthy relationships. I wish he'd taken a loan from a bank."

As for me, I wasn't angry with Gary for soliciting and accepting money from my family. But I was haunted by the specter of possible damage, both profound and subtle, to my relationships with my mother and brothers should Stonyfield fail. How would my mother's financial loss affect her retirement? Would my brothers blame me for jeopardizing her future? Would they blame Gary?

Fortunately, Gary's and my relationship with my mother and brothers remained unaffected by their significant investment (though that might not have been the case had Stonyfield failed). My relationship with a couple of old high school chums, however, has grown more complicated. Neither of my friends is entrepreneurial by nature, but both regretted not investing in the yogurt company. So they jumped at the opportunity to put money into Gary's second venture: the restaurant O'Natural's (later renamed the Stonyfield Café).

Ten years later, the Café is still finding its way as a business, and its survival is not a sure bet. My friends have expressed anxiety about the fate of their cash, and all of us wish they had never invested. As a result, my relationship with one has grown more distant and prickly. I remain in frequent contact with the other, but finally I had to recuse myself from discussing the status of the Café with her, despite her frequent inquiries. I've known her most of my life, and this is the only subject we simply can't discuss.

A BUSINESS FOOTING
*Layering a professional relationship
onto a personal one*

Entrepreneurs who opt for family money over more impersonal sources can mitigate some of the emotional risk by keeping the proceedings as businesslike as possible. Though entirely stripping sentiment from friend-and-family transactions is unrealistic, company founders should provide family investors with as much information as they would a loan officer. Likewise, they should discuss with them the same hard questions a professional investor would ask. For example, any investment, even of friendly money, puts the entrepreneur on a path to sell, sooner or later. She must be clear about her intentions and explain exactly why she is in business. Is it just to cash out? Or is it a lifestyle/identity choice? Ideally, the answer should help determine how much money she takes in, and from whom.

The information supplied may scare off friendly investors, which can put its own strain on relations. Usually it's the rejected entrepre-

Nancy Hirshberg, Gary's sister.

neur who feels disappointed. But if the company goes on to thrive, thwarted investors may have their own reasons to feel frustrated. In 1985, my sister-in-law Nancy wanted to put money into Stonyfield. But the minimum investment was $5,000, and Nancy had just $12,000 in savings. Gary made it very clear that she had to be prepared to lose her money. "He was so convincing that I instead put that money into Calvert," said Nancy. "Ten years later my Calvert investment was still worth about $5K. Biggest financial mistake I ever made."

Seth Goldman, Founder of Honest Tea, based in Bethesda, Maryland, actively discouraged a few early investors who were parents of his sons' baseball teammates. "I figured we were going to see these guys for a dozen more years," he told me, "so it would be awkward if I lost their money." But Seth wound up changing his mind. He explained:

> A couple of them persisted, and as the business—and my cash needs—grew, my resistance broke down. You don't want to insult someone by saying, "You can't invest." I came around to feeling, if this business goes under, I'm going to have a lot more problems than a few awkward moments with these guys—even though one of them was going to put in his son's college money. In the end, the baseball dads' network was lucrative—we raised more

than a million dollars from that extended group. I'm glad to say that the one father will have no trouble paying for his son's education now.

It's important to remember that who-ever invests will have a say over how you exit: the greater the investment, the greater the say. One benefit of bringing in friendly (versus institutional) investors is that you can usually retain a measure of control over your business, without promising a definite exit. But just because someone loves you doesn't mean they won't fight like hell for what they perceive

The Goldman family in a tea garden in India.

to be their own self-interest. Money can reveal unexpected—and often unpleasant—sides of people we thought we knew well. Even when the business is prospering, relationships can sour, as happened with my friend whose parents tried to force a liquidity event. She advises that if you must take money from relatives, get them in and out quickly, with short-term debt. Whenever possible, structure the transaction as a loan rather than as equity so valuation does not become an issue. If you do give up equity, make sure to press for a shareholder agreement and get a right of first refusal on the stock.

Friends and family will also likely have opinions about how to run your business. As long as they have cash on the table, you need to listen. Gary avoided letting investors unduly influence his thinking about Stonyfield. Everyone had ideas, and often they conflicted: the yogurt's too sweet/it's not sweet enough; the cup shape or design needs to change/it's perfect the way it is; the company is too concerned/not concerned enough with environmental impacts. Gary listened respect-fully, but he always trusted his instincts and never changed direction solely because of an investor's opinion.

After Stonyfield became successful, Gary endured a different kind

> Friends and family will also likely have opinions about how to run your business. As long as they have cash on the table, you need to listen.

of pressure. Several of his investors launched start-ups of their own, and they expected him to invest. After all, they'd dug into their own pockets and cast a vote of confidence during Stonyfield's bad old days. Shouldn't he reciprocate? Irrespective of the merits of what these people were attempting, Gary chafed at being guilt-tripped, and there were some awkward moments. (He wound up investing in one business—on its merits—but not in the others.)

EMOTIONAL RETURNS ON INVESTMENT
Financial commitment can pay off in closer ties

Occasionally an investment by friends or family not only works out financially but also changes personal relationships for the better. In 2003, Lisa Calhoun was languishing in a San Antonio advertising job. Then her younger brother and only sibling, Vince, offered her the $4,000 she would need to fulfill her dream of moving back to Georgia and starting a PR agency (Write2Market, in Atlanta, is now a thriving business with 14 employees.) Lisa described the unexpected changes in their family:

> Money is a big deal in my family because we never had much of it. Four thousand dollars should be slap-around-able, but at that time it was very significant. My brother, who had been sleeping on a twin mattress on a friend's floor, also surprised me by buying his first house so that I'd have a place to move back to. He charged me a little rent, and I paid him back the full loan within a year.
>
> Vince had been someone I bossed around all my life: my adorable sidekick. This experience changed our

dynamic. We're closer now. And he's easily an equal—I'm no longer patronizing. I'm glad he took the opportunity to step forward and take charge. When my parents saw him do that, they started treating him like a man, no longer a boy. Mom was very grateful—she cried. Dad felt like it was a family leadership baton passing to Vince. So in a way, Vince grew up too.

My personal story had a happy ending as well. The constant pressure from my family's investment lifted in 2001 with the sale of the non-employee stockholders' shares in Stonyfield to Groupe Danone. (Gary still runs the company and retains majority control of the board.) Gary recalled his relief when the deal was signed:

> I remember the lump in my throat melting away. Now I could once again be part of your family instead of the person who held their financial destiny. Money is this funny substance—it's fungible, liquid, a concept. But when it belongs to someone else, then it becomes personified. It's a presence in the room. The investment altered the DNA of my relationship with your family—before, I couldn't be totally honest about what I was going through. I don't remember the burden as much as I remember the relief I experienced from not having it anymore.

My mother is at ease in her retirement. Her risky investment in Stonyfield secured college educations for all her grandchildren. Our family is as close as ever and feels great collective satisfaction at having been part of building a thriving business. And Gary's success has spawned entrepreneurial dreams in other members of the clan. Some of what our family made on Stonyfield stock has been invested in my nephew Jon Cadoux's start-up, Peak Organic Brewing Company, based in Portland, Maine. These days when we all reunite for Thanksgiving, it is Jon's hide on the carving platter instead of ours.

Things to Talk About

- How much additional stress will you endure from putting loved ones' capital at risk along with your own? Is it worth it?

- You may be counting on relatives and friends for emotional support during the difficult start-up period. Will taking their money make that support harder to get? Can you handle it if relationships become strained?

- When an entrepreneur taps her spouse's family and friends, the spouse may find his loyalties hopelessly divided. How will such an act affect the marriage?

- Investors have a say in how the company is run and in when and how to exit. How willing are you to open yourselves up to such (usually non-expert) interference . . . I mean advice?

Things to Do

- The entrepreneur should clearly state the risks of the investment. Don't sugarcoat. Be transparent, and warn friends and family that future rounds of financing could dilute their investments or even change ownership of the company. Make sure they understand that this asset will be illiquid indefinitely.

- Get a good lawyer and document everything. Make sure even close family members sign a minority shareholder agreement; explain to them that this protects you both. Provide a mechanism to resolve disagreements. Make sure you have a right of first refusal on the stock so that investors are not able to sell it to whomever offers the most (which could wind up being a competitor).

- Be very reluctant to accept anyone's retirement or college-fund money.

- Identify the amount of money you can take from friends and family and still feel comfortable with the investment. As Gary put it: "You need to avoid being immobilized by fear, but able to look yourself in the mirror and not feel like a schmuck."

Chapter 3

To Love, Honor, and Report To

Sometimes, romance is born in the office.
Unless entrepreneurs who work with their spouses are careful,
romance can die in the office too.

As I mentioned in the first chapter, when I moved to Stonyfield Farm in the mid-'80s to live with Gary, I immediately went to work in the yogurt business. I worked part-time in the office and in sales, and part-time as a yogurt maker. Back then our "factory" consisted of some jury-rigged machines in our barn; turning out good product required improvisation and luck. But my sales job was just as taxing, in personal ways I hadn't anticipated. That's because I reported to Gary.

Working with my husband amplified aspects of both our personalities that had remained muted during two years of courting. We'd always known we had different problem-solving styles. I'm slow, linear, and methodical, while Gary is fast and goes on gut. Those contrasts had seemed complementary—even charming—in our personal relationship. In a business context, they made us bristle.

At home, we always tried to deal with problems as they arose. I had assumed we'd do the same thing in the office. But it turns out there are

no don't-go-to-bed-angry policies in human resources manuals. In the
midst of running a start-up, Gary didn't have time to salve my injured

feelings or negotiate a compromise over some point

of contention. Often when instructing me on the

handling of clients or suggesting shortcuts for busi-

ness trips, he would speak quickly and skip details.

He'd get impatient with my confusion and god-

awful sense of direction. As for me, I personalized

everything and felt hurt by his abruptness. I was

unable to compartmentalize or live with ambigu-

ity—critical skills for couples that work together.

> There are no
> don't-go-to-bed
> angry policies in
> human resources
> manuals.

Gary and I were, to use a favorite phrase of my father's, young and
stupid. Any seasoned advisor—probably anyone with a passing understanding of human nature—would have cautioned us to get better
acquainted before jumping into business together. Some amount of
mental and emotional recalibration is inevitable in any new marriage
as spouses let down their guards to reveal irritating habits and unbe-
coming traits. The daily operation of a business expedites the departure
of bloom from rose. Working together can reveal quirks that might
never have surfaced in domestic life.

Even long-married couples encounter unpleasant surprises. When
one friend of mine, married 20 years, joined his wife in her business, he
discovered that "she wasn't just a witty, sharp-tongued, funny woman.
She was actually mean and abusive. We stopped liking each other."
The couple eventually divorced.

One reason spouse-employee arrangements sour is that so little
thought goes into them. Bosses interview job candidates to assess their
skills and interests. Working conditions and responsibilities are defined
up front. Spouses, by contrast, may have to alter their shapes to fit whatever hole the company needs filled. Sometimes it's a match: the onetime accounting major takes over the books. Sometimes it's not: I was a
literature major who made yogurt and helped with accounts receivable.

I started working for Gary for the same reasons that most spouses
get swept up into entrepreneurial ventures. I was available, capable,

and cheap. My role grew out of expediency, not because I possessed any particular skills or an abiding passion for the job. In situations like ours, subjects like compensation, flexible hours, and titles are often not raised. How long will the arrangement last? Is the spouse just helping out or putting her own aspirations indefinitely on hold? Is she simply another employee or entitled to special treatment?

More profoundly, how will the couple shift back and forth between competing professional and domestic spheres without their relationship falling to tatters? The wear and tear will likely be greater on the spouse. She may be dedicated. Her future, after all, depends on the company's success. But she is not an equal partner living a dream of joint creation. And so she suffers a comparable level of stress without enjoying the same measure of personal fulfillment.

The marriage isn't all that's at risk. Even when the work relationship goes right, if the company itself goes wrong both husband and wife are out of jobs. There's no separate income to fall back on for house payments or insurance. Often home equity loans are used to fund businesses, and couples risk everything they own. If the spouse has been "helping out" for years, she may never have had the chance to accrue experience and credentials in the line of work she trained for, making it harder to find another job. When both partners rely financially on their business, they greatly raise the stakes in what is already a high-risk venture.

Still, the entrepreneur stands in his wobbly canoe, hand extended, a look of pleading in his eyes. "All hands on deck," he says, "until we're under sail or at the bottom of the drink." What loyal spouse could refuse?

WHEN A MARRIAGE OF EQUALS SUDDENLY ISN'T
You are not the boss of me

Most marriages are punctuated by small skirmishes for the upper hand. When couples joust over whose choice of paint color or vacation locale prevails, the playing field is level-ish. Working together upends that parity. The power differential is impossible to ignore: it is spelled out on business cards and reinforced every time a customer or employee comes looking for an authoritative answer. Even when one spouse doesn't report to the other, the entrepreneur usually acts like the boss, which is not ideal when you're trying to sustain a marriage of equals. A husband assumes he will be "working in our business." Instead he finds himself "working for my wife."

If the company is big enough, couples can mitigate the queasiness of a boss-employee relationship by having the spouse report to someone other than the entrepreneur. But that arrangement can be awkward—not least for the person interposed between the two. Jill Wolfe works as the Mindbody Finder program manager at Mindbody, Inc., a San Luis Obispo, California–based company that provides software for the health and wellness industry. Jill's husband, Rick Stollmeyer, founded Mindbody, but Jill reports to Rick's partner, Bob Murphy.

Rick Stollmeyer and Jill Wolfe
working on contract language.

One reason people get married, of course, is so they'll always have someone to vent to, and Jill naturally tells Rick about her occasional frustrations with a work project. She asks her husband to "listen as my lover, not my coworker" and requests that he not bring up the issue with Bob. Still, Rick usually finds it impossible to react dispassionately, and soon he's on the phone to his partner. Lately, Jill has been trying to avoid those marital gripe sessions, limiting expressions of work concerns to office conversations. "It's complicated, but the three of us are learning how to play together in the sandbox," Jill told me.

A better strategy than building buffers into the org chart is building consultation and respect into the business relationship. Spouses who work together should make clear to everyone—including each other—that they are collaborators pursuing a common goal, in business and in life. That's true even if one plots strategy while the other restocks shelves. The entrepreneur should never command her spouse to perform a task at work any more than she would at home: courtesy and consideration should guide interactions in both spheres. So should respect for the other's time. There may be no faster route to upsetting your spouse than behaving as though your time is more valuable than his—even if from a revenue standpoint that happens to be true.

Many spouses, no matter their titles at the office, will also expect a seat on the entrepreneur's kitchen-cabinet of advisors. Given their unique insight into the leader, familiarity with the business, and interest in the company's success, they deserve to have one. Formally or informally, the entrepreneur should routinely seek her spouse's judgment about business issues and not hide the fact that she does so from the rest of the company. That doesn't mean the entrepreneur makes decisions by marital consensus. She is merely acknowledging that she values her spouse's opinions and weighs them as she would those of any other talented colleague.

For more than 30 years, Ruth Harms has worked at Harms Engineering in Pasco, Washington, a consulting business founded by her husband, Leonard. Her title there is office manager, but she functions as CFO, human resources administrator, and purchasing director. "I can't be his Girl Friday during the workweek, then his partner at home," said Ruth. "I have to be his partner all the time." At the office, Len confides in his wife, and Ruth has veto power over big decisions that fall in her areas of proficiency. When she needs to talk to Len, he stops everything and gives her his full attention. That lets her know she is more important than any project or client. "I don't feel like he

Ruth and Len Harms.

is 'allowing' me to have a say in our business," Ruth said. "I feel like he really depends on my perspective and expertise."

When authority flows in one direction all day, it doesn't easily reverse course at knock-off time. Often the entrepreneur has trouble making the transition from an autocracy into a democracy, with all its attendant chaos, conflict, and need for compromise. A woman who works with her husband told me she occasionally tells him to "stop CEOing it" at home. And one long-married man wrote: "My wife is the boss at home too. I now feel like I work for her 24 hours a day."

> When authority flows in one direction all day, it doesn't easily reverse course at knock-off time.

The entrepreneur's temptation to maintain control at home is understandable. After all, it's more efficient to rule by fiat. During the day, the entrepreneur is in the flow, getting things done by delegating tasks and deploying people where they can be the most use to him. At night, a brief transition may be necessary for mental realignment. Driving home, the spouse could lead the conversation about what the couple has planned for that evening. Once through the front door, visual cues help—for example, prominently display a calendar that assigns household chores to spouse and entrepreneur alike. If the entrepreneur has a home office, the spouse should, ideally, lay claim to a comparable private space.

Some couples seek balance by giving the spouse authority over matters domestic. That delineation has eased tension in both domains for Staci Bejcek, who works with her husband, Behfar Jahanshahi, in his IT consulting business, InterWorks, based in Stillwater, Oklahoma. Now that she makes final decisions on such critical matters as family expenditures and the upbringing of their daughter, Staci is more comfortable with her husband's buck-stops-here stance at the office. "I no longer personalize work arguments or feel like I'm being attacked if he disagrees with something I do at work," she said. "I know that he has based this decision on what he ultimately feels is best for the company, even if that goes against what I think is right." Meanwhile, Behfar increasingly helps with chores like laundry and food shopping, "just like I help him at work," said Staci. "We back each other up."

The turf division reminds Staci that "this business is his brainchild, not mine, and my role in it is to help make his dream come to life." She is further placated by Behfar's assurance that if she wants to pursue her own entrepreneurial dream someday, he will wholeheartedly support her and celebrate her achievements as she does his. As for Behfar, the arrangement, while imperfect,

Behfar Jahanshahi, Sophia, Staci Bejcek

imposes some order. "Things are moving fast and we don't necessarily always have time to talk," he said. "With a framework in place, we can make decisions without discussion."

A different division of labor benefits couples who try to act as equal partners. Amy and Shawn Kelly are Founders of PicFlips, a Fort Worth, Texas, company that makes custom flipbook party favors. In the early days of the business, both spouses wanted to do everything. Finally, weary of arguing about the specifics of how they conduct their business, they separated the company into two domains. Shawn is in charge of the programmers and licensing deals. Amy coordinates with event planners who want to feature PicFlips products. "Now that we're no longer two chiefs sharing one tipi," Amy said, "we're less inclined to kill each other." Still, the Kellys may only be postponing the inevitable. Separate but equal is rarely sustainable. As companies add employees, hierarchy rears its ugly head. Ultimately, streamlined decision making requires that one person be the boss.

TAKING THE COUPLE OUT OF THE OFFICE AND THE OFFICE OUT OF THE COUPLE
Leave it at the door

Hierarchy isn't the only stressor that trails couples home. Even outside the office, spouses find themselves defaulting to a single topic: work. Dinner table conversation picks up where the afternoon huddle left off, and home ceases to be a sanctuary. In the early days of Stonyfield, our living quarters were about 10 feet from the office. Sometimes after my shift in the yogurt factory, I would meet Gary back in our apartment to make supper. Still in my hairnet and sweaty from the incubator, I'd fret about our endless production problems while his brain clicked away on how to meet that week's payroll. Sitting at the dinner table, we were in no mood to pose that sweet inquiry of the other: "Honey, how was your day?"

It's not just work talk that breaches domestic boundaries; it's work feelings too. For spouses who are frustrated with one another at the office, petty grievances, like one of them forgetting to take out the trash, escalate from misdemeanors into capital crimes. The annoyance that couples suppress in front of other people can explode once they're in private. A different but related problem: after 10 or 12 hours of acting tough and impervious—that is, professional—spouses have trouble segueing into the kind of candid, sensitive communication that nourishes marriages. Problems at work demand yes-or-no solutions that are often arrived at quickly and served up with no explanation. At home, conversation, compromise, and nuance matter.

> "Work can de-energize a romance. Just because a couple gets along in bed doesn't mean they'll get along on the factory floor."

An entrepreneur friend described the dissonance well when he said that working with his wife eroded the "soul quality" of their relationship. "Work can de-energize a romance," he added. "Just because a couple gets along in bed doesn't mean they'll get along on the factory floor."

For some lucky couples, the work

relationship infuses fresh energy into the domestic one. Roger Wellington, who used to work with his wife in her design business, shared her passion for the company. Roger described talking shop with her as being "like a drug."

> Married couples often don't talk together much as the relationship matures. They've heard it all before, all the stories. So when there's this new gush of energy, it's sexy. She valued my opinion and was engaged and interested. I couldn't remember the last time my wife actually wanted to hear what I had to say.

The drug, unfortunately, was not strong enough medicine to remedy other ailments in the couple's marriage. They eventually divorced.

Sometimes, the business relationship threatens the marriage, and the couple has to make a choice. Personally, I never blanched at the prospect of parting ways with Stonyfield. But if the spouse loves her job and sees herself as part of a family business, that choice can be fraught. I spoke with one couple that has realized their marriage would be healthier if the wife eventually leaves her husband's company. But the wife is engaged in some challenging projects and is reluctant to go. The husband worries that if his wife quits for the sake of the relationship, she'll resent him for the loss of what she sees as her dream job.

For those hanging in there, it's important to accept that "work-life balance" is a fantasy. Compartmentalize, yes, but be realistic about how much you can do so. You can't make your home into a clean room, with a protective airlock at the entrance to keep psychic contaminants out. If the business is top of mind for each of you, you're going to discuss it. But try to limit your conversation to a recap of the day's highs and lows and the sharing of creative ideas that excite you both. Avoid conversations that double-down on the stress you're

> Try to limit your conversation to a recap of the day's highs and lows and the sharing of creative ideas that excite you both.

supposed to be escaping. Don't nag each other about work left undone. Don't dwell on mistakes made during the day. And most importantly, eschew impromptu performance reviews.

I also find it best to steer clear of topics that require critical or detailed thinking, especially when only one spouse is heavily invested in the subject. If the husband says he'd rather analyze relativity theory than last week's sales numbers, his wife needs to take the hint.

YOUR MARRIAGE ON PUBLIC DISPLAY
We rave at the office

The company-home membrane is permeable from both sides. Starved for time alone, spouses at work understandably lapse into discussions—sometimes heated ones—about kids and mortgage payments. Couples track their domestic lives into the office like muddy footprints.

That's dangerous, because employees have their noses in the air for any whiff of drama. Marital strife is inherently interesting, and sometimes it's a clue to the state of the business. When raised voices are just discernible behind closed doors, staff can't tell whether a couple is riled up about impending layoffs or an impending visit from an in-law. Either way, visible friction is a distraction and ineluctably erodes the sense of professionalism. "You need to keep emotions hidden at the office," said Michael McMillan, sales director at Chicago-based Answer Center America, who works with his wife in his mother's company. "Even if my wife and I are arguing about work issues, the employees assume we're having problems at home."

Ruth Harms, of Harms Engineering, thinks some disagreement between spouses in the office is healthy, so long as it's restricted to work matters. She's found that employees who see her disagree with her husband, the company's president, are more comfortable voicing their own dissenting opinions. Several employees have told Ruth they appreciate and have learned from the couple's collegial differences. Still, Ruth restricts contrary comments to noncritical issues:

> If we are in a staff meeting and he suggests we have the company picnic on the second Tuesday of June, I am very comfortable saying I think we should consider another day because Tuesdays are bad for one reason or another. However, if he announces some new company policy that I'm not comfortable with, I won't challenge him in front of everyone else. If I have real concerns about it, I will talk about it to him at home. If I strongly challenge him about something important in front of others it feels like a put-down to him—*because I am his wife*. It feels different to him than if an employee had said the same thing. And I think it feels different to the employees too.

For Nicole and Peter Dawes, public debate is more robust. They have vigorous, open disagreements—which they ultimately resolve—about work issues while they are at the office. The couple said employees at their small company, Late July Organic Snacks, in Barnstable, Massachusetts, understand that they are engaging as coworkers, not as husband and wife. Peter's view is that the company wouldn't be as successful if he and Nicole didn't stick to their guns. "When every penny of your life is invested in something, it's pretty scary," he said. "We have different perspectives. We get passionate. But then we'll have coffee and go for a walk."

The spouse's unique relationship with the entrepreneur also affects her treatment by the rest of the staff. The CEO is lonely at the top; by association, his spouse is also isolated from peers and colleagues. Even when the spouse takes pains to show she gets no special privileges, other workers are always aware that she—unlike them—doesn't have to worry about losing her job. The (usually correct) perception is that the spouse has the boss's ear, and so employees may tiptoe around her for fear of saying or doing something that gets them in trouble. Alternatively, they may try to curry favor with the spouse so as to win an influential advocate.

Some spouses find themselves occasional pawns in political chess games. At Mindbody, both Jill's husband, Rick, and her boss, Bob, will sometimes tell her things they don't want the other man to know. More frequently, they use her as a go-between when they'd rather not discuss an issue directly. Although this arrangement puts Jill in an awkward position, it can work to the company's benefit. Acting as a diplomat, she softens the message, making it easier for both to accept information they need to hear.

Entrepreneurs can't—and shouldn't—pretend their spouses are just like any other employees. But neither should they go overboard trying to avoid shows of favoritism. Struggling to appear all business, CEOs can be abrupt or officious with their spouses, giving shorter-than-normal shrift to their opinions and ideas. One spouse complained to me that her husband is often impatient with her at work. He never acts that way at home or with other employees. His behavior makes her resentful, and the employees—who, of course, notice everything—uncomfortable.

Ideally the couple at work will model a healthy, warm, respectful relationship. That, in turn, affects how other employees treat one another, their suppliers, and their customers. Who knows? They may even be nicer to their own spouses at home.

THE SIDEKICK'S LAMENT
Making room in the spotlight for two

I've been explaining how couples can work comfortably together inside their companies. But out in the world, the prestige differential may rankle even when the power differential between spouses does not. Although not all entrepreneurs seek the celebrity of a Steve Jobs or a

Richard Branson, the limelight seems to find them. Some couples—Lucille Ball and Desi Arnaz, Tim and Nina Zagat—successfully conjoined their identities on the company marquee. But often one light burns brighter in public, even if in private the couple shares power more or less equitably. In the business community, at social functions, and even within the company itself, people see the entrepreneur (creative, dynamic, visionary) and his "helper" (emotionally supportive, administratively practical). The spousal designation ("This is my wife, Eve. She handles marketing.") can be deflating when colleagues or customers suspect Eve earned her place by walking down the aisle.

Even long-standing, key contributors may be relegated to second-class status. Aileen Calligaris has been Vice President of her husband's eponymous satellite-electronics company, based in Kingston, Ontario, for 20 years.

> Marco won a sales contest, and I thought, "Gee, I closed most of those sales." It wasn't his fault. It's just the way people think. They see you as the boss's wife and not as an equal partner. They will joke about the wife being the "real boss"—wink, wink. Once we went to meet a sales rep in downtown Toronto, and the rep suggested I go off shopping with his wife. At cocktail parties people will say, "Oh, you work for your husband." I like to think that we work together. The business wouldn't be here without me either.

Aileen admits that her modesty has contributed to the misperception. She handles most of the company's critical and strategic work and is responsible for planning, budgeting, financing, marketing, and human resources. Yet when people ask what she does, her instinct has been to sabotage herself

Marco and Aileen Calligaris.

and respond, "I do the books" or "I work for my husband." "It's easy
to discount your own worth," she told me. Recently, Aileen has been
pushing back when she and Marco meet with employees and customers, and defining her own role more assertively. "Now I try to answer
people by saying, 'I have my own business, in custom electronics. I
work with my husband.' People pick up on cues."

Aileen recognizes that in the past she's played into a gender stereo-
type. It's unfortunate, but still true, that even within equal partnerships
the wife is often assumed to be subordinate. A friend who started a
chain of natural foods stores with her husband experienced a twinge of
resentment when he was recognized as a "Businessman of the Year" in
a White House ceremony. "I was in the audience, applauding, and felt
proud," she said. "My husband knew I deserved the award too.

"A woman's role in business is usually unofficial," my friend added.
"Most often, it's the woman who's busting her ass privately. Along the
way I've always had to tell people, 'Hello, I did this too!'"

Men who work for their entrepreneurial wives may suffer from
reverse expectations. Feeling unfulfilled as a trademark lawyer, Ron
Abrams joined his wife, Sandy, in her company, Moisture Jamzz, a
Beverly Hills maker of skin-conditioning gloves and socks. "It doesn't
bother me when my poker group gives me a hard time, teasing me
for being a tagalong who helps his wife make her feminine-sounding
product," said Ron, who's responsible for invoicing, shipping, and software. "Sandy and I are making a living doing something we enjoy,
while being present for our kids. I checked my ego at the door."

Dr. Kathy Marshack, an Oregon psychologist who has counseled
and written about entrepreneurial couples, said that both men and
women have a difficult time with role reversals in a marriage. When
the wife is the boss, she's apt to be overly deferential to her husband,
fearing that he'll balk at taking direction or mischaracterize leadership as bossiness. The fact that these days more men act as helpmeets
does not mean they feel tranquil in that role. "I see the distress in my
office all the time," said Dr. Marshack. When she points out to her

male clients that their discomfort stems from antiquated social norms, they become conscious of being bound up by convention and are more likely to work on changing their attitudes.

Gender issues notwithstanding, it boils down to the fact that both spouses who work in the business in a serious way derive part of their identities from their jobs, just like everyone else. They want their contributions and achievements recognized. Semantics matter. "Cofounder" (assuming that designation is accurate) says volumes more than a mere job title does.

THE BEST OF ALL POSSIBLE COLLEAGUES
So happy together

Despite all the angst, a lot of couples love working together in a family business. Though in a sense indentured to their own creations, they have the flexibility to set their own hours and schedules. There are other practical benefits: the ready-made carpool buddy, the ability to synchronize vacations. Married colleagues sympathize with each other's stress; understand the need to work evenings or answer business calls on weekends; and offer each other wise and informed counsel. And they avoid the long hours of separation typical in entrepreneurial ventures.

Perhaps most importantly, these husbands and wives enjoy the ways their spouses' minds work. They fantasize and brainstorm together and get a kick out of watching each other in action. They value time spent in the company because it is time spent in each other's company. The intensity of the shared experience strengthens their bond. As Nicole Dawes of Late July Organic Snacks put it, "I can't imagine doing my life's work with another person."

On the job, spouses may gain new respect for each other. A wife or husband can appear better organized, more focused, more dynamic than at home. You experience a frisson of excitement seeing the one

you love looked up to by others. Gloria Sharrar went to work with her
husband, Dave, when—following a layoff—he started City Parking,
in Richmond, Virginia. In more than 30

> On the job, spouses
> may gain new respect
> for each other.

years of marriage, she had never seen him
so energetic and motivated. "I feel like I
rediscovered Dave," she told me. "I asked
him, 'Were you always like this, and I just
never noticed?'"

For some, the prospect of working together may sound like a little too much "us time." As one couple put it, "We reached our 40th
anniversary in 12 years." But just because you're in the same company
doesn't mean you sit in each other's laps. I spoke with a woman who
designed her baking business so that she could manage it from home,
while her husband works at the bakery. "We don't want to be judging
each other's every move," she said. Another couple, in the printing
business, joke that the carpeted section of the office is her domain, and
the concrete floor area, housing the presses, is his.

Packed agendas, as much as office blueprints, prevent many spouses
from scoring more than quick "visuals" of each other during the
day. Yet that's enough to make them feel connected. Every glimpse
reinforces the message: we are doing this
together. Jo Ann Rossi, who runs Zooom
Printing, in Richmond, Virginia, with her
husband, Ben, put it this way:

> Working together is a blessing. I like
> the fact that I see him a lot, that our
> lives are so intertwined. I do real-
> ize, though, that we often confuse
> together time at work for intimate
> time as a couple. People think we're
> together all day, but our schedules are
> completely different. It's like we're
> running a race side by side. If he

Ben Rossi and his daughter, Nora.

worked these long hours away from me and our family I'd get sad, and that would turn into mad and resentful. I'd feel abandoned. We may not have much quality time together, but we get to see each other frequently during the day. Even the dog comes to work with us.

There are times, too, when the companies—like children—hold together couples that might otherwise break apart. Of course, neither offspring nor business can be expected to glue a truly bad marriage together indefinitely. Nor should they. But sometimes the very thing that puts the greatest burden on a marriage can provide a reason to save it when other ties fray. A wise person once told me that marital reconciliation is possible as long as both spouses aren't out of love at the same time. For company owners, I would add: as long as both spouses aren't out of love with each other *and the business* at the same time.

One woman who works in her husband's business told me that in times of stress she used to fantasize that an appealing job would materialize for him, tempting him to sell his company. Recently, though, she's realized that company building and life building have become the same thing. She compared her change of heart to the moment when a person starts thinking of an adopted city as "home." "This business has become an integral part of who we are as a couple," she said.

But that never happened for Gary and me. One spring morning, two years after I joined Stonyfield, we had our last business meeting in his office. By mutual agreement, we decided I should leave the company. Our business situation at the time was dire, and when I got pregnant, I became concerned that our chronic, extreme stress would affect the baby's health. Also, we had both learned something important. Though personally compatible, we did not work well together. We chose to protect our relationship, which had existed before the business and which we wanted to exist long after it.

We smiled and embraced. I turned on my heel and walked the 10 feet back home.

Things to Talk About

- You can't avoid talking about work at home, but you can avoid subjects that provoke palpitations. Identify topics that are permissible (new ideas, long-term plans, highlights of the day) and those that aren't (worst-case scenarios, ad hoc performance reviews).

- Personal relationships don't always translate neatly into professional environments. How will you behave toward each other in the workplace? Is it OK to question or criticize each other in front of employees? Should all personal subjects be verboten?

- How will you distribute responsibilities at home to achieve a reasonable balance with your roles in the company?

- Entrepreneurs tend to attract outsize attention. Spouses often feel eclipsed. How can the entrepreneur ensure that her spouse receives due credit in the eyes of others?

Things to Do

- Whether this arrangement is permanent or just for now, establish job definitions and working conditions upfront. Titles, responsibilities, reporting relationships—all the things that are spelled out for new hires should be addressed.

- After six months or a year, step back and evaluate the arrangement. This isn't a performance review. It's a relationship review, with the option of reconfiguring either spouse's role.

- Find a mentor, a therapist, or a business coach to mediate when you disagree seriously over something related to your jobs.

- Agree on some rituals—lighting a candle, turning off your computer, just changing your clothes—that signify to each other that the workday has ended and family time has begun.

Chapter 4

Bed and Boardroom

Employees in the kitchen. Customers in the
bathroom. There's nothing like a home-based
business for amping up the family stress.

W hen I moved up to the farm in 1986, I was newly engaged
and fresh out of living alone in my own apartment. I adjusted
easily to cohabiting with Gary. It was shacking up with his
business that was hard.

As I mentioned in the first chapter, for four years Gary and I
shared a dilapidated farmhouse with Stonyfield Yogurt. The huge,
wood-heated building housed the company's offices and yogurt
works, as well as an apartment for us and another for Samuel, Louisa,
and five of their six kids.

Living with Stonyfield, we had zero privacy. Trucks groaned up
our narrow gravel driveway at all hours. Employees were ever present,
glancing at what was for dinner and frequently using our bathroom
when the public one was occupied. (The employee restroom was the
only one with a bathtub. I love a good soak, but if I tried to grab one
late at night a worker's more urgent requirements would invariably
send me scrambling.) When our best yogurt maker had to work the
night shift and couldn't find a babysitter for her son, yours truly would

rock the boy to sleep. Our kitchen table overlooked the yogurt works, so we couldn't get through a meal without distractions from outside. (Did that guy really just throw a lit cigarette into the Dumpster?)

Hosting guests was a challenge. Friends and relatives anticipating a relaxing weekend in the country would inevitably get caught up in the madness. Kicking back chez Hirshberg might involve grabbing a shovel to dig out a truck stuck in the mud or off-loading pallets— before going to bed and nearly freezing to death in our unheated spare bedroom.

One afternoon, I walked into our kitchen cradling bags of groceries and found a young man I didn't recognize removing cutlery and plates from our cupboard. I stopped in the door-way and stared. "We have a lunch meeting in the office," he explained nonchalantly. I was speechless, feeling invaded at the most basic level. This was my kitchen. My *stuff.* Then I chided myself. These people were keeping the company afloat, and we all believed in using fewer disposables. Why couldn't I feel good about sharing? Why was I being so uncool? Still, I thought, there have to be boundaries. The only question was, where did they lie?

> There have to be boundaries. The only question is, where do they lie?

That question was answered a few months later. One Sunday morning while Gary and I were in bed, an unfamiliar teenager strolled into our room. He announced that he'd been hired to clean the offices, and did we know where to find a broom? By Monday night, our apartment door had a lock on it. But that bit of iron was mostly symbolic, a finger in a leaky dike. Employees, job applicants, investors, and suppliers still flowed freely through our home. Only now they knocked first.

In 2007, the most recent year for which there are statistics, there were more than 18 million home-based businesses. (Most likely those numbers have swelled along with unemployment.) The major-ity of new companies spend at least some time under the founder's roof, for obvious reasons. Home-based businesses are rent free, and the entrepreneur can usually take a tax write-off for a home office. They make it easy for entrepreneurs who still have other jobs to cram start-up activity into odd hours. Parents can be there for children after school or establish their company's proof of concept before springing for day care. And, of course, the commute is achievable in slippers. On its face, then, starting a business from home is the one low-hassle element in a notoriously hassle-rich venture.

But that assumes the company remains a part-time-one-person-one-computer affair. And how likely is that when an entrepreneur is behind the wheel? As home-based businesses grow, they gobble up square footage as hungrily as they devour hours and mental turf. Born in the corner of a dining room or basement, they expand their footprints to accommodate inventory, technology, and packing stations. Employees make the scene, blocking the spouse's car in the driveway and storing their lunches in the family fridge. As operations crank up, the circadian rhythms of personal life cede to the unrelenting pace of production and sales. If you're not careful, what started as a home-based business becomes a business where you and your family also happen to live.

> If you're not careful, what started as a home-based business becomes a business where you and your family also happen to live.

For most families, space is a less emotional subject than is time. Piles of marketing collateral stacked on the dining room table probably won't, by themselves, provoke tearful recriminations. Still, incursions on the family's property and invasions of their privacy are yet another straw laid across the camel's back. And, given all the pressures entrepreneurial families endure, that is already one deeply stressed-out camel.

Admittedly, there is romance in launching a start-up from home. After all, the official "birthplace of Silicon Valley" is David and Lucile Packard's rustic one-car garage, where Hewlett-Packard got its start. (Bill Hewlett lived in a shack next to the garage. I would have loved to ask Lucile how they managed the bathroom situation.) But whether the company is a permanent fixture in the home or just there for gestation, the entrepreneur and her family must establish rules if they hope to cohabit with it successfully.

BECAUSE IT'S THERE
Why not work 24 hours when you can?

Of course, certain hazards of living with a business apply to anyone with a home office. The problem with the office being footsteps away is that the office is footsteps away. We're all familiar with that slippery slope of nipping in after dinner—just to clean up a few emails—and emerging at midnight. A friend of mine who frequently found herself making middle-of-the-night visits to her home office eventually put a sign on its door—"Get a life"—to remind her somnambulating self that she was being obsessive and whatever it was could wait until morning.

Because this problem of working nonstop is universal these days, I won't belabor it. But I will suggest that the temptation is more irresistible for company owners than for regular salaried folk. A company founder is not "putting in hours"—she is building what to her is something new, exciting, and wholly her own. The entrepreneur working in an outside office recognizes that, much as she hates to tear herself away, at some point she has to pack up and go home. The entrepreneur already at home faces no such artificial deadlines.

But the ability to work until fingers crab and eyeballs pop out on springs is not the boost to productivity many imagine it to be. Paul Houck and his wife, Kate, own a financial planning consultancy in Richmond, Virginia, that they formerly ran from their home. Paul described how much more effective he became after moving to an office several miles away. The off-site location—specifically, the need to leave it—set boundaries around his workday. And boundaries, he argued, are good for focus and creativity. "If you go to an art class and they say 'do something,' you are stumped," he explained. "But if they say 'paint within this space,' you suddenly have a structure to work with, and the ideas start to flow." Productivity may not be the only thing at stake. There are good reasons why we limit the hours of pilots and truckers and question the alertness of doctors toiling long shifts. Errors made by exhausted entrepreneurs may not threaten lives, but they can certainly threaten livelihoods.

No commute also means no transition from work to family, and therefore no time to decompress. One entrepreneur's spouse complained to me that after her husband started working from their home, his interactions with the family changed. "He used to come home tired but happy to see me and the kids," she said. "Now he passes me in the hallway and doesn't even see me because he's thinking about work."

Then there's the danger that home-based entrepreneurs will go overboard making themselves accessible by phone or email. That's partly because they draw no distinctions between work and home, and partly because they want to prove that their enterprise is no less professional than one housed in an office. Amy Gray, who runs the agency New Leaf Speakers out of her Massachusetts home, is careful not to let the ability to write her own rules become the freedom to write her own prison sentence. Although she

Amy Gray.

now adheres strictly to a nine-hour workday, Amy said it was years before she mustered the courage to do so. "Earlier in my career, I wasn't confident enough in myself to believe that people would still want to do business with me if they couldn't reach me 24/7," Amy said. "You don't want to wind up envious of those who *don't* have home offices."

Home, too, is full of distractions. The spouse constantly (justifiably) complains when the business-burdened entrepreneur claims an exemption from household chores. But she also worries when she finds him loading the dishwasher or folding laundry instead of trying to rustle up sales. Entrepreneurs are as prone to procrastination as anyone else, and such trivial, undemanding chores offer the chance to scratch off a couple of To Do list items without having to buckle down and prepare those PowerPoint slides for investors.

Some women entrepreneurs must also contend with outmoded gender expectations and the additions to their workloads that result. Women with home businesses are regularly expected to somehow find time to cook, shop, and clean as well as run the business enterprise. The spouse needs to understand that although he is gone during the day and his entrepreneurial wife is in the house, she is still *working*. It's not OK for him to come home and nonchalantly ask, "What's for dinner?"

FAMILY AS AN INTERRUPTION
I love you. Now scram.

It sounds idyllic at first. While the business operates from home, the entrepreneur's family will actually see more of him. Eager to secure his spouse's buy-in on the new business, the founder waxes Norman Rockwell-ish about how he'll be able to make the kids breakfast, greet them when they come off the bus, help with their homework. Those images overcome the spouse's reservations. Spending so much time at home, her husband will be more accessible to her and the children than ever. Who said that entrepreneurship was hard on families?

Home-based businesses are a big tease. They dangle the entrepreneur before his loving family (Dad's home!) and then immediately snatch him away (Dad's locked his door!). It's especially rough if the entrepreneur is coming off a normal job outside the house. A friend who wrestles with these issues observed that in the minds of most people, including his wife and kids, the notion is ingrained that work is something you leave home to do. So they assume that if he's home he ought to be available to the family. Sometimes, his wife pokes her head into his office to see if he'd like to take a break and have lunch together. "She doesn't understand that I just don't want to break the work spell," he said. "I'm in the zone and need to stay there. But she takes it personally."

Children feel the snub more profoundly than they do a parent's absence because they actually *see* her rejecting them. The entrepreneur doesn't mean to be insensitive. She's got to give the business her all, and that means all her attention. And the more interruptions, the longer she'll have to work—not just because it takes time to answer this question or resolve that argument but also because every time her concentration is broken she must refocus. One home-based entrepreneur told me that when her kids are around it takes twice as long to cover the same ground. Another said she is so bothered by noise that even though she can afford a nanny she sends her kids to day care all week. I understand why she does that. Still, it seems sad that the children need to vacate their home so the business can live there instead.

Those who keep their kids home become masters of the anguished shush. Don Lever is a house designer who lives with his wife and six children near Salt Lake City. He operates his business out of a coat closet near the living room of his 1,200-square-foot home. Don described for me a typical workday scenario: "I can't count the number of times I've been on the phone with a client and given my kids the death-stare followed by the finger-across-the-throat signal, or angrily pulled an imaginary zipper across my lips and mouthed the word *Silence.*" Even when he manages to restore

The Lever family (with their sixth child on the way).

quiet, Don worries that clients on the other end of the line sense his distraction. But after he's hung up the phone, Don often feels contrite about his agitation with his kids. "Sometimes I'll go back to them and say, 'Dad didn't handle that very well,'" he admitted. "I regret that my children have to share my work space. But what do you do?"

On the subject of the death stare, I sympathize with both Don and his kids because I have both given and received it. Often I've walked into Gary's home office while he's been on a business call only to see him wince at my intrusion. Now that I work full-time from home, I find myself reacting the same way. When Gary or one of the kids interrupts me on the phone, I brush them off with that frantic wave that is more desperate dismissal than greeting. Such behavior inflicts small hurts, little bits of damage that accumulate.

One spouse complained that her husband expects her to keep the kids quiet all the time—even when they're playing outdoors since the clamor is audible though open windows. "We can't always tiptoe around," she said. Her children enjoy having their father home, but "they've gone from appreciating what he does to hating what he does, because they can't bring their friends home," she told me. "They always ask me if Dad's around, because his presence defines what can happen in the house."

One advantage to owning your own company is the freedom to choose those with whom you'll do business, as well as when and where. Home-based entrepreneurs can often work with people in similar circumstances, who will likely cut them some slack. One entrepreneur described to me a phone conversation with her publicist during which the entrepreneur was playing farm with her kids and the publicist was playing parking garage with hers. Such moments are better than a morning on the golf course for building rapport.

WHOSE HOUSE IS IT ANYWAY?
When business interests dictate

It's one thing to accommodate an entrepreneur-spouse at home, another to accommodate her company. If the family doesn't already resent the business for absorbing so much of the entrepreneur's time and attention, they can become irritated by the interloper's intrusion into their previously private terrain.

Demands on space are an obvious challenge. Fifteen years ago, when Sandy Abrams (whose husband, Ron, was mentioned in chapter 3) launched Moisture Jamzz, she filled every room of her Los Angeles apartment with fabric rolls and shipping boxes. The dining room table was piled high with packing tape and stationary. One day an earthquake tumbled the fabric and boxes in front of the door. Sandy and Ron spent 10 terrified minutes clearing a pathway so they could exit.

Sandy Abrams, with her sons Clay and Brock Abrams.

Still, physical intrusions are a relatively small annoyance. You can stub your toe on a packing crate, but the crate won't walk in on you while you're in the tub. As the company develops, the entrepreneur, who may have begun as a soloist with few connections, will increasingly deal with other people. The more people who circulate through the founder's home, the bigger the pain it is for the family.

Home designer Don Lever frequently meets with clients at his house. During those times, Don needs his wife, Rachael, to keep a lid on his kids' noise. He feels bad about imposing on her, but, he explained: "Imagine pitching a client on the design for their new home at my conference table—read, 'kitchen table'—and then having three of the kids decide that it's Kung Fu Panda time in the bedrooms." In some instances, Don encourages clients to bring their own children along, thus converting the homey, family-filled setting from a liability into a benefit. The hitch: while Don conducts business with the adults, he expects Rachael to babysit both broods. Rachael wants to help Don, but she considers being dragooned into the nanny role a questionable breach of the work-life barrier.

Entrepreneurs who routinely see clients at home are also, understandably, concerned about appearances. If they don't have a fancy office to show off, they at least want visitors to sit on couches free of cracker crumbs and use bathroom sinks un-streaked by dried toothpaste. Consequently, they expect their families to keep the house cleaner than is perhaps natural for households without a professional maid service. Spouses automatically assume more work by dint of entrepreneurs' packed schedules and frequent travel. Informing them they must also maintain the house at the level of an *Architectural Digest* spread is, many would argue, beyond the pale.

I spoke with Anna Breyer whose husband, Matt, runs a construction company in Reading, Pennsylvania. Matt would like Anna to keep the kitchen clean for employees and visiting clients, but she balks at that expectation. "It's my house, too," she told me. "I don't want to always make sure the dishes are done. I realize we have to make sacrifices. But this is a house with kids. It's lived in."

Lisa Johnson.

If the battle against creeping chaos can't be won, the entrepreneur may choose to keep customers or clients away rather than risk their good opinion. Lisa Johnson of Norwich, Vermont, produces her Yummy Yammy dips and sauces in her home kitchen. She used to hold tasting parties in her home and would carefully straighten up before guests arrived. But Lisa lives in an old New England house cluttered with coats and plants and baseballs and boxes of sweet potatoes stored on every available surface. Despite the bleach and hairnets she trots out on production days, and her home caterer's license issued by the state of Vermont, her kitchen is never going to be the reassuring vista of gleaming stainless steel most people expect from a food-production facility. She finally stopped hosting the parties, worried that the informality might cause customers to question the quality of her products. (This issue will likely soon be moot, since Lisa plans to co-pack her products at a professional facility.)

When the home is hopelessly inhospitable, entrepreneurs generally suggest some public spot for meetings. If Don Lever senses clients may question his professionalism when confronted with his coat-closet office and his very homey home, he diplomatically asks whether they'd prefer to meet at a coffee house or in their own homes. Chicago business consultant Amy Riley, whose desk occupies a corner of her dining room, conducts client meetings at the local Peet's or Panera. But increasingly she finds that the clanging of dishes and shouted greetings can be as distracting as the commotion in her house.

All these problems go away if the entrepreneur owns a house and can afford to build a separate entrance into a room set aside for the company. If a good fence makes a good neighbor, a closed door makes a calmer family.

EMPLOYEES OVERRUN THE HOUSE
Could you ask them to flush?

The home-based entrepreneur may entertain a customer once, or once in a while. Employees, however, can seem like nine-to-five housemates. Of course, many companies move out when it's time to start hiring. But the bootstrapper's credo calls for keeping costs as low as possible as long as possible. Entrepreneurs who might be considered ready to fly the nest instead keep cramming in additional squawking fledglings.

While entrepreneurs may not feel compelled to keep their environs as pristine for staff as they do for clients, the intrusion on their privacy is greater. When a business owner is sick, she may feel like a prisoner in her bedroom. A trip to the kitchen for tea risks an encounter with an employee who's there on the same mission. The boss may not be in the mood to deal with business questions or even be well enough to force small talk while waiting interminably for the water to boil.

When employees work in your home, they automatically are privy to many details of your life and the life of your family. You may be able to keep some big secrets confidential. (That's not always so easy, however. One entrepreneur trying to hide a significant medical problem told me she had to make excuses and run to her bedroom every time a doctor's office called.) But the trivial, the distasteful, and the embarrassing will eventually reveal themselves.

These revelations are, of course, awkward for employees as well. They are acutely aware of the inherent asymmetry: they have a window into your intimate life, but you don't have a reciprocal window into theirs. They don't know your secrets because they earned your trust over years of devoted friendship, but because you (or your spouse) cut their paychecks. They know when you are sick, how often you scream at your kids, what groceries you buy, what brand of toilet tissue you use. They know what you are having for dinner, whether your spouse is mad at you, how often your mother-in-law visits, and that you clean frantically just before she arrives. You wish they did not know these things. They wish they didn't either.

> What family wants to literally air its dirty laundry to strangers?

Families have an even worse time of it, and most spouses have at least a few war stories to tell. Anna Breyer, wife of construction company owner Matt, has experienced aggravations similar to what I went through at Stonyfield. She is irked that trucks and trailers are always parked in her yard. Workers have free reign of the family's kitchen and

The Breyer family.

bathroom. "Sometimes I'll have to sign for an early-morning lumber delivery while I'm still in my PJs and the dog's barking and my kid's screaming," Anna told me. She feels awkward having employees walk through her house when it's piled high with dishes and soiled clothes. What family wants to literally air its dirty laundry to strangers?

Fortunately, over time, many of these "strangers" become trusted colleagues and even friends, at which point the discomfort diminishes. Still, not all good workers are also pleasant. They may not even be safe—a serious concern, especially for parents. Anna told me about a couple of employees who made her distinctly uncomfortable. Occasionally they would show up at her door, looking for a paycheck, on a Saturday morning when she was alone with the kids. Matt eventually fired them. None of our Stonyfield workers ever gave me the creeps. But we had our share of oddballs that, under other circumstances, I probably would have given a wide berth. Instead, I would emerge from my bedroom clad only in a bathrobe and collide with them on the way to the kitchen.

BUILD UP THIS WALL!
The importance of setting boundaries

Running a home-based business requires erecting invisible boundaries—of time as well as space—and then enforcing them. Be disciplined about not letting your work overrun everything else. Think of your business not as home-based but rather as dining-room-table-based or back-corner-of-the-basement-behind-the-furnace-based. Resist co-opting part of the house that the family uses regularly. It's psychologically a good idea to keep your work space out of the bedroom, if that's possible. Set business hours and keep them—no customers or employees before 8:00 AM or after 6:00 PM. Let every family member know when outsiders will be on the premises. Above all, don't make the house any less a home by, for example, forbidding children from having friends over lest they turn up at the same time as a client. You can insist that your kids behave during business hours. But you can't flick a switch and shut them off.

Regarding kid behavior: we all know that children—especially young ones—can be unpredictable and hard to control. You can't give them an employee handbook and expect compliance. So it's best to establish a few very simple, very strict rules right from the start. For example, if Mommy's door is shut, then don't enter unless something or someone is on fire. Make sure the nanny or babysitter knows under what circumstances she may interrupt you and when to just let the kids duke it out.

One entrepreneur uses her outfits to telegraph approachability to her family. She wears business clothes when she doesn't want to be interrupted, sweatpants if it's OK. "Dressing for work also keeps me mentally on my game," she said. "Somehow the PJs, sweats, and sloppy jeans send my mind a different signal than if I'm in business attire."

Family members are often eager to help out with the business. In a home-based company, that willingness is easy to exploit. The entrepreneur must remind himself that just because his wife and kids share space with his business doesn't mean they work there. They are not free labor to fall back on whenever the founder needs someone to type labels or collate copies.

As much as possible, keep employees segregated from the family, for the benefit of both. Even small gestures help. For example, things improved for Anna and Matt Breyer when she put a coffeemaker and microwave oven in the garage for employee use, so the workers didn't have to come into the kitchen. At Stonyfield Farm, Gary and I eventually built a cheap bathroom with a tub where I could bathe in peace.

Finally, get innovative. Kayme Pumphrey owns a placement service for in-home child care in Chicago. She works out of her own home, so she can be with her children, and leases office space for her staff of seven. Kayme starts each workday with a two-hour phone conversation with employees and views their email stream in order to monitor their work. Maybe once a quarter she'll go into the office. Amy Gray of New Leaf Speakers does not have children, but her use of technology could be advantageous to those who are trying to sequester work from family life. Amy and her single employee, who works in another state, keep Skype open all day so they can see each other or IM whenever they need to. "I still feel like I work with her," said Amy. "Because of Skype we can see each other's facial expressions and have that human interaction, that nonverbal communication."

Every family will have to perform its own calculus—based on its limitations and activities—to find a solution to the home-business equation. But if the entrepreneur locates her office at home solely to save money, then she and her family are more apt to consider it an invasion. Though cost-savings is an excellent reason in itself, other perks help tip the scale. For example, the ability to stay home with one's children can make all the hassle and intrusion worthwhile. Or, being liberated from what would otherwise be a long, tension-filled, and frustrating commute. One reason my memories of living at the farm are mostly disagreeable is because there were few personal benefits to being there for Gary and for me. While it was a relief to have our rent paid by the business, that was cold comfort on those mornings when I woke up to the stench of plant effluent.

TWO PEOPLE, TWO VENTURES, ONE HOME
Parallel play

These days, Gary and I are learning to cohabit with each other's enterprises. He often works out of his home office, and I am a full-time writer and frequent speaker. I'm not an entrepreneur—not in the sense Gary is, anyway. I don't own a company. The biggest thing I risk is my time. Still, I get what it means to do something I'm passionate about, and to do it in an environment where I could keep doing it 24 hours a day if I was physically able. Working from home, I routinely find myself ignoring some of the guidelines described in this chapter. I'm typing this sentence while propped up with pillows in my bed, on what could otherwise be a mellow Sunday morning filled with newspapers and popovers. So much for keeping strict work hours and banishing the computer from the bedroom.

Gary has been very tolerant of my work mania. He knows that the pot is in no position to call the kettle black. Imperfect as our arrangement is, we have devised our own rules for making it work. For example, if one of us is on the phone, we each deliver messages by silently slipping into a room and placing a sticky note in the other person's line of sight. And we have trained ourselves to distinguish between physical presence and availability. Though my eyes tell me that Gary is in his home office, he is not, for my purposes, at home. He is not available for figuring out where to meet friends for dinner or how to celebrate Danielle's birthday. And now that I'm working hard in my own home office, Gary accepts the same rules. I don't take it personally anymore. Nor does he.

> Any family that shares space with a company must create the mental and emotional equivalent of physical distance.

Home-based businesses are usually a mixed bag: somewhat convenient and somewhat onerous. Any family that shares space with a company must create the mental and emotional equivalent of physical distance—the gap that keeps their worlds from colliding. Sometimes, all it takes to make things work is a closed door or a second microwave or some sticky notes to place in front of your spouse. It might not hurt to scrawl—as my friend did—"Get a life" on one or two of them.

Things to Talk About

- How will everyone in the house feel about sacrificing some privacy?

- What is reasonably appropriate behavior for children sharing a house with a business?

- What, if anything, are family members expected to do for the business? Pitch in, in a pinch? Work harder to keep the place presentable?

- How long will this situation continue? The entrepreneur and spouse should agree on milestones for moving the company into a home of its own.

Things to Do

- Set work hours and, as much as possible, stick to them.

- Set up a work space in a part of the house that gets little people traffic. Try to contain inventory and office supplies to that area.

- Establish rules about when the entrepreneur may or may not be interrupted. Agree on some signals: perhaps he hangs a necktie on the door when he's on an important phone call or dons sweats when he wouldn't mind a few minutes of company.

- Let employees know what parts of the house are off-limits.

Chapter 5

Sharing Gary

The entrepreneur's business always wants to steal
his time. Now it has a sexy little accomplice in
the form of a smartphone.

Her name is Bond Girl.

She sleeps on Gary's bedside table and wakes us each morning. When he reaches to silence her, he can't resist scrolling down her sleek silver body to check for last night's emails. When we dine at restaurants, she reclines close to his hand, purring randomly. She knows all Gary's secrets and contains all his memories. She alone knows where he'll be today, tomorrow, and ever after.

My normally calm husband turned quietly frantic when he misplaced Bond Girl a while back. She turned up after a 15-minute search, and I joked that it would be interesting to see just how long he could live without her. Not missing a beat, Gary replied, "I think you just did."

Over the almost 30 years that Gary has been in business, we've marveled at each new technology. I remember my amazement at our first PC in 1985 and first fax machine in 1987. Then cell phones came along. But none of those affected the texture of our relationship the way Bond Girl has. Although the barrier between work and the-rest-of-life has been eroding steadily, it's taken the smartphone to shatter it altogether. Her incessant buzzing—Check me! Check me! It just might be important!—slices into our family cocoon. Bond Girl gives Gary constant access to the world. But more disturbingly, she gives the world constant access to him.

Of course the preoccupation with all things digital is not unique to company builders like my husband. It spans all ages, all professions, and, increasingly, all nations. I recently read an article in the French magazine *Elle* about a woman driven mad by her husband's BlackBerry use. One evening, after he checked messages during a romantic dinner *à deux*, she grabbed the device and plunked it into his ice water.

> "Never-off" is a natural state for entrepreneurs because they are never done building their companies.

But business owners are especially wedded to their devices. "Never-off" is a natural state for entrepreneurs because they are never done building their companies. There are always 10 more calls they can make, 20 people who need something from them, 50 tasks that could be done or done better, 100 things that could be going wrong. When the CEO gives a client her personal phone number, it sends a powerful message: this company will always be there for you. But then the client uses that number, and the CEO must snap to, even if she's strolling to her seat at the theater. And snap to she does because the client expects immediate access and answers. Like a harried physician, the entrepreneur is always on call.

Most people who check their smartphones obsessively do so because they can't help themselves. Entrepreneurs can't help themselves either. But many also have a reasonable fear of missing something important. It's a vicious cycle. The easier an entrepreneur makes it for customers, employees, and suppliers to reach him, the more those people will email, text, and call. That, in turn, plays to his sense of importance. While he may groan about interruptions, the persistent ringing and his swelling inbox reassure him of his centrality. "I think, therefore I am" gives way to "I communicate, therefore I lead."

So, for entrepreneurs, smartphones are simultaneously the masters who summon them, the servants who do their bidding, and the sycophants who remind them they are leaders. No wonder company owners find them indispensable. And now, of course, we have tablets. I loved entrepreneur Paul Graham's observation on his blog: "Several people have told me they like the iPad because it lets them bring the Internet into situations where a laptop would be too conspicuous. In other words, it's a hip flask."

DON'T LET FREEDOM RING
Time off while still on call is time on

Technology's intrusion into the lives of families like mine is especially irksome, because we have already been invaded. The business takes over our homes, our weekends, our plans for the future. We cohabit with our spouses' work in ways relatives of people in "normal professions" do not. Smartphones and their ilk ensure that there is no crack or crevasse where the demands of the company do not intrude. Our battle for the entrepreneur's undivided attention is lost before it is begun.

Nowhere is this conflict more evident than in the smartphone's assault on leisure time. Entrepreneurs know it's important to occasionally kick back and hang out with loved ones. Still, they see an opportunity cost to every moment they are not working on the business. This is where Bond Girl and her sister sirens get devious. They beguile with the illusion of freedom. With a BlackBerry nestling in the entrepreneur's pocket, he can spend time with his family *and* be accessible to work and consequently manage guilt in both arenas. "I can give you your life back," Bond Girl promises.

Gary believes her. Accompanied by his electronic Girl Friday (more accurately, Girl Sunday through Saturday) he can finally take vacations with an easy conscience. But I would argue that his laptop, my former nemesis, freed him more effectively than Bond Girl has. This is not hairsplitting. Before the BlackBerry, Gary would work on his computer each morning to lighten his load before we left to play for the day. Because the laptop is comparatively bulky and doesn't mix well with sand, sea, and piña coladas, he would leave it behind in the afternoon.

By contrast, Bond Girl goes everywhere with us. She's in the restaurant, on the tennis court, and at the beach. On the surface, these family times "count" as leisure spent together. But in my mind, Gary's not truly in nature if his BlackBerry hitches a ride up the mountain on his hip. If his BlackBerry's at the dinner table with us, then he's not. The way some mourn the loss of wilderness, I grieve the loss of quiet space, free of electronic intrusion and interruption.

The best I can say for this third wheel in our relationship is that she's reasonably unobtrusive. A friend took a trip to Tahiti with her CEO spouse in the pre-BlackBerry dark ages. She described to me how her heart sank as she watched him pacing the white sand of this dreamy Polynesian island, bulky satellite phone in hand, desperately searching for a signal.

In the old days, if Gary expected a call while we were on the beach, he'd bring his cell phone and leave it zipped away in his backpack. But Bond Girl is no mere phone. She is an irresistible superwoman who brings email, instant messages, and the Internet. She is an alarm clock, Rolodex, camera, and calendar keeper. Now while Gary waits for his calls, he can't resist checking his messages and catching up on other tasks. Bond Girl is powerful because entrepreneurs must do everything, and she is a tool for doing everything. She is simply too big to fire.

A BRIEF PAEAN TO THE USURPER

Can't live with her. Can't live without her.

Still, I have to be fair to the other woman. While Bond Girl distracts Gary, he'd also be distracted without her—wondering when and whether to check in with coworkers and business associates. She also helps him dispense with important items quickly and ignore the rest. After Gary took Danielle college shopping, he told me that without his BlackBerry he'd have squandered hours of precious father-daughter time taking work calls. Bond Girl kept those interruptions minimal.

What confounds me is this: the very device freeing Gary to leave work for this trip is the same one ensuring that he's always working. Bond Girl is the solution to the very problem—24/7 connectivity— that she creates.

The paradox is especially problematic for female entrepreneurs. Who needs to be on tap more than a mother with a business? Julie Gordon White, who has three children and a business brokerage firm in Berkeley, California, said she is "guilty of thinking that my beloved BlackBerry allows me to have it all. I have even negotiated deals with six-figure fees at stake from the soccer field." Beth Lang, CEO of Alexa's Angels, based in Windsor, Colorado, texts jokes and quick I-love-you's to her children when she's traveling. At home she must be reachable at odd hours by the Chinese factories that produce her jewelry and accessories. "I'm the parent who's expected to go to the soccer practice and the Valentine's Day party at school," said Beth. "The BlackBerry is what makes that possible."

Julie Gordon White.

Another female CEO observed wryly that financial deals always seem to close during vacations. Her BlackBerry lets her go to the beach with her partner and kids, and discreetly do her work. "Sometimes you can't step out of your business," she said. "So I gladly put up with the burdens of constant connectivity in order to enjoy that walking-around freedom."

Male or female, when you are the one the buck stops with, work can't be limited to normal business hours or times when you are physically present. Most business owners would agree that it is better to escape the office encumbered with electronic devices than to hunker down there interminably. So I will now pause and offer up a heartfelt thank-you to those metal, glass, and plastic familiars that have been making entrepreneurs' lives easier for more than a decade. OK, that's enough of that.

CONNECTIVITY AS A QUALITY-OF-LIFE ISSUE
This is your brain on tech

I hope the previous section proves that I am not a Luddite. I have my own smartphone, although it (he?) does not play the role of superhero in my life (cabana boy, perhaps?). Still, while I love to rag on Gary about Bond Girl, the fact is that I, too, frequently get stuck in technology's Web. Rabbi Steven Kaye of Denver had written me about similar concerns, so I followed up with a phone call to ask him what price he thinks we all pay for our enslavement to devices. Rabbi Kaye said that when he does premarital counseling he finds intrusive technology to be a stressor in most relationships. "People are not present for each other," he said. "You can dwell with someone but still be isolated."

It is probably unfair to blame technology for emotional distancing. The culprit isn't the BlackBerry but rather our behavior in response to it. Smartphones don't kill relationships. Smartphone owners do.

Ehren Weiss and Kelly Gray.

That almost proved true for Kelly Gray. Kelly, a partner in a marketing and advertising firm in Boulder, used to be a BlackBerry addict. At the gym, she would grow nervous about leaving the device in her locker while she worked out. As time passed, her anxiety grew: prolonged absence from her smartphone induced panic attacks. Meanwhile, she was sabotaging her relationship with her boyfriend, Ehren, by taking calls during their purported leisure time together. Kelly explained the problem this way:

> Whether or not you want the person to feel second best, they inevitably will. When I take those calls, not only am I excluding Ehren, but he's hearing a different side of me. Your partner hears you switch into work mode, which can be a little aggressive and foreign. Ehren became not only alienated from the conversation, but alienated from me. Often after these calls, I would start venting about work problems, which steered our conversation away from personal matters and toward business.

Children are even more vulnerable to hurt because their sense of security derives from the love and nurturing of adults. Strangers to the competing fascination of work, they sometimes demand better treatment. Last year, Julie Gordon White's 11-year-old daughter staged a BlackBerry intervention. "My daughter asked me to come sit down at the kitchen table," Julie recalled. "She then said, 'Mom, when you're on your BlackBerry, you're not paying attention. You are nodding, but you're not really listening.'"

Julie apologized and agreed to turn off the device between 5:00 and 9:00 PM. "I don't want them to grow up and say, 'My mom was very successful, but she was always on her BlackBerry,'" she told me. "As parents, we think if we're in the room with them we get points for that. But it doesn't mean we are really present for them." As another CEO mother said, "It's awful to be ignored because someone is playing with a piece of technology."

> "It's awful to be ignored because someone is playing with a piece of technology."

Entrepreneurs also agonize that their behavior enables their children's own addiction. These parents feel hypocritical telling their kids to take a break from screens when they are so patently unable to follow their own advice. During family dinners, they surreptitiously check their phones when they think no one is watching. But of course the kids are aware that their parents have zoned out of the conversation. (This reminds me of the children's book *Danny and the Dinosaur*, in which the titular brontosaurus believes he is successfully hiding behind a telephone pole.) Parents are supposed to be role models. What they model by constantly fiddling with their devices is rudeness. "Do as I say, not as I do" is not an effective parenting strategy.

PUTTING TECHNOLOGY IN ITS PLACE
The no-phone zone

Clearly, entrepreneurs and their families need strategies for dealing with the technology creep. Although there are books on cell-phone etiquette, few rules have become ingrained as social norms. That is likewise true in the world of work, where people keep their smartphones on during business lunches (an entrepreneur I spoke with compared this behavior to scanning the horizon at a cocktail party to see if someone more important walks in). And it is especially true at home.

One place to start is with Steven Covey's admonition (in *The 7 Habits of Highly Effective People*) to distinguish between what is *important* and what is *urgent*. More than 20 years after that book was published, Jody Giles, CIO of the athletic apparel company Under Armour, in Baltimore, still distributes it to employees. "Urgency addiction is nothing new," he said. "But technology has become the great enabler." Jody urges the company's college interns to screen out interruptions that are less than true emergencies. A great many things are important, he said. So, as a rule of thumb, make the most important thing whatever you are doing *right now*. "In meetings or discussions, it's critical that everyone emerge with perfect clarity about what they are going to execute," said Jody. "People can't do that if they've been distracted from the conversation by their BlackBerry."

But prioritizing is a slippery slope. When it's your company, "important" can get upgraded to "urgent" in a twinkling. Entrepreneurs may have better success by simply eliminating temptation. A radical example is Yvon Chouinard. Yvon, the Cofounder (with wife Malinda) of the clothing company Patagonia, based in Ventura, California, does not own a smartphone—or even a computer. He finally broke down and bought a cell phone but leaves it in his car for emergencies only. "My company is as wired as any other," he told me. "I just personally decided to have nothing to do with it. I'm trying to simplify."

> Yvon Chouinard, Cofounder of the clothing company Patagonia, does not own a smartphone—or even a computer.

Yvon believes most non-face-to-face communication is intrusive and a waste of time. His assistant triages incoming emails and prints out those that need a response from the boss. Yvon then dictates his replies. (Maybe a trustworthy assistant who can effectively screen emails is the best productivity tool an entrepreneur can buy.)

Yvon Chouinard.

Most business owners can't imagine going to Yvon's extreme. A reasonable alternative is to carve out technology-free zones both in time and space. Let's start with space. "First and foremost," urged Rabbi Kaye, "unless you are a physician, keep the BlackBerry out of the bedroom!" Many entrepreneurs also banish electronic devices from the dinner table, giving the family precious uninterrupted time to share stories from the day.

My nephew Mike Cadoux and his wife, Brit Liggett, have banished not just technology but also all electrical devices from one room in their apartment. They go there to read and think, to play guitar and talk. Visiting friends are drawn in by the soft glow of oil lamps. Most nights the couple eats dinner there, by flickering candlelight. They relax easily there, said Brit, because "there's nothing to fiddle with."

The need to escape devices also influences the choice of vacation spots. Entrepreneurs and other harried professionals have effused about taking a high-mountain trek or deep-canyon rafting trip where the scenery was magnificent and cell signals weak to nonexistent. (Perhaps hotels are missing a trick. Those catering to vacationers should stop advertising "Wi-Fi" under amenities and instead advertise "Lack of Wi-Fi.")

The other dimension entrepreneurs can regulate is time. There's no need to physically run away from technology if business owners are disciplined about how often and how long they use it.

Babs Smith and Dan Sullivan have founded a company that trains business owners to exert that control. The Toronto-based Strategic Coach shows entrepreneurs how they can increase business productivity while simultaneously improving their quality of life. The couple—who are married—introduce clients to the concept of "Free Days": 24-hour periods during which the entrepreneur does absolutely nothing related to work. Not even a fleeting glance at a smartphone is allowed.

To prevent withdrawal, the entrepreneur increases his number of Free Days gradually. After three years in the program, the average participant logs 150 a year. Babs said that clients report better relationships with their families and also improved business performance. By regularly and completely checking out of work culture, entrepreneurs free up their brains and reduce the tension in their personal lives, which frees up their brains even more.

(I proudly confided in Babs about how cleverly Gary and I compromised during vacations, by limiting his work to mornings only. She told me we were deluding ourselves. "It's not just a couple of hours in the morning," she said. "It's the hours before, when you are thinking and preparing, and the hours after, when you have to decompress.")

Akin to Free Days is the idea of a "technology Sabbath," described to me by Rabbi Kaye. He quoted another rabbi, Eric Yoffie, who wrote that during the Sabbath, "We are asked to give our kids, our spouse, and our friends the undivided attention they did not receive the rest of the week. . . . During the week we pursue our goals; on Shabbat we learn simply to be." Parting from our smartphones for a day makes those worthy Sabbath goals easier to achieve.

EXPERIMENTS IN DIGITAL DISCIPLINE
Giant strides begin with baby steps

You know a subject isn't trivial when it makes the curriculum of an Ivy League business school. A few years ago I sat in on an MBA class about work-life integration and leadership, taught by Stew Friedman, a professor at the University of Pennsylvania's Wharton School. Stew and I grew up in the '50s and '60s, when there were three ways to communicate: letters, phone calls, and visits. In a brainstorming session, Stew and his students came up with 17 different ways people now communicate, and Stew pointed out that this proliferation of choice has in fact made us less choosy. Today we grab whatever media is handy, reaching out with personal missives to those we love in the same way we dispatch a random bit of business. (Most of us have received sensitive email messages that would have been better delivered face-to-face.)

This issue is appropriate for a business course because, as Stew points out, people who give their families, communities, and personal lives the attention they deserve are ultimately better leaders. Each semester he asks his students to try some experiments to better align their personal values (to spend more time with friends and family, for example) with how they actually spend their time (mostly working). Not surprisingly, many start by placing limitations on their smartphones.

I spoke with one of Stew's former students, Sam Allen, about this issue. He's the Cofounder and CEO of ScanCafe, an online photo-scanning company based in Burlingame, California. Sam told me that

The Allen family.

his experiment was to turn off his iPhone and ignore work for two hours when he got home to his wife and young son. "At first, I thought this would stress me out even more," he said. "But it helped me focus, and I was rejuvenated by the break. And my wife was happier." Sam has maintained this discipline while building the company to 625 employees.

In the years he's conducted this exercise, Stew has found that smaller, less ambitious experiments are more likely to stick. Those who boldly vow they won't check their smartphones at all on weekends end up sneaking peeks, like dieters nibbling from a cache of cookies hidden behind the wheat germ. Soon they're back gobbling the digital equivalent of ice cream and fries.

Small improvements are fine, but Kelly Gray, the woman whose BlackBerry abuse threatened her health and her relationship, felt she had to take more drastic action. So she inaugurated her own version of a 12-step program. First, she apologized to Ehren, acknowledging that he "makes me a better person and the world a better place—not my BlackBerry." Next she banished all computers from the bedroom and started muting her phone during dinner. If Kelly expects an urgent call, she warns Ehren in advance. Once the call is over, she swiftly steers the conversation back to him. Her message to her boyfriend is implicit but unmistakable: he matters most.

Kelly has also stopped hiding behind technology. Now all her serious conversations—both personal and professional—take place in person. She sleeps on problems rather than indulging in the imperative of instant communication. As a result, she comes up with better solutions. She has lost weight, restarted yoga classes, and begun teaching kickboxing and cycling during her lunch hour to other professionals seeking balance. Her relationship with Ehren has healed and deepened.

Obviously, simply reducing BlackBerry use didn't turn Kelly's life around. But regaining control was a totemic act representing a fundamental reordering of priorities and a refusal to succumb to stress. An endless torrent of calls and emails may make an entrepreneur feel powerful. But enslaving herself to an inanimate object makes her weak.

> An endless torrent of calls and emails may make an entrepreneur feel powerful. But enslaving herself to an inanimate object makes her weak.

Inspired by what I learned in Stew's class, Gary and I decided to try some experiments of our own. He turns Bond Girl off during dinner and warns me in advance if he needs to take a call while we're together. For my part, I'm trying to mentally recast Bond Girl as Miss Moneypenny—an indispensable sidekick, but not one to make me jealous.

Things to Talk About

- The first step in a 12-step program is admitting you have a problem. Relatives should discuss with the entrepreneur—without rancor or recriminations—the effect her technology abuse has on the family.

- What values and priorities are the children learning from their parent's/parents' constant technology use?

- The entrepreneur should make a realistic assessment of which matters must be urgently dealt with and which can wait. Can he limit his accessibility and delegate more to employees?

- Is it desirable to plan vacations or getaways where connectivity is not ubiquitous?

Things to Do

- Work with your family to limit technology use for everyone. Banning devices during meals is a good place to start.

- Designate certain areas—the bedroom, the family room—as technology-free zones, and keep them that way.

- Set aside whole days in which you do nothing work-related. Gradually increase the number of those days as it becomes clear your company isn't suffering.

- Hire an assistant, or establish rules that discourage employees from calling about anything that can wait. Be extremely selective about which clients get your home or cell phone number.

Chapter 6

Minding the Kids

The entrepreneur is the most important person in the world
to her company and to her children. How can she give both
the best part of herself?

When my daughter, Danielle, was in fourth grade, her teacher
sent students home with invitations to a holiday concert. The
announcement, decorated with adorable snowmen in scarves,
included the time and date of the event and instructions that the young
performers leave their jackets "with parents or in cubbies." Before handing Gary and me the invitation, Danielle emphatically penciled around
the word "parents" and added her own scribbled note: "Actually I would
not add plural because DADDY'S NOT COMING!" Even at age nine,
our daughter knew enough anatomy to locate Gary's Achilles' heel.

Like many entrepreneurs, Gary traveled frequently during Stony-field's early, rapid-growth years. He became a familiar face to flight attendants and could make his way blindfolded around dozens of airports as he schlepped to visit customers, attend trade functions, and give talks and media interviews. Too often, he was stuck ironing tomorrow's collared shirt at a Marriott somewhere, while hundreds of miles away Danielle giggled through a birthday slumber party, Ethan received a purple belt in karate, or Alex got an assist during his soccer game.

Gary worked hard to make up for his chronic absence from our lives. If he couldn't be there consistently, he wanted at least to be consistent about some things that were meaningful to the kids. When he was home, he would rise with them, make yogurt smoothies for breakfast, and drive them to school. When he was away, he constructed crossword puzzles, which he faxed to them from the road. He coached their soccer teams—sometimes three teams in a season since all our children played. If anything, Gary overcompensated for his absences by applying to the kids' sports the same mania he displays in business. "I didn't allow myself to absorb the guilt," he told me. "I knew I was providing for them in other ways."

Now that our three kids are grown and out of the house, Gary and I have been reflecting on how we raised them. Curiously, it had never occurred to us to ask them, when they were younger, how they felt about our company and its endless claims on Gary's presence and attention. We both hoped that their father's achievements had justified the sacrifice, and that his efforts to spend time with them when he was home had atoned for his absences. But we didn't really know. So recently I posed the question to each of my children: what was this like for you?

What surprised me most was how differently they responded. The boys weren't much bothered by Gary's absences, mental or physical. "Dad was there for things I cared about, like my soccer games and teaching me to ride a bike," said Alex, who is 23. "All I remember now are the things that he was able to do." Ethan, 21, said "I think Dad's absences put a lot more pressure on you than they did on us."

Danielle, 19, had another view.

> It was great that he coached my soccer team. But during those times, he was my coach, not my dad. Our games and practices were just part of his busy schedule. You feel like you're just another thing on his calendar. You know, "It's 4:00 PM, time for Danielle's practice." Sometimes I felt bad when he came to soccer games, because I knew there were more "important" things he should be doing. . . . For Dad, there's no no-work zone. His mind is always working, even when he's sitting sipping tea. He's busy, then he gets busier, and then he doesn't notice when he gets too busy.
>
> At this point in my life, I appreciate his mission and what he's doing to support organic farmers. But the world is never going to be saved, so there's no end to Dad's work. No finish line, no winner. Sometimes I think, "Why does my dad have to be the guy who saves the world?" Sometimes you need to be the guy who chills out. Let somebody else save the world for a while.

"Sometimes I think, 'Why does my dad have to be the guy who saves the world?'"

Unfortunately, when it's your own company, often you're the only one who fits into the tights and cape.

WHERE'S DADDY?

Every minute apart deepens the guilt

The subject of children is laden with anxiety for many working parents—not just entrepreneurs. According to a 2006 study by the Work Life Institute, 60 percent of adults with families are stressed out by conflict between their professional and parental roles. But company owners experience extra dimensions of guilt. I hate to belabor the your-company-is-like-your-child analogy, but there's truth in it: the entrepreneur creates, and so is uniquely responsible for, both. Thus he sets up a perennial tug-of-war between two constituencies to whom he owes everything.

Also at fault is the myth that entrepreneurs are free to design their own lives, a proposition especially attractive to the "sandwich generation" charged with caring for both children and elderly parents. Many company founders believe self-employment will allow them to control when and how much they work. Theoretically, being your own boss gives you flexible hours. But how flexible can hours be when you're working 16 of them every day?

No measure of success in business can compensate for the feeling that you are failing as a parent. The bond between parents and children is primal, sensory, and emotional: it withers in absentia. The child grows up without the father's strong hand helping to steer her bicycle, the mother's warm voice murmuring a story at bedtime. Every moment missed is a moment lost: this is a sacrifice the entrepreneur implicitly accepts when he throws his all into the company. The parent knows, when he makes his excuses, that the child doesn't hear "This is all for you" but only "This is instead of you." No wonder entrepreneurs feel so guilty.

Barry Edwards was formerly the CEO of an audiovisual equip-

The Edwards family.

ment company in Louisiana. One day, his wife, Susan, pulled up to the office in the family car with their two-year-old son, Cody, in the backseat. The boy excitedly pointed at the building and exclaimed, "Daddy's house!" "That comment changed my husband," Susan told me. Across from his desk, Barry hung a poster of a little boy who looked like Cody. Printed in bold at the bottom was the word *Priorities*. "It became his daily reminder of the need to shut down and go home," she said.

But it's not just the long hours. It's also the travel. Particularly in the beginning, entrepreneurs take most meetings themselves, wher-ever those meetings may be. Making sales, building trust, establishing camaraderie with partners and suppliers—such matters can't be left to the bloodless interchange of email or Skype. But physical distance hurts and confuses kids, especially very young ones.

Khary and Selena Cuffe.

Selena Cuffe is the Cofounder, with her husband Khary, of Heritage Link Brands, a Los Angeles–based company that imports to the United States wines produced by black South African vintners. She recalled a trip to Cape Town she made several years ago when her first child (she now has two) was just 18 months old. "I gave Kalel a teddy bear with a recording of my voice embed-ded in it," Selena said. "I thought it would make him miss me less. But my mother-in-law told me whenever he heard it, he would go all around the house looking for me and cry when he couldn't find me. It was heartbreaking."

That deceptively chirpy epithet "mompreneur" notwithstand-ing, the guilt and strain are especially hard on women. Amy Cueva is Cofounder of a technology-design firm called Mad*Pow, in Ports-mouth, New Hampshire, and the mother of three young children. Last year, Amy worried constantly that she was failing them.

> Before I cut back on my work hours, I sometimes didn't even feel like a woman. I didn't have time to nurture my kids and be there the way my mom was. At one point, my daughter emailed me with a detailed plan for her 11th birthday party. I didn't know whether to be proud of her

organization and tech-savvy or depressed that she knew
that email was the best way to get in touch with me.

When her five-year-old asked that Amy pick him up from school
every day, "like all the other moms do," Amy tried fetching the child a
few times. But she ultimately delegated the task to a babysitter because
"work was screaming louder." As time passed, the kids grew more
accepting of their mother's busyness and distraction. While that was
a relief, it saddened Amy that they had stopped asking for her time
because they knew they wouldn't get it. "People used to tell me how
amazing it was that I accomplished all that I did," Amy told me. "But
I felt like I was screwing up every day."

THE ANGST OF SINGLE PARENTING
IN A TWO-PARENT FAMILY
Alone again (unnaturally)

The spouse, meanwhile, is caught in the middle, trying to allay the pain
and resentment of a child while soothing the entrepreneur's inevitable
guilt. She makes excuses for the absent parent and constantly con-
veys reassurances of his love. She assumes an outsize share of child
care and home maintenance, even if she herself works. And when her
spouse manages to be home—really home—for a few precious hours
or days, she regretfully sacrifices her own claims on his attention. The
kids need him more.

Kathleen Hafey said that her sons, 9 and 11, describe their father
as "someone who has to go away." Glenn Hafey, owner of a marine
design and construction company near Vancouver, has spent four to
eight months on the road every year since
his children were small. Life was harder
for Kathleen in the early days: she was
frequently exhausted, lonely, and jealous of
Glenn's diaper-free life away from home.
As the boys grew, Glenn understandably

> The boys describe their
> father as "someone who
> has to go away."

chose to spend his brief sojourns with them having as much fun as possible. So Glenn became mountain-biking parent; Kathleen was clean-the-garage-mow-the-lawn parent. This lopsided distribution of responsibility irked Kathleen. But the family spent so little time together, she wasn't going to waste it arguing.

Today, of course, life without Glenn has become standard operating procedure. Yet his absences still, occasionally, sting. More often than not, Glenn misses the boys' birthdays, which fall during his busy season. Kathleen worries that a big hoopla will only remind them that their father is not there, so instead she "under-compensates": making the boys special dinners but saving the big celebrations for Glenn's return.

Kathleen (who calls herself a "Skype wife") has learned to function as a single parent—maybe a little too well. While the family misses Glenn and loves having him home, his sudden reappearances can arouse a "power thing," Kathleen told me. "This has been my house," she said. "I've developed my own parenting style in his absence, and suddenly he comes home and starts telling the kids about the proper way to use a fork. It alters the dynamic in our home. The readjustment is hard."

Theoretically, entrepreneurial spouses want nothing more than to share the burdens of raising a family with their partners. But when you make decisions unilaterally 75 percent of the time, it's not easy to share authority. A few years ago Kathleen put into place a strategy to ease Glenn's homecomings. "We instituted a semiformal telephone powwow to discuss our expectations and mind-set for when he walks in the door," Kathleen said. "It gives him insight into how I've been running the house, and I can tell him whether I've developed new discipline strategies or routines. It's better for him, too, since he doesn't feel out of the loop as much."

Although these calls have helped allay tensions with Glenn, Kathleen does worry that forced single parenting has affected her relationship with the boys. Her older son is now interested in girls and wants his mother to loosen the leash a bit. "I've had to reassess my attachment to the boys," she told me. "Why do I want to hold on to them so tightly? Because I'm by myself?"

As for me, I'm not sure what I expected when Gary and I started having children. Our first arrived two years after I moved to the farm, and the second and third two and four years after that. I had not signed on for single parenting, and I confess I was not always a paragon of patience. As with Glenn Hafey's travels, Gary's absences skewed the developing relationships with the kids for both of us. Predictably, I assumed the role of disciplinarian: the parent who said no, who scolded, who took things away, and who sent kids to their rooms. Gary was the fun parent, bearing presents and laughter. So, naturally, the children would hector me about when their father would be home. And occasionally—despite my better angels—I would burst out in frustration: "I don't know! And don't ask me again." It was hard, and I didn't always have the strength to conceal that.

My vexation was complicated by my difficulty deciding whether my feelings were even justified. Many of Gary's trips didn't seem strictly necessary to me. I'd question why he didn't delegate more: why someone else couldn't meet with that account, or deliver that Rotary club talk. But as a mere observer—and a far from disinterested one—I knew I was in no position to make those calls. So I endured the double whammy of irritation over Gary's absences and irritation with myself for doubting decisions of his that might have been unavoidable. Was I sitting through this parent-teacher meeting alone because Gary *had* to be somewhere else or because he *chose* to be somewhere else? Absorbed in the enormous challenge of his own occupation, did he underestimate the challenge of mine?

And of course while I missed Gary for the children, I also missed him for me. He tried, sweetly, to soften the sting of his absences. I'd find shaving cream hearts on the mirror (which I'd superstitiously refrain from wiping off until he was safely home) or little notes in unexpected places. When he finally returned, I didn't know which I wanted more: to catch up with him over a glass of wine or to lock myself in our bedroom, alone, away from the kids' needs and demands. Often I chose the latter. Back then, my ideal Mother's Day present was not a lopsided handmade candy dish or charred pancakes served to me in bed; rather, it was a day of blissful solitude.

The McDonnell family.

As happened with Kathleen, my life as a quasi-single mom became easier as the children got older. My friend Jill Kearney—married to Stephen McDonnell, Founder of the natural meat company Applegate Farms, in Bridgewater, New Jersey—described how her family dynamics evolved over time:

> In the early years, I was absolutely livid over Stephen's lack of engagement with the kids, and particularly incensed whenever he used the analogy that the business was like his child. But I have come to see that what he built was hard and extraordinary, and also that parenting has its seasons. He's a very engaged Dad now. Perhaps we didn't both need to be on deck at the same moment. If I could have seen into the future, I would have cut him some slack.

It's of course easy to say this now, in retrospect, but I agree with her.

A CHILDHOOD HOME HAUNTED BY MONEY FEARS
Keep out of reach of children

Many busy professionals agonize about being absentee parents. Entrepreneurs' consciences also suffer a more distinctive torment. Company founders feel guilty for exposing their adored, vulnerable children to extraordinary financial risk without the children's understanding or consent. When a parent loses a job, she can (usually) get another one. But when she loses a company, she may lose everything.

Parents are supposed to make decisions that keep their kids safe.
Starting a company is not that kind of decision.

If you can't keep your children safe, at least you can protect them
from knowing how shaky things are. Children require stability. Parents whose fortunes are ebbing and flowing, then ebbing and ebbing
some more, can provide no more than the semblance of it. Maintaining
the fiction that all is well may require a feat of playacting reminiscent
of the movie *Life Is Beautiful*, whose hero weaves a happy fantasy to
shield his son from the horrors of a concentration camp. Hiding your
own fears to prevent your children's can be exhausting.

During the early years of our company, Gary and I didn't want to
burden our kids with the ever-looming threat of bankruptcy, a concept
they were too young to understand anyway. We reserved the topic of
our financial woes for hushed discussions at night, after they'd fallen
asleep. Fortunately, kids are naturally myopic when it comes to the
adult world, so we were able to maintain their illusion of security.
Gary and I might be swinging from the chandeliers emotionally, but
as long as the kids had their house, their friends, and their toys, they
were happy.

I'm grateful our three were too young to pick up on our anxiety. If
they'd been older, I'm not sure what we would have told them. Parents
can reasonably disagree about how much to shield progeny old enough
to absorb the implications of business uncertainty. (And what is "old
enough" anyway? 8? 10? 14?) One CEO told me about the frequent,
tense exchanges he has with his wife about what to reveal to their
daughters, nine and six. He doesn't want to distress the girls. But he
does want them to understand that his company has ups and downs, so
the family's limited resources can't always stretch to cover trips or toys.
His wife, by contrast, prefers to protect her daughters. She grew up in
a household burdened by chronic financial pressure and hates the idea
of them suffering the insecurity she experienced as a child. "My wife
shushes me when I talk business problems in front of the kids," the
CEO told me. "She brings *more* tension to the situation when she does

that." Acceding to his wife's wishes, he now tries to keep their money talk private. But that hasn't been easy. Like employees who fear impending layoffs, the girls sense tension and stick close to their parents to find out what's going on.

> "My wife shushes me when I talk business problems in front of the kids. She brings *more* tension to the situation when she does that."

Protecting kids becomes even more difficult when the company is located in the family home, which commonly occurs during the start-up phase, when the entrepreneur's fortunes are especially precarious. I spoke with one teenager whose parents ran a catering business out of their kitchen. When the parents saw their daughter hanging around, they would warn her that if she didn't help prepare food for their customers, then the family might not be able to afford food for themselves. The teenager knew they were kidding. But she also knew there was some truth in the joke. Forced to bear personal witness to the company's struggles, she found these comments more troubling than funny.

Most entrepreneurs are more cautious about exposing kids to financial woes. Yet no matter how much we try to protect them, in an environment suffused with worry, children can't help but inhale secondhand stress. I spoke with a woman in New York whose husband has spent a fruitless year trying to raise money to launch an alternative energy company. The family has been living off their retirement fund and the college funds for their three children. While the kids' future education hangs in the balance, many of their present desires go unsatisfied. They can't join clubs or dues-paying sports teams. They get to go to camp for only one week while their peers spend the hot summer months swimming, hiking, and singing around a campfire. "When I was a kid we just played kick the can," this woman told me. "But these days kids are more scheduled, and their activities can be expensive. I just don't want them feeling different from their friends. They didn't choose this life, but they are affected by it. I sob about it at least once a day." Recently, her oldest, a seventh grader, blurted out: "Why does Dad have to start his own company? Why can't he just work?"

Of course, business founders who have children can simply choose to risk less. For entrepreneurs, however, the instinct to invest money in their business is almost as powerful as the urge to reproduce. But the cost-benefit analysis of taking out a line of credit against a home changes when children's bedrooms, toys, and memories reside under that roof. Lisa Johnson (the yam-dip maker from chapter 4) is trying to grow her business, but like most early-stage entrepreneurs, she is starved for cash. Lisa has considered mortgaging the house, but she hesitates because of her two young daughters. "I've been thinking that if it weren't for the kids, I'd get the loan and move on it right now," Lisa said. "But having the kids makes me both more conservative and creative, and forces me to think of other ways to grow my company." The prospect of paying college tuitions has given Lisa a growth trajectory and a financial goal for her business. But even in pursuit of that goal, she's not willing to risk consigning her family to Vermont winters spent shivering in a tipi.

A COMPANY WHERE KIDS ARE WELCOME
It takes an office

Earlier in this chapter, I called the design-your-life theory of entrepreneurship a myth: alluring but usually unattainable. In most cases that is true. But some founders do find ways to construct work worlds that coexist harmoniously with family ones. Rocio Romero, for example, used to be on a plane every other week, traveling to sites where clients were erecting her elegant prefabricated homes. Since giving birth to twins in 2009, however, Rocio scarcely travels at all. Instead, "I'll work with customers remotely, using pictures and site plans, or have them hire a local architect for that part of the work," she explains. "And I have no problem asking customers to come to me. I suggest it all the time now. People understand."

For years, Rocio commuted from her house to her office. After the twins were born, though, she moved her family to a three-story home in downtown St. Louis. There, she established her office on the first floor and work and meeting rooms for employees on the third floor. On the second floor are the living quarters, where the babies spend the day with their nanny. "I can spend the whole day moving easily among these three worlds," Rocio said. "I'm downstairs doing emails in my office. I walk up two floors and I'm with my three employees reviewing designs. Then on the way back down I can stop for 15 minutes and play with the children."

Entrepreneurs can make outside-the-home offices hospitable to young children as well, with benefits accruing both to employees and themselves. Nicole Dawes (the organic cookie and cracker manufacturer from chapter 3) is the daughter of Steve Bernard, Founder of Cape Cod Potato Chips, and she practically grew up at her father's company. She has come to believe that "it takes an office to raise a child." Today, Nicole and husband Peter bring their children to work at Late July Organic Snacks when they need to. Workers also have peace of mind that if child care falls through and they are unable to work from home, their children are always welcome at the office. The company has a large playroom equipped with toys, books, and puzzles. One employee can help with the kids in a pinch. "It's surprising that it's not disruptive, but it isn't," said Nicole. "Plus the kids love it. And their presence brightens the office mood."

Nicole Dawes and her sons, Stephen and Benji.

The Holy Grail of child-friendly workplaces would have to be Portland, Oregon-based gDiapers, where Kim and Jason Graham-Nye have opened an on-site day care center. The founders of this manufacturer of biodegradable diapers had sound business reasons for shouldering the substantial financial and regulatory burdens such a project entails. The center helps them attract and retain people they ordinarily couldn't afford to hire. But the Graham-Nyes also have the luxury of being present for their own kids' milestones, seizing moments with them throughout the day and watching them develop friendships with the children of colleagues. Unfortunately for the rest of us, such centers—virtually unheard of in entrepreneurial companies—are no more than pretty dreams.

THE UPSIDE OF ENTREPRENEURIAL PARENTS
The kids are alright

Entrepreneurs like Nicole Dawes and the Graham-Nyes are as creative at adapting their family lives to entrepreneurship as they are at building their businesses. They make their companies bright spots for their children, creating a positive aura around the image of entrepreneurship. When the children of such people become adults, they often reflect fondly on their experiences growing up in the family business. They recall their parents' companies as second homes, backdrops for some of their fondest memories, and tantalizing windows into the adult world of work.

Entrepreneurs are in a great position to inspire, educate, and excite their offspring. How much cooler is Bring Your Daughter to Work Day—for both parent and child—when "Work" is a business her father created and where he is the leader, respected and admired by others? Salem Samhoud, Founder of &Samhoud, a consulting firm in the Netherlands, brings each of his three children, separately, to work for one day every six months. The kids look forward to getting out of school and spending a special day with their father. They bask in the attention paid them by employees, and their own respect for him swells as they watch other adults seek his direction and counsel. The knowledge that when Dad is gone he's not just gone—he's somewhere else doing something important—makes those frequent absences easier.

Company owners also have extraordinary latitude to involve older kids in their work. In those circumstances, children can actually spend *more* time with their parents while gaining an early education in business. Packing boxes after school or counting inventory on weekends can be a terrific first job. Children feel closer to their parents and proud of the family business: this is ours! We are making this! Our own kids spent some summers working in Stonyfield's offices and plant. Laboring side by side with people whose livelihoods depended on the company's continued success, they understood the pressure Gary was under and realized that, though they didn't always like sharing him, at least they were sharing him for a good cause.

Before Wangene Hall, 19, left for college, she regularly worked beside her Kenyan mother in the kitchen of her family's business, Mel's Gourmet World Cuisine, in White River Junction, Vermont. From her parents, she has learned practical skills—for example, how to prepare chicken stew—but also life lessons, such as the importance of hard work. Wangene values the easy, wide-ranging conversations she had with her mother as they cooked, cooled, and packed the food. "We would talk about Kenya, about our ambitions, about school and my social life," Wangene said. "We would never have had those exchanges otherwise. They brought us closer. I understand her better."

Working, or just spending time, in a parent's company bestows another benefit on children: it demystifies business. Economic literacy is a potent weapon against the kind of money-grows-in-ATMs mentality that underlies many kids' mindless consumerism. Children see how things are made and marketed, how problems are analyzed and solved. They come to understand the hard work and complex decision making that goes into the manufacture of a pair of sneakers or a video game.

Nicole Dawes remembers being riveted as an elementary-school student when her father taught her about gross margins. Today, Nicole's own children weigh in on Late July's latest products. "Sometimes the kids surprise me," says Nicole. "They'll offer an opinion and I think,

'Oh my god, why didn't I think of that?'" At food shows, her eight-year-old son, Stephen, glad-hands visitors who drop by the company's booth and doles out his own business cards, embossed with the title "Boy on the Box" (a reference to Late July's logo, on which he is featured). During dinner, Stephen will often raise subjects like why the company can't afford more advertising, even though his parents would prefer to talk about his day at school.

A company-building parent can also shape a child's career choice. After seeing Gary's labor, stress, and sacrifice, our daughter concluded the entrepreneurial life is not for her. "When I was a kid," Danielle told me, "I thought it would be cool to have Dad's job. But as I got exposed to what it's really like, I'm just like, ugh."

Wangene Hall, by contrast, has inherited the entrepreneurship gene from her parents. Despite the unrelenting demands of business, Wangene harbors "wildly ambitious plans" to start a biotech company, a science-communication company, a music-marketing company, *and* a fashion-design firm. Intimate exposure to her parents' business—wild ride notwithstanding—has created an optimist. The fear of failure only makes her want to work harder. "People say you can't do this or that," said Wangene. "I reply, 'Watch me.'"

MAKE THE MOST OF THE TIME YOU HAVE
Being there

It is gratifying for company founders to contemplate their children growing up with and in the business. Still, the vast majority of family life takes place outside of work. Children have rich worlds of friends, hobbies, activities, learning, and adventure that parents—even those shoulder deep in their businesses—must try to share or at least to accommodate. Fortunately, there are a few fairly simple ways to tip work-life balance a bit more in the kids' favor.

Many entrepreneur-parents simply learn to delegate better. Amy Cueva, the CEO who gave up collecting her five-year-old from school, no longer works nights and weekends now that she's made some key hires. These days she drives her kids to sports practices and events. "With my time has come my attention," she said. "My kids seem happier and more comfortable. I told them that my working less means we will make less, and maybe not go to Disneyland this year. But they get me instead."

The less you delegate, the better you must become at scheduling: packing your days as adroitly as a parsimonious traveler trying to avoid excess baggage fees. While many scheduling strategies—such as plotting family and work events on the same calendar—are no different than those of any career family, company owners have so many claims on their time that they may require contingency planning. For example, entrepreneurs may need to incorporate work time within designated family time. That's OK if it relieves stress and reduces distractions. Our family has always made vacations a priority, even if we took six months to pay off the Visa bill. But we also recognized that Gary would have to work at some point each weekday, so we cordoned off a few hours for that in the mornings. That way, Gary was less burdened by guilt, and the kids and I could relax knowing we'd have his full attention for big chunks of the day.

Another strategy that's successful for some entrepreneurs is to alter their work schedules to better fit their children's needs. If both parents work, it's usually possible to stagger hours so one is home for the kids in the morning and the other when they return from school.

But while scheduling is necessary, it is not sufficient. Even when the entrepreneur is home, she's often not *there*. Struggling to keep pace with the overwhelming demands of her business, she succumbs to the lure of multitasking. Her "together time" with her

> Her body is with her daughter at the Girl Scout meeting, but her mind is mulling margins.

son consists of sitting in his room while he plays video games and she reviews payroll. Her body is with her daughter at the Girl Scout meeting, but her mind is mulling margins. And she shouldn't delude herself that the kids don't notice.

So commit to giving your kids your full attention while you're with them, no matter how fleeting and mundane those moments may be. Many parents told me some of the greatest conversations with their kids take place in the car, in the 10 minutes it takes to get to school or a sporting event. You might go quietly crazy sitting on the floor with your five-year-old, intoning The Little Engine That Could's mantra "*I think I can*" while what you're really thinking is "*I think I should* go check email." Control yourself. Your child is soaking up both the story and your attentive presence. Return the favor by delighting in his company. The winds of your business will always be howling. Physical and mental multitasking mean doing more things less well.

When I asked the teenage daughter of an entrepreneur how her dad could show he cared for her, she replied, "I wish he didn't run to his home office to squeeze in a phone call or an email every time there was a pause in the conversation or a minute between things. When he's at work, he's in the flow. That's how I'd like to see him at home too. More spontaneous and in the flow."

OUT OF THE MOUTHS OF BABES
Concerned you're screwing up? Ask the kids.

That teenager's comment made me think back to the afternoon, described at the beginning of this chapter, when I asked our three children about growing up with Stonyfield. After those "interviews," I realized that the best authorities on what children need are often the children themselves. I wished Gary and I had consulted our brood about what is and isn't working back when we were all going through this together.

Would we have acted differently toward Danielle if we'd known how she felt at the time? Gary tried to treat all three kids equitably. But maybe his daughter needed something more from him—or at least something different. When employers want to illustrate how flexible their work policies are, they invariably drag out the cliché that employees are free to attend soccer games and school plays. Somehow, we've come to accept that bearing witness to our kids' achievements is synonymous with good parenting. Certainly, being at such events is important. But sitting in an audience with 100 other parents is not the best way to get to know your child, or for your child to get to know you.

Since that conversation took place, Gary has been enjoying unscheduled, unstructured hang-out time with Danielle when she's home from college. The lesson for us is that you can't let your child feel like an item on a To Do list, even if you've made her a repeating event on your Google calendar. The other lesson: if you want to know what your children need from you, ask them.

> If you want to know what your children need from you, ask them.

Salem Samhoud, the consultant from the Netherlands, makes a practice of asking his children that question every few months. Stealing a trick from the manager's tool kit, Salem holds quarterly "360 degree reviews" with his wife and three children, aged 22, 16, and 11. The reviews show him where he's falling down as a parent and also where he doesn't need to sweat it. "Recently they told me I spend too much time on my iPhone," Salem told me. "They were right. Now I switch it off on weekends. Because of their feedback, I already feel more relaxed and focused. They asked me to do it for them, but it's also better for me."

At the Samhoud clan meetings, the kids get reviewed as well, by each other and by their parents. As a result, they might pledge to bicker less or empty the dishwasher more. Salem believes it's important for children to understand that they share responsibility for the happiness of the family. And happy families, he concluded, contribute to healthy companies by supporting the entrepreneur emotionally and helping him to model balance. "The boss doesn't set a good example if he's always stressed out," said Salem. "Maybe during the first few years it's understandable. But after that, you have to organize your life. If you can't do that, how can you organize your business?"

Cindy Pierce, owner and manager of Pierce's Inn, in Etna, New Hampshire, also participates in regular family meetings with her husband and children, ages 14, 12, and 10. These gatherings take place

The Lingelbach-Pierce family.

almost every week. The family kicks things off with expressions of appreciation by each person for the others. At first, Cindy said, those declarations were awkward and perfunctory, but now they are thoughtful and sincere. Family members also record their irritations in a book, which is reviewed at the meetings, and the complaints are usually resolved.

> When the kids have recorded issues with our parenting or authoritative approach in a situation, we listen and usually accept the feedback if it is legit—it almost always is— and ask if a variety of alternative approaches would have been better, or we change the decision. We make ourselves pretty vulnerable and open, so they feel empowered. They really respond well to this. The meetings have become our centerboard. There is now a place where all kinds of truth can fly.

I admire Cindy's communication strategy, and I like her attitude just as much. When the subject turns to children, most entrepreneurs regret what they've missed and lament what they expect to miss in the future. Cindy, by contrast, survives by setting the bar low. She's resigned herself to living with messes—both literal and figurative—and refuses to feel guilty or to judge herself by others' standards. The priorities she sets each day reflect her greater mission: to develop a relationship with her children—not manage them. She believes that her travel and work schedule have taught her kids independence and made them more responsible. A little benign neglect, said Cindy, is a good thing. As another entrepreneur put it, "The truth is, some days the kids get the best of me and some days the company does." To me, that sounds like a pretty healthy perspective.

Above all, remember that work-life balance is a chimera. At any given moment, you will probably be shortchanging someone. But in the bigger picture, your child is living with someone who's going for it. You are giving her something of enormous value: a front-row seat on what it means to live a passionate and engaged life.

> "The truth is, some days the kids get the best of me and some days the company does."

Things to Talk About

- The founder of a company, especially a start-up, will be extremely busy much of the time. But that doesn't mean she can simply out-source parenting to her spouse. What will be the entrepreneur's parental responsibilities? What kind of relationship does she want with her children, and how will she achieve it?

- Depending on children's ages, most parents will want to protect them from financial fear and insecurity. How much information about the company's ups and downs will you share with the children? If times are lean, what will you ask them to sacrifice?

- Kids are free labor that can be engaged by the business or exploited by it. How, and how much, will you involve the kids in the company? Should you expect them to work after school and during the summer?

- What child-friendly policies will make your workplace more hospitable for both you and your employees?

Things to Do

- From time to time, have your children spend a normal day at work with you, even if it means taking them out of school. Consider bringing them along occasionally on a business trip.

- Make family dinners a priority. If the kids eat before you get home, ask them to sit with you for 10 minutes while you dine so you can hear about one another's days. Ban all electronic devices—including your own—from the table.

- Spend relaxed, informal time with your kids. Soccer games and school plays are important, but so is just hanging out. (See ban on electronic devices above.)

- Try holding regular family meetings to discuss, among other things, whether the kids feel they are getting enough and the right kind of attention. Ask how you can do better and suggest ways they can contribute more to the family's well-being.

Chapter 7

Left Behind

The spouse accepts that the entrepreneur needs to work long days. But shouldn't he spend his free time with her and not run off to play?

Back in the '80s, when Gary and I were living the full catastrophe (young kids, new business)—when 80-hour workweeks were commonplace, dinners together a luxury, and most conversations an endless list of To Do's—one commitment remained inviolable: Gary's tennis dates. Often he and his friend Rick would meet at a local court at 10:00 PM, and by the time Gary returned to the farm, I was long asleep. As a non-jock, I was mystified and more than a little resentful of the choice he was making: to sacrifice precious catch-up and connection time with me in favor of smashing little yellow balls over a net. I felt abandoned and pretty far down on his priority list. And at the end of my long day, I wasn't exactly gracious about being left with three screaming little people while he was off working up a cathartic sweat.

For families of entrepreneurs, the issue of leisure time is often a flash point. Spouses can usually—albeit grudgingly—reconcile themselves to the demands a business makes on the entrepreneur's days. (Hence my uneasy detente, described in chapter 5, with Gary's BlackBerry.)

The long hours Gary puts in satisfy his drive and sense of mission, but they also benefit the entire family.

What has irked me is the manner in which Gary chooses to spend his paltry fund of discretionary time. When you marry an entrepreneur, you accept that the business will require his frequent, sometimes extended, separations from the family. At the same time, you assume that his views on the best use of his scant free time will correspond with your own. When he *can* spend time with his family, he *will* spend time with his family. The spouse pictures the entrepreneur's life as a simple pie chart. The wedge that isn't the business ought to be her and the kids.

> The spouse pictures the entrepreneur's life as a simple pie chart. The wedge that isn't the business ought to be her and the kids.

Often the entrepreneur thinks otherwise. *Inc.* magazine features a department called "Passions" that chronicles the extracurricular activities of some of its CEO readers. The articles present a kaleidoscopically fascinating assortment of pursuits, ranging from glassblowing and knife-throwing to gold-prospecting and competitive cattle-herding. But the one thing all those pursuits have in common is this: there is no mention of family members participating. It's easy to see how the spouse's repressed resentment can flower in the fertile loam of the entrepreneur's regular jaunts to the golf course or the gym—or the foundry or the ranch, as the case may be.

Work is necessary. Leisure pursuits are a matter of choice. Voluntary abandonment stings in a way that obligatory leave-taking does not.

FINISHING THIRD
The angst of being nudged out by a hobby

Which brings me back to tennis. When I've confronted Gary with my frustrations, he's pointed out that for him, then and now, sports are a necessity, not a luxury. They lower his blood pressure and clear his head. He gets creative ideas while engaged in physical activity, away from the clamor of people and the bleeping of computers and smart-phones. "Doing sports makes me a nicer person," he told me recently. "I can't make the stress go away. But after the tension release of playing tennis or skiing, I feel more hopeful—I feel revived. Better that than bringing the stress backwash home."

It's true that I've learned to gauge Gary's stress level by counting the pairs of sports pants in the laundry hamper. Yet I confess I felt a frisson of anger when my husband returned home on a Friday night after 10 days away on business and announced his plan to go skiing the next day. Right on anger's heels came "The Lecture" I gave myself: "This is good. He needs this. The more he sweats, the more he smiles. Everyone needs to stay healthy, have fun, and find ways to wring out life's dirty dishwater."

Tennis and skiing, however, are only two of Gary's many voluntary pursuits. He is also politically active, serves on several boards, and travels frequently to give speeches. The crux of the problem, he has pointed out to me, is that entrepreneurs are overly optimistic about how much they can take on without sacrificing something important. When you over-pack a suitcase, some item must come out or the lid won't close. It hurts when the item Gary chooses to remove is time I'd hoped to share with him.

I've talked to the spouses of other entrepreneurs about this, and many sympathize. My friend Kit Crawford, who owns the Emeryville, California-based energy-bar company Clif Bar with her husband, Gary Erickson, told me she once wrestled with the same issue.

Gary Erickson and Kit Crawford.

All Gary's adult life he's taken an annual two-week intense bike trip. Right after our third child, Lydia, was born in 1994, Gary left on one of his trips. I thought, "You are kidding me." I rolled with it, but it was hard. He'd call me from the road, and I would weep. I felt lonely, overwhelmed, and resentful. He came home early from that trip, and then I felt guilty that he cut his trip short because of me.

In such instances, it's not just loneliness and the sense of desertion that rankle. It's also the fact of not being chosen. The spouse feels hurt that other priorities rank above her. Where, exactly, does she stand? At the risk of perpetuating gender stereotypes, I believe women feel the slight more than men. Certainly I've heard far more women talk about it. Their common complaint is they not only want their husbands to spend time with them; they also want their husbands to *want* to spend time with them, and they seek expression of that desire in both words and deeds. Without it, wives torture themselves with the question: how can he be content when he sees so little of me?

Lee Williams doesn't make excuses for himself or for his entrepreneurial peers. The CEO of Digital Connections in Nashville observed that when a spouse feels like she's in second place, it's because she is, in fact, in second place. Lee, who is on his third marriage and has thought a lot about what went wrong with his former ones, said that an entrepreneur may profess that he loves his spouse deeply. But if he's physically AWOL all the time, "his actions speak so loudly that she can't hear what he says. There's talking the talk and there's walking the walk," said Lee. "I was distracted by too many things. I won't make that mistake again."

Women also suffer more from perceived abandonment because they tend to adopt the role of caretakers of relationships. Consequently, they are less likely than men to assume their marriages can roll along indefinitely on cruise control. They know that relationships take work, and they become frustrated if they are the only ones putting in the labor.

I spoke with Alder Yarrow, Founder of the San Francisco consulting firm Hydrant. On top of running his business, Alder devotes 10 to 25 hours a week to his acclaimed wine blog, *Vinography*. His wife, Ruth Lieu, refers to herself as a "blog widow." Alder believes that the time and activities the couple shares are enough to maintain a healthy and loving relationship. But Ruth said she would feel more connected if they did more together, talked more, and spent more time with friends. "We have many interests in common—we met rock climbing," Ruth told me. "But now we don't make the opportunity to share things that used to form the foundation of our relationship."

Alder Yarrow, Ruth Lieu, and their daughter, Sparrow.

At least for Ruth there's an upside to Alder's hobby: the pleasures of sharing a home-cooked meal paired with a bottle of amazing wine. But she jokingly told her husband that if she were rich she'd pay his hourly consulting fee so she could have more of his time. "I've often said to him that if he devoted some of that overachieving energy to our family life, he'd knock it out of the park, the way he does everything else," said Ruth.

If the marriage is strong enough, most spouses learn to grin and bear it. Hurt gives way to habit as the entrepreneur's time-for-himself becomes a ritual of family life. Robert Massie, Founder of Marketing Informatics, a market-research company in Indianapolis, has long claimed as his exclusive preserve what for many families is the social nexus of the week: Saturday night. On those evenings, "I make a pizza, I crack open a bottle of wine, and then I go out to my garage and listen to *Prairie Home Companion* and finish it off with a cigar," said Robert. "I've done that for 20 years. My wife can't stand it, but she gives me that."

IT'S ONLY FAIR
When do I get mine?

Left-behind spouses crave entrepreneurs' time and attention. But they are also after parity. Over the years, I've noticed that many families use a kind of unarticulated "point system" to track individuals' domestic contributions. The more points each spouse earns doing chores and running errands, the more time off he or she feels comfortable claiming.

Spouses of entrepreneurs build up credit fast. They pay the bills and make the budgets. They meet with lawyers, insurance agents, and financial-planning professionals about the household's affairs. They become the couple's sole representative at community activities and family events. And nowhere do points count more than in child care. Parents don't actually talk about points, but you see the complex calculus at work when a couple argues over who should take the twins to the park.

> **He:** "I made them breakfast this morning, so they've already seen a lot of me." (Breakfast prep + shared meal = 2 points.)
> **She:** "I'm still beat from taking them and their two friends to the zoo yesterday." (Two car rides + 90 minutes zoo time + snack + gift shop tantrum + two extra kids = 22 points.)

As one spouse put it: "The way I thought about it was, 'I had the kids last Saturday. You take them this Saturday.' It's the human inclination to even the score."

But this system starts to crumble when one spouse is an entrepreneur. The business is so important to the family that it awards the entrepreneur a bucketful of extra points. And because entrepreneurs must stay physically and emotionally well to attend to that business, they don't expend as many points as the spouse when they take off on their own for some fun. Thus the currency of time is allowed to float, and the spouse finds herself running an eternal deficit.

Naturally, the spouse's feeling that she'll never earn enough guilt-free leisure causes resentment. And that resentment is amplified by a phenomenon peculiar to entrepreneurship: the double-dip effect. Building a business is hard as hell. But it's not a mere job; it's also a thrill. The company is the entrepreneur's bag—his *thing*. So when he spends his nonwork hours boxing or doing aerial photography, then he's got *two things*. It's not that the spouse wants the entrepreneur to be miserable at work. But when he excitedly describes his brilliant performance at a sales pitch followed by his brilliant performance on the basketball court, she starts to reflect on all she is sacrificing without equivalent recognition and reward.

> The currency of time is allowed to float, and the spouse finds herself running an eternal deficit.

Entrepreneurs also get away with not expending points on time spent with employees, even if, to the spouse, those activities look a lot like pure socializing. Company founders claim that late-afternoon happy hours or early-morning hoops are important for developing culture and boosting morale. How can the spouse argue with that? Still, because he's enjoying himself with other people—people the spouse may barely know—she feels not only abandoned but also excluded.

Even extra office hours can raise hackles if their purpose is ambiguous. Two or three times a week "Josh," CEO of a telecom equipment supplier in New York, meets after work for several hours with a handful of managers. "That's when the growth happens, as far as creativity, problem resolution, and new idea development," he told me. His wife, however, sees those gatherings as a convenient excuse for Josh to hang out with work friends. "I think she resents that they are getting and giving something that she wants to be a part of, but can't be," said Josh. "My wife and I are not on the same team."

Entrepreneurs can make things somewhat better by blurring the work-hard/play-hard line that so often divides their lives. By building a little playtime into their workdays, they can ease the need to relax on their spouses' clocks. Cindy Pierce, the New Hampshire inn owner I mentioned in chapter 6, is a frequent speaker on the college circuit. Whenever she's on the road, Cindy makes sure to do something for herself, such as exercising or going to a movie. That way, her homecomings don't coincide with the immediate need for decompression—something a chaotic domestic life doesn't easily afford. "Many people think that when they travel for work, they have to grind the whole time they're away," Cindy said. "But then they come home spent. Both spouses feel pissed off and like they need a break, particularly if they have young kids."

THE ZEN OF "WE"

Laying a foundation of togetherness

Josh's "same team" comment gets at the heart of the abandonment problem and also suggests at least a partial solution. Dr. Gary Lewandowski is an associate professor of psychology at Monmouth University in New Jersey who has studied how the attempt to accumulate knowledge and new experiences—"self-expansion"—factors into relationships. His research shows that an individual's outside interests and pursuits can expand his spouse's universe, strengthening the couple's bond in the process. But he cautions that solitary activities can also foster isolation. The way such situations play out, according to Dr. Lewandowski, depends on whether the couple has established a sense of "we-ness"—of being on the same team. When spouses identify strongly with each other, each derives joy from the other's success and gratification. The more they are united, the more time they can spend apart without damaging the relationship.

Tammi and David Wilson have worked hard at creating we-ness.

The pair own Braveheart Sports Network, a portfolio of sports-related websites, based in Pelham, New Hampshire. A couple of years ago their relationship broke down because they weren't nurturing a life together outside of work. Stretched for time, each felt hurt when the other chose to spend a rare free hour apart. Dave liked to go biking but stopped because he assumed that Tammi disapproved. When Tammi went out for a facial or massage, she felt under the gun to get home quickly. "We'd eye each other warily," said Tammi. Resentment deepened as each drained pleasure from activities the other most enjoyed.

Then David suggested the couple start a book club—for just the two of them. They selected *Intimacy and Desire* by Dr. David Schnarch. Separately, they read a chapter a week. Then, for one or two hours over lunch, they shared their reactions to specific passages. Those discussions drew them closer. "Before we started this, we weren't sharing completely honestly," said Tammi. "Now that I understand him better, I get 100 percent enjoyment out of his enjoyment—even if it means he's off playing fantasy football on a Saturday." The foundation laid, the couple no longer needs to commune over a book. They continue to meet regularly, but now it's just to talk—often about their relationship.

The nice thing about the Wilsons' book/conversation club is that it was compelling enough that both spouses willingly committed to it, but not so time-consuming that they couldn't still pursue their separate interests. And now they do so with one another's blessing.

Of course, it's easier to foster a sense of we-ness if you have interests in common. "Date night" is important, but relationship by appointment isn't wholly fulfilling. By contrast, when couples share a genuine passion for the same pursuits, they spend time together naturally, united by enthusiasm, adrenalin, and maybe even good-natured competition. Gino Venditti met his wife, Sarah, on a social bike ride. He is Vice President of Operations in his family's commercial kitchen equipment company in Pittsburgh; she is a medical resident. Despite these exhausting and time-gobbling occupations, the couple still rides together as, presumably, they would have ridden separately had they never met. They also both love to camp and work in their gar-

The Stewart family.

den, and they make time for those activities as well. "It's more than just hanging out in the same room," Gino said. "When we achieve something together, we share a sense of accomplishment."

Dan Stewart inadvertently came up with a neat solution by starting a second business that combines his own favorite pursuits with family time. Dan is the owner of Lifestyle Crafts, a crafts and scrap-booking supply company near Salt Lake City. A zealous bike rider, he was indulging his own interests when he founded Rockwell Relay, a business that hosts events for cyclists. But he also wanted to create a company that his wife, Melanie, and their six children could enjoy. The kids help out at events by serving hot chocolate and pancakes. The entire family now enjoys bike outings together, with the older kids riding and the younger kids rolling behind in trailers.

Other couples have found comradeship in philanthropy, which many profit-driven entrepreneurs experience as a deeply satisfying diversion in its own right. My friend Jill Kearney, who I mentioned in chapter 6, is a professional writer. She and her husband, Steve McDonnell, Founder of Applegate Farms, started a nonprofit to help Ecuadorean cacao farmers find markets for their chocolate in the United States. Through their collaboration, Jill learned to value Steve's business skills in a new context, and the two developed greater mutual appreciation. Similarly, Lee Williams, of Digital Connections, works with his wife to help underprivileged kids afford college. "What it does for our relationship is simply amazing," Lee said. "As a couple, we feel great that we're not just taking all the time. We respect the goodness in each other."

DO YOUR OWN THING
The spouse gets out there

A spouse hell-bent on equalizing the couple's "points" can try to limit the entrepreneur's extracurriculars. But a more salutary approach is to find things she enjoys doing alone or with friends. Parallel play, the natural behavior of toddlers, has a role in healthy marriages as well.

(Of course the child-care burden complicates such autonomous larking. If no relatives live nearby and paid babysitters aren't an option, I suggest seeking out similarly positioned parents with whom you can swap extended playdates. I've even seen versions of point systems deployed between families. "We had Katie Morrison here for lunch and a video. But the Morrisons let Josh sleep over when I came back late from the ballet, so we owe them an afternoon.")

Gary Erickson's commitment to his biking made his wife, Kit, mad, but it also made her think. Having passions was a good thing, she realized. The solution wasn't to deny Gary his but, instead, to pursue her own. So, with Gary's encouragement, she started painting and resumed horseback riding and biking—hobbies she enjoyed before her kids were born. "My resentment sprang from the fact that I wasn't taking care of myself," Kit said. "We do a lot of things together. But doing what we love individually has ultimately made us stronger as a couple."

> "We do a lot of things together. But doing what we love individually has ultimately made us stronger as a couple."

Like Kit, I believe it's important for both spouses to do what they love. Now that I have my own fulfilling work—writing and teaching—I sympathize more with both of the Garys. I've come to understand that professional gratification is not the same as personal fulfillment. Nor are "work-life balance" and "work-family balance" identical. There's more to personal life than just family. People must claim the time they need to feel restored.

We all need to take care of ourselves and give back to our communities.

For me, gardening, traveling, reading, and serving on nonprofit boards (and yes, even exercising—thank you, Gary) are not just leisure pursuits. They have come to feel necessary. Ideally, couples will create strategies together that give them the time they need as individuals. As Dr. Lewandowski points out, "self-expansion" is a distributive principle. Each spouse is enriched and, in turn, enriches the marriage.

Nancy Rosenzweig, Lori Johnston, and their children Harper and Isabella.

Nancy Rosenzweig put it more philosophically. She is a serial entrepreneur and CEO, and the mother of two small children. The fact that she also devotes significant time to volunteer work has sometimes caused tension at home. Paraphrasing the poet David Whyte, Nancy asserts that the antidote to busyness is not rest but rather "wholeheartedness."

She said that her community commitments don't deplete her—they energize her. Nurturing ourselves by doing things we're passionate about allows us to wholeheartedly nurture others—including our families and our companies.

A SEPARATE PEACE

The search for a truce continues

So when Gary is off playing tennis, he is replenishing his body, mind, and spirit, and I benefit from that. I get it now.

But here's the deeper truth: my understanding is more in my head than in my heart. I know I shouldn't chafe at Gary's rightful and healthy decision to do things he loves—things that are not financially compensated but that bring him joy and growth. Still, the extent of his voluntary commitments rankles. We enjoy our respective leisure activities in very different contexts. My work is largely confined to normal business hours and requires little travel. When I take up a new interest, our family life is not materially affected. The demands of Gary's business, by contrast, consume his mind and his time. Long before he snaps on that ski boot, his cup hath already run over.

There will always be more new things that Gary and I want to explore. Ideally some will be interests we share. But many will not be. And as our combined calendars fill up, the white spaces that represent our unscheduled time dwindle. Without conscious brakes and limits, heedlessly adding commitments can create a cycle of escalating busyness, a mutually assured (if unintended) destruction of togetherness.

Balance remains elusive. But Gary and I do better when we both grab the eraser and reclaim some of those calendar squares for the two of us.

> Gary and I do better when we both grab the eraser and reclaim some of those calendar squares for the two of us.

One recent Valentine's Day we woke up, ate a wonderful breakfast, and watched a movie we had rented. It was a lovely, lazy start to a wintry Sunday, and I was looking forward to a rare day together. Then came the backhand volley. Gary: "I'm playing tennis with Adam at 3."

I winced but immediately rallied and lobbed myself The Lecture: "This is good! He needs this!" Then up piped a wee voice in my head: "Isn't this out of bounds?"

Absent an umpire, I wasn't sure. I served up, "OK, but it would have been better if we'd talked about it first." Gary agreed. Neither one of us cried fault.

We both got the point.

Things to Talk About

- Many spouses are reluctant to admit resentment because they fear seeming bitter or petty. Repressed anger grows poisonous. Put the subject out there.

- Entrepreneurs spend all day interacting—often intensely—with other people. Spouses should understand that the desire for peace and solitude is not a personal rejection.

- What sacrifices will the entrepreneur make to ensure his spouse gets the time she needs to pursue her own interests?

- What interests do the entrepreneur and spouse share that they can develop together?

Things to Do

- Entrepreneurs who plan to recreate for more than a few hours should block out time on the family calendar and give their spouses plenty of warning.

- Spouses should cultivate their own interests. Try something new or return to a long-abandoned hobby. Become involved in philanthropic work. Take up a physical activity; it lowers stress.

- Find non-taxing, non-time-swallowing activities you can do together. Read and discuss the same book. Find a long-running series you missed on television and watch one episode a night.

- Make child-care-sharing arrangements with other time-strapped parents.

Chapter 8

Breaking Up's Not Hard To Do

Only half of small businesses survive past five years.
Entrepreneurs' marriages are almost as vulnerable.

A business school professor I know invites entrepreneurs to his classroom when he teaches case studies about their companies. Before the guests arrive, he challenges his students to read their biographies, ask some discrete questions, and deduce from those clues how many times these accomplished businesspeople have been married. The idea is to impress upon students early that relationships pay the price when entrepreneurs fling themselves—body, brain, and heart—into a start-up. The professor hopes that when his students return to the class to discuss their own successful ventures they won't be dragging a string of exes in their wake.

No one, as far as I know, breaks out divorce statistics for entrepreneurs, but I'd wager that they're higher than the U.S. average. Fortunately, my husband and I are not among that number. The demands of Gary's business have created periods of distance and suffocating tension between us. But our marriage has survived the occasional stony silence and slammed door. Still, given the extraordinary pressure company founding exerts on families, it could easily have been otherwise.

Common causes of divorce include financial strain, neglect, lack of communication, and divergent goals. Postmortems on the remains of entrepreneurs' marriages turn up all those grievances in abundance. Other professions keep people away from home and preoccupy their thoughts, but they don't produce the toxic cocktail of resentment and anxiety created by putting the family's security constantly at risk. Then there's that green-eyed minx, Jealousy. How often have you heard an entrepreneur describe her company as her "passion"? How often have you heard one say the same thing about her spouse?

Particularly in already strained marriages, there is no tension that owning a business can't make worse. The intensity of the entrepreneurial experience amplifies unhealthy marital dynamics. For one thing, company-owning couples have so many more issues to argue about. Even if a couple isn't fighting about sacrifice, frequent absences, or the pain of living with uncertainty, the spouse won't hesitate to fire that ammunition during whatever battle they *are* fighting. Many of the stories I tell in other parts of the book—pushed to their logical, harrowing conclusions—would be equally at home in this chapter.

When marriages are weak, the pressures of company building can act as a catalyst, speeding an outcome that would probably have happened anyway. Arguably, a quicker split is not always a bad thing, because it saves time and prevents additional heartache. But it's equally possible that, absent the contention introduced by a company, the couple might have cruised along with a lot less turmoil. Newlyweds would have had time to get better acquainted: to recognize one another's breaking points and develop mechanisms for handling conflict. Time, shared history, and more skillful communication may increase the couple's desire to keep the marriage alive.

"Alienation of affection" is the charge brought by a deserted spouse, usually against the "other" man or woman implicated in a divorce. It's a wonder no start-up has ever been named as a defendant.

. . . LET NO BUSINESS PUT ASUNDER
The company resets expectations

Combining a company with a marriage reveals a fundamental paradox. Marriage is about doing things together, while business building—assuming the spouses are not cofounders—is largely a solo journey. So the couple divides into two individuals traveling separate paths. After a while, they know each other less well than when they first wed.

One cause of distancing is that the pair communicates less—and not just as a function of spending less time together. When family life gets rocky, entrepreneurs often take physical, mental, and emotional refuge in their companies, which present a set of problems more easily resolvable by their analytical talents. Entrepreneurs in high-anxiety situations—domestic as well as business ones—tend to work more and talk to their spouses less, according to Dr. Michael Komie, a clinical psychologist in Chicago and professor at the Chicago School of Professional Psychology who counsels high-level executives and business owners. That psychological isolation often causes trouble in a marriage.

> Entrepreneurs in high-anxiety situations—domestic as well as business ones—tend to work more and talk to their spouses less.

Couples don't always communicate about the business either. The entrepreneur is probably aware that openness and honesty are critical for healthy relationships. But as problems bubble up, he keeps them to himself, either to shield his spouse from concern or because he knows the revelations will ignite conflict. The spouse, for her part, knows ignorance isn't bliss but assumes knowledge will be anguish; she steers clear as an act of self-preservation. Thus, a start-up can become a marriage's third rail: the subject couples dare not touch for fear of shockwaves. "Entrepreneurs have people freaking out on them all day long," one company founder told me. "We don't want the same thing at home. If I'm worried about meeting payroll some week, I need her to hold my hand and ask what she can do to help, not run from the room screaming that she can't believe I had gotten us to this place." So the entrepreneur worries silently about the company. The spouse worries about the entrepreneur who won't tell her what he's worrying about. Unshared, their burdens are twice as heavy and ultimately unbearable.

The entrepreneur's evolving priorities—or what the spouse believes are his evolving priorities—can also cause disillusion and dismay. The spouse finds that, even if she remains first in her husband's heart, she is no longer first in his mind. So the relationship devolves into a series of skirmishes that come down to a choice: the business or your family? The business or me? If the entrepreneur repeatedly chooses the business, chances are the marriage is doomed.

The tipping point where differences shade into irreconcilable differences varies from couple to couple. But the death spiral of the marriage of "Kevin" and "Jessica" is typical. Kevin told me he had detected fissures in the relationship even before he started an electronics manufacturing company. Afterward, those fissures widened into canyons. Jessica never took the business seriously and doubted openly that it could support them. His wife's negative attitude made Kevin—already preoccupied with the start-up—even less eager to spend time with her. So he neglected her, poring over business plans when she wanted to chat.

Resentful, Jessica decided that if she couldn't compete with the business for her husband's attention she would compete with it for his resources. If Kevin bought a tool for his company, Jessica would go out and buy jewelry of equal value. "Once I bought an oscilloscope, and in return I had to buy her a Corvette," Kevin told me. "She considered my stuff toys. Playthings." The couple divorced after two years.

Sometimes, company building changes people, and not always for the better. As the entrepreneur gets comfortable with leadership and secure in her achievements, traits such as bossiness, self-importance, and impatience often intensify. I'm not talking about situations like those described in chapter 3 in which the entrepreneur, by virtue of her role, assumes a dominant attitude at the office (when the spouse also works in the company) and then unconsciously sustains it at home. I'm talking about personalities and priorities changing, about egos swollen by success and personal relationships devalued if they don't contribute to that success. I'm talking about waking up every morning next to someone who is increasingly a stranger.

> "The seeds of our dissolution were already there. But they were like popcorn. The heat of the business made them pop up all over the place."

"Ray" said building a company made his wife of 23 years feel so powerful and confident that she became dismissive of him. She expected that her vision and needs would dominate their lives. "The seeds of our dissolution were already there," said Ray. "But they were like popcorn. The heat of the business made them pop up all over the place."

Ironically, Ray said, the thrill of starting a business had initially reinvigorated their relationship. But over time, as his wife's workaholism continued, Ray asked if she really still wanted a husband. "She replied with some version of, 'Not now; maybe later.'" The couple divorced before later had a chance to arrive.

YOUR MONEY OR YOUR WIFE
Arguments over finances create permanent rifts

In chapter 2, I described how money creates tensions between the entrepreneur and her friends and relatives. Money can also ram a wedge between the entrepreneur and her spouse. In fact, financial troubles fall above infidelity (although below poor communication) on most rankings of reasons for divorce.

Disagreements over whether to allocate limited cash to business or family needs rapidly deteriorate into whose-money-is-it-anyway, a game that can turn really nasty when the spouse's earnings and savings are also in play. One entrepreneur I spoke with made a chunk of change selling a condo he had purchased before his marriage. Later, he planned to invest that money in his new business. His wife wanted it safely banked. She said the money was "theirs." He said it was "his" and acted accordingly. "You might as well break up the relationship when you do that," he said. They divorced shortly afterward. In retrospect, the entrepreneur said, he wishes he'd sat down with his wife and calmly discussed what to do with the funds.

Entrepreneur-invests-in-business: spouse-gets-mad is the usual formula for the money-wrecked marriage. But sometimes the spouse wins the battle over finances, causing both to lose the war. By refusing to spend the family's money on the company, the spouse telegraphs her belief that the entrepreneur is pursuing a lost cause—and, by extension, that she has no faith in him. While the entrepreneur is begging for another transfusion, the spouse is issuing the DNR order. I spoke with the former wife of an entrepreneur who termed "gut-wrenching" her decision to refuse to sign a home equity loan that would have salvaged her husband's business. The business went under. The couple never recovered.

Traditional wedding vows ask couples to take one another "for better, for worse; for richer, for poorer." But when an entrepreneur consistently sweeps the possibility of "for better" and "for richer" permanently off the table, it's hard to blame the spouse for rethinking the deal. "Paul," a software and media entrepreneur, admits he subjected his wife to "eight years of damn-near abject poverty and suffering" while he struggled to produce and sell a TV show. Finally, "she couldn't take it anymore," he said. "Two kids in diapers and wondering where next month's mortgage payment was coming from," Paul's wife delivered an ultimatum: the TV show or her. "I said the TV show," he told me. "That was the day the love died." The marriage died with it.

Paul, at least, noticed and understood his wife's sacrifice. But sometimes spouses are willfully blind to each other's suffering. "I don't think my entrepreneurial activity had anything to do with our divorce," said "Eric," founder of half a dozen companies. "She seemed to enjoy business vicariously." Eric told me that his ex-wife, "Lisa," never took responsibility for their financial health, always assuming that he would find a way to pay for their lifestyle. Their home was perpetually collateralized, but he said Lisa never seemed bothered by that fact. "I couldn't have started all those businesses had she been concerned about security, houses, all those things," Eric said.

Speaking with Lisa separately, I heard a wildly different story. "At one point, he told me we could lose everything," she said. "That level of tension, exhaustion, and fear can make you crazy. I had learned not to get hysterical in the face of insecurity. I knew that panicking wasn't going to improve things." It was hard to believe we were discussing the same marriage.

TWO DEADLY SINS
Marriages laid low by jealousy and envy

Infidelity, of course, is a common cause of divorce in general, and there's no evidence that entrepreneurs or their spouses are more likely than others to succumb. But entrepreneurs are away a lot. And sometimes absence makes the heart grow fonder of someone else. To the entrepreneur on his travels—or even working late at night with an attractive consultant or employee—the world of his business and the people who populate it are sometimes more real and more vital than the spouse he barely sees. Meanwhile, the spouse, feeling neglected and increasingly alone, is also vulnerable to temptation.

"Jack" described to me what happened when he moved his wife and two children to Britain so he could run a joint venture for his family's business, which produces supplies for the steel industry. He thought he and his wife had struck a "bargain." He'd supply the shekels; she'd raise the kids in

"It was classic. The business was my mistress."

their lovely home. But Jack spent more than half his time on the road, leaving his wife in an unfamiliar country with no support network. "It was classic. The business was my mistress," said Jack. His wife had an affair, eventually leaving Jack for the man who was there for her.

Jack's personal life wasn't all that suffered because of the divorce. During the split, he was so enervated and distracted he lost several big contracts. The constant trips required by his business became torture. "It's hard traveling when you know someone else is with your wife," he told me. "I was consumed with wondering what was going on at home and felt terrible that there was nothing I could do about it."

In the previous section, I described Eric and Lisa's disconnect over money. But finances were just one factor in the dissolution of their marriage. Eric's business took him out into the world and endowed him with a kind of glamour. His natural charm, embellished with a CEO's cachet, attracted the attention of other women. "I understood that he needed to network," Lisa told me. "But at events, I was shocked as women would come up as close as they could, flirting, sighing, eyes all sparkly. I'm there thinking, 'Oh shit.' I wanted to tell him that I was already his fan, that he was already famous with me." Preferring the flattery and attention of his admirers to the rancor and criticism at home, Eric had affairs, and the marriage went under.

Not quite so destructive as jealousy—but still plenty destructive—is envy. Entrepreneurs with successful businesses often develop prestige, power, and their own spheres of influence. They are featured in newspapers and magazines, star in television commercials, receive awards, deliver speeches, and chair boards.

Unless the spouse enjoys a comparably flourishing career—and if she's managing a family, that's unlikely—a status gap opens between the two. The spouse feels unappreciated and reacts sourly to the entrepreneur's accolades.

This envy can become especially corrosive when the successful entrepreneur is a woman. Sorry as I am to say it, there are still husbands who, provoked by the collapse of gender stereotypes, resent rather than celebrate their wives' entrepreneurial successes. The CEO of a thriving PR agency said that she split from her husband when he became emotionally and physically abusive in response to her growing independence. "He would tell people I wore the pants in the family, just because of my income," she said. "I didn't understand why he wasn't happy for us."

Of course, accomplished women in any profession risk similar backlash. But female entrepreneurs—by definition leaders of others—pose a particular threat to vulnerable male egos. Insecure men confuse a woman's sense of authority with a desire for superiority. As one female entrepreneur said, "I think most men are put off by businesswomen who act the same way men do in similar situations. It de-feminizes us in their eyes."

> Female entrepreneurs pose a particular threat to vulnerable male egos.

MOM-AND-POP. SUBTRACT POP.
Keeping the business together
as the owners separate

Spouses who own and run a business together may have a better shot at avoiding rupture. After all, they have extra incentive to make their relationship work—the business equivalent of "for the sake of the children." They are also less likely to follow divergent paths or disagree about where to invest their money. In fact, a business can keep a wobbly marriage on its feet by providing powerful, shared experiences. One woman told me that she and her ex-husband formed their closest bonds celebrating company successes and commiserating over setbacks. But the business was all they had in common. Ultimately, it was not enough.

Just as company building can lead to divorce, divorce can destabilize a company. It can even sap brand equity if the business trades on a family image. Chris Blanchard grows 20 acres of vegetables at Rock Spring Farm in Decorah, Iowa, a stone's throw from the Minnesota border. In his original marketing materials, he and his now-ex-wife,

Kim Keller, were the literal face of the farm. They still smile together in newspaper articles, from brochures, and on posters in natural-food

Chris Blanchard.

stores. "We had this public image of the idyllic farm family, and that was part of what we were selling," Chris told me. He hasn't lied about the end of his marriage, but he hasn't broadcast it either. "Look, my customers want a good story with their vegetables," he said. "They want a narrative. This divorce just doesn't belong in a Smith & Hawken catalogue. And I have a business to run."

Today, things are better between the two. Chris missed Kim's skills and perspective so much that he hired her back. But she's an employee now, and no longer a source of thousands of hours of free labor. Furthermore, farm capital improvements and the financial implications of the divorce forced Chris to renegotiate his equipment and real estate loans, assuming considerable debt and putting the farm on shakier footing. As a farmer, Chris understands how vulnerable life is to outside forces. There are droughts. There are floods. And now there is divorce.

Spouse partners who leave the business suffer too. Kim put 10 years of sweat equity into their farm; her only way out of an unhappy marriage was to leave that investment behind. She emerged without a job, her own credit history, or even a job title to list on a résumé. "I didn't want to destroy the farm by asking for half of it," Kim told me. Ray, the man whose wife thought she might want a husband later, lost his CFO spot along with his marriage. "I'd made a huge contribution, and that identity was stolen from me," he said.

Kim Keller.

Severe marital conflict is also distracting and unnerving for employees. They work for a company whose existence began with the union of two people. Absent that union, they worry whether anything will be left. One former couple, founders of a California food company proud of its familial culture, postponed for almost a year telling staff that they had divorced, hoping to tamp down anxiety. They eventually let the news leak out, rather than announce it, to downplay its significance.

Other co-preneur couples, however, choose to string a clothesline across the office and hang their dirty laundry there for all to see. A woman I'll call "Jane" described how, before they divorced, she and her now ex-husband would sit through meetings seething at each other. Once he rammed a product design through to completion even though he—and all the employees—knew Jane would disapprove. The employees were afraid to tell her. So they tiptoed around the furious couple, "hoping Mom and Dad would hold it together," Jane said.

If Mom and Dad can't keep it together, dividing up the business may be harder than dividing up other commonly held assets. After all, you can always buy another house. But a company is the one-of-a-kind product of the creativity, energy, and vision of both spouses.

I spoke with one business owner whose husband tried to take the entire company, claiming that he had written the software it was based on. He also went after his ex-wife's retirement fund and—until she sued him—her IRS refunds. Jane's husband threatened to sell his 50 percent ownership in their business to a competitor when the pair divorced. Jane agreed to pay him $1.5 million over 10 years to buy back half his stock, and her accountants assured her that cash flow would cover it. But she failed to consider that those annual $150,000 installments would be siphoned from post-tax revenue. Payments to Jane's ex contributed to the company's eventual descent into chapter 11.

I asked Jane why she'd agreed to this deal. "I did the thing women do," she told me. "I thought, 'I want to get this over with. I just want out, and I don't care what it takes.'" Jane also worried that unless she dispensed with the matter quickly, investors, lenders, customers, and employees might see the business as shaky. And she was alarmed at the prospect of a judge determining the value of her company.

Jane's story might have had a happier ending if she'd had a shareholder agreement. "I'd be remiss if I didn't ask my client how he or she will address marital problems from a business perspective," said Alan Reische, a New Hampshire corporate attorney who specializes in corporate succession planning. Even cofounding couples with cloudless marital horizons should create such an agreement, spelling out how to value the business should they divorce and specifying a maximum payout period for the non-active spouse. If one spouse owns a minority share, the agreement should establish an automatic buyout mechanism in the event of a split.

> Jane's husband threatened to sell his 50 percent ownership in their business to a competitor when the pair divorced.

Alan cautions entrepreneurs against being miserly in their assessment of the company's value in an attempt to minimize payout, lest the court overturn the valuation and impose its own. If a couple splits without an agreement in place, the division generally falls to divorce attorneys. As Jane can attest, that is not a happy prospect.

Though divorce threatens a business, it can also have upsides. After all, there's relief in finality. Following the announcement (or quiet one-on-one conversations), rumors and gossip briefly spike, then die out. The knot of accumulated tension in the workplace is undone. The owners can finally back-burner their personal lives and focus all their attention on the business. Work returns, more or less, to normal.

And, amazingly, plenty of couples labor together peacefully and productively post-split. Katie Paine, CEO of Berlin, New Hampshire-based KDPaine & Partners, which measures the effects of marketing campaigns, recently hired her ex-husband (they divorced in the mid-'80s) to run her business. They work well together, Katie told me, although she struggles against relapsing into old marital patterns. While Steve Demos and Pat Calhoun were founding WhiteWave, a maker of tofu and Silk soymilk in Broomfield, Colorado, they were in the midst of a divorce. Starting up a company while winding down a marriage may sound like dangerously incompatible activities. But, said Steve, "we shared a mission and a work ethic. She is still one of my closest friends."

Katie Paine.

DOING BETTER NEXT TIME
The entrepreneur promises reform

Like most people who divorce, entrepreneurs vow not to repeat the same mistakes. Many accept blame for their skewed priorities. And if they remarry, they promise their new spouses undivided attention. There is much talk of date nights and shared hobbies. The next marriage—like the next company—will benefit from lessons learned in the failure of the first.

But although entrepreneurs may be teachable, they are not wholly reformable. As I spoke to divorced company founders, I heard underneath the grace notes of good intentions a common bass lick: the business will still come first. As Chris Blanchard put it, "Anybody I get involved with will have to know that I already have one wife—and it's the farm. Relationships rarely seem as urgent as anything in the field."

At least these entrepreneurs are being honest with themselves. And hopefully they will be equally honest in their next serious relationships: providing full disclosure about the role their businesses played in the dissolution of their marriages.

Still, divorce attorneys might want to stamp indelible caveat emptor—buyer beware!—warnings on entrepreneurs' hands as they leave the office. As one divorced entrepreneur put it, "My priorities haven't really changed. I still have big plans."

Things to Talk About

- If the divorcing couple works together and plans to continue doing so, how will they collaborate amicably?

- The spouse's earning potential may have suffered because she postponed her career while the entrepreneur built the business. What reparations can be made?

- If custody is not shared, will there be an ongoing role for the children in the business?

- What went wrong? Relationship autopsies are often not productive. But as the entrepreneur and spouse move on to new relationships, it may help to understand what role the business played in breaking them apart.

Things to Do

- Even if the cofounding couple swears their love will last forever, the company's disposition is too important to leave to divorce attorneys. Craft a shareholder agreement that spells out what happens in case of a split.

- When drawing up the agreement, don't rely on a formula that will underestimate the company's value.

- If the divorcing couple co-owns the business, make a plan for informing employees, customers, suppliers, and other stakeholders. Try to anticipate their questions and come up with reassuring answers in advance.

- Entrepreneurs try to prevent their families from feeling the turmoil of their business lives. Similarly, they should try to shield their companies from tumult in the domestic sphere. Don't forget, employees take their cues from the mood of the leader.

Chapter 9

Death of the Dream

It's all over. The company failed. Emotionally drained,
the entrepreneur and his spouse are left to
pick up the pieces of their finances,
their reputations, and their relationship.

Gary and I have lived through so many crises, I must be a masochist for dwelling on the one awful thing that *didn't* happen. Still, I can't help wondering what our lives would have been like if Stonyfield had failed.

As I've mentioned, our company flirted with bankruptcy for the better part of a decade. Both Gary and I were uncomfortably familiar with the poor odds of any small business succeeding. Still, Gary believed we'd be the exception to the rule. I, by contrast, was pretty sure we had "rule" stamped on our foreheads. Had my prophecy come true I don't know if we could have recovered. The loss of Stonyfield would have meant the loss of everything: our home, our lifestyle, our ability to put three children through college. More profoundly (and this is where my exercise in alternative history gets really scary), it could have meant the loss of my confidence in Gary. If his big bet—his promise to me and to our family—had not worked out, would I have looked at him differently? Trusted his judgment less? Forever questioned his ability to assess risk?

Over the years, I've talked to entrepreneurs about some tough topics, including divorce and catastrophic illness. But no conversations have proved as wrenching as those concerning business failure. Perhaps it's a matter of culpability. In divorce, the blame is usually shared. When someone gets sick, it's nobody's fault. But when a company goes down, responsibility sits squarely on the shoulders of the entrepreneur. "It's just too raw and emotional for me," apologized one entrepreneur who backed out of an interview. "I don't know if I could make it through your questions, for I might just cry and cry." It's not surprising that a recent loss would be so overpowering. But this woman's business went under almost a decade ago.

The entrepreneur's company is the crucible in which his character is both forged and revealed. The only heat more intense is produced by the business going up in flames. In the wake of its loss, the founder's belief in himself falters, even shatters.

Business failure also takes a wrecking ball to the entrepreneur's relationships built on trust. He feels responsible for everyone: his now jobless employees; friendly and institutional lenders who may be owed substantial sums; the investors who bet on his idea, sure, but first and foremost on him. Worst of all, he knows he has kicked his family's fortunes back to square one, or past that to square 0 or −3. For perhaps the first time, he wonders, by what right did I ask this of them?

In any business failure, sorrow and worry are a given. It's the family's reaction to the loss that determines how their relationships will fare. Is the entrepreneur able to dust himself off and recover his optimism? Can the spouse muster more sympathy than resentment for a serious setback that was not of her making? Can the children adapt to their altered circumstances?

Most at risk is the entrepreneur's marriage. A failed business consumes a couple's assets until there is nothing left. In the worst case, it does the same thing to their love for each other.

There but for the grace of God . . .

FOR BITTER OR WORSE
The spouse gets mad

Traumatic events can deepen relationships or damage them. Deepening is often the result of a fully shared experience. Damage is more likely when people experience a blow in different ways, as occurs when the business of one spouse fails.

For the entrepreneur, business failure is mostly about the future. He may ask himself what he could have done differently, but his greatest suffering comes with the harsh realization that his vision and destiny will never be fulfilled. For the spouse, business failure is mostly about the past. True, she is crushed that there will be no payday. But much more than the entrepreneur, she looks backward and wonders, "Was all that sacrifice really for nothing?" The entrepreneur shrinks from the prospect of long, lonely days and nights without his business, while the spouse dwells on the memory of long, lonely days and nights without her husband. He grieves for what will never be. She grieves for what never was.

The couple may also suffer from changes in the spouse's attitude toward the entrepreneur. If the sailing has been less than smooth (a given), chances are that resentment and doubt have been fermenting for some time. During rough patches, the spouse worries that the entrepreneur is on a vision quest, has delusions of grandeur, or is perhaps indulging a hobby dressed up as a company. Her faith in him erodes, and with it, her respect. Still, she represses her feelings until her suspicions are confirmed. Then, when worse finally comes to worst, she lets loose not only with the anger and fear of the moment but also with recriminations—over scrimping and postponing and single parenting—that she's been rehearsing in her head for years.

In his darkest moment, the entrepreneur desperately needs his spouse to remain strong, comforting, and encouraging. He wants her to tell him, "It's OK. You did the best you could." But, at least initially, the spouse can only splutter, "How could you?"

> "Losing our company has made me question my values. Do things have to work out in order for me to still love my mate?"

Among the ruins of the family's fortunes, the spouse may also discover some unwelcome truths about herself. If her affection and respect hinged on the entrepreneur's financial success, she wonders what that says about her. "Losing our company has made me question my values," one spouse put it to me baldly. "Do things have to work out in order for me to still love my mate? I was good with the marriage before, when we were doing well financially. I would hate to think that's what kept us together."

"Cynthia" experiences a slight twinge as she recalls the words she spoke to her husband, "Stephen," when he voluntarily closed down his Manhattan-based company. "You got us into this mess," she told him. "Now you've got to get us out." Although it was not her proudest moment, Cynthia believed Stephen was ultimately responsible for the financial and emotional strain that the company's liquidation placed on their 14-year marriage. "The ordeal sucked a lot of life out of our relationship," she said.

The business—an online social network—was all Stephen's baby. It had begun to gain traction, but not quickly enough to support the couple and their two children. As the financial noose tightened, the pair jointly set benchmarks for the company's continued existence: benchmarks it failed to meet. Stephen was left to mourn largely on his own, just as during his company's short life he had kept Cynthia at arm's length from it. His goal, then, had been to shield his wife from worry.

> I wanted to be closer to her, but she didn't want to know. She's more emotional and reactive than me. When I share with her a small ride I'm on, she goes on a big ride. You don't want to treat your spouse like a child, but you need to be sensitive to the fact that she has a different risk profile.

Neither Stephen nor Cynthia anticipated how the company's loss would affect their marriage. Most couples don't. The spouses don't feel they can safely express the depths of their despair to one another. So they wind up huddled in opposite corners, nursing their wounds. Fortunately, Cynthia eventually accepted that Stephen's decisions were consistent with the character of the man she loved. She came to see his willingness to shutter the business before he was forced to as testament to his commitment—first and foremost—to his family.

Some spouses take longer to forgive. Dr. Kathy Marshack (the Oregon psychologist, mentioned in chapter 3, who specializes in counseling entrepreneurial couples) said a spouse's anger, confusion, and anxiety are both natural and usually temporary as the couple assimilates the lessons from the crisis and starts to rebuild. "Dealing with loss is a process," Dr. Marshack advises entrepreneurs. "Don't freak out because your partner is upset. She should be upset. It doesn't mean that your marriage is going to fall apart."

> "That's what crises are for couples—an opportunity to change things."

When I asked whether there were fewer recriminations when couples took the entrepreneurial plunge together, Dr. Marshack set me straight. Yes, a noninvolved spouse can fault the entrepreneur for mismanaging the family's money and security while the entrepreneur accuses the spouse of being unsupportive. But even a couple that runs a business together may endlessly and venomously debate which one ruined everything. "The list goes on and on with ways that loved ones can blame the very person they should be turning to," said

Dr. Marshack. "Such victimizing never works. The key is to drop the blame and work on solutions. That's what crises are for couples—an opportunity to change things."

A GLOOM OF ONE'S OWN
The entrepreneur gets depressed

It's a vicious cycle. The entrepreneur, wrapped up in his ever-more-demanding company, grows distant from his family. Though a bundle of energy, he has little time for activities that don't advance the business. Then, the company folds. His obsession, the subject of most of his waking thoughts, is gone, reduced to a puddle of regret. And so, the entrepreneur succumbs to depression and remorse. No longer overwhelmed by work challenges, he sees the days stretch empty before him. His energy gone, he grows even more distant from his family. And now that distance is more troubling because he is alienated instead of preoccupied, and the light at tunnel's end is extinguished.

People cope with loss differently. Some entrepreneurs mourn their failed companies briefly and, a month later, are drawing up new business plans. Others become so enervated they can't lift the page to see the next chapter.

"Eve," whose husband's business failed, told me that "Philip" now spends most of the day moping around the house in sweatpants, trying to figure out what to do. Every day the couple loses ground, depleting their children's college funds and their own retirement money. They lose ground psychologically too. The children give their father a wide berth, sensing his sadness and fearing his emotional volatility. They wonder why he is at home so much, and Eve worries that Philip's apparent aimlessness will, in her words, emasculate him in their eyes. A crack is forking through the family, with Philip on one side and Eve and the kids on the other. "My mommy thing has kicked in," Eve said. "I'm gathering my children around me with my wings and protecting them with my feathers and asking him, 'Why did you put all this at risk?'" Making things worse, neither spouse is sleeping well. Not surprisingly, "couple time is not a priority," Eve said.

While Philip wallows, Eve swings between resentment of her husband for letting her down and anger at herself for letting it happen. Eve works, but her teaching job doesn't pay nearly enough to support the family. That never troubled her before because, as she now admits, she simply assumed Philip would always be the primary breadwinner. "Why didn't I know better?" Eve asks herself. "Why didn't I prepare?" (Personally, I think Eve is being hard on herself. If the entrepreneur is fully engrossed in pursuing Plan A, it seems unreasonable to expect the spouse, who is managing everything else in their lives, to also be chugging away on Plan B.)

Although the spouse is also depressed, she can't afford to retreat from the world. She may be forced to act as the couple's public face, constantly apologizing for her husband's absence or behavior and absorbing the unwelcome questions or commiseration of others. When "Jim" sank into a depression after his company failed, he stopped going to social events and attending family functions. His wife, "Ellen," was left to perform the social niceties on her own. Ellen's parents, meanwhile, badgered her with questions about why Jim didn't "just get a job," and they accused her of being a doormat for staying with him. Even though she had no decision-making role in the business, Ellen felt like a failure by association.

> "I thought moving and starting with a clean slate would make a difference. But the trail—the history of why we are in this situation—followed us here."

The couple finally moved across the country, eagerly grabbing a job offer as an opportunity to start fresh. Yet they remain estranged from each other and are on the verge of divorce. "I thought moving and starting with a clean slate would make a difference," Ellen told me. "But the trail—the history of why we are in this situation—followed us here. Our problems didn't change with the landscape."

The entrepreneur's misery will be especially intense if she believes that the failure has thwarted her dreams for good. Sure she can blame things on a bad economy, bad luck, or bad timing. But unless she is

Jason Jacobs.

in complete denial, she must also blame herself. Even if she has her spouse's support, who will believe in her next time? She thinks back on the long hard slog of raising money and envisions repeating it wearing the albatross of bankruptcy around her neck. She cannot imagine finding the strength to try again.

Such sentiments, however, are mostly the depression talking. Many entrepreneurs who have lost their businesses pick themselves up and start again (including, by the way, the woman I mentioned at the start of the chapter who refused to talk to me for fear she would cry). Older and wiser, they avoid the mistakes that previously brought them down. Investors often recognize that fact and are not put off. Jason Jacobs lost his retail software company in 2009, forced out by his venture investors. When he launched a consulting business in upstate New York in 2010, "I was concerned that I'd be damaged goods with VC firms," Jason said. "But I'm not. They've reached out to me."

Lanny Goodman, a New Mexico management consultant, recalls being told by one investor that he *preferred* to see a business failure on an entrepreneur's résumé. "It told him that the entrepreneur had moxie enough to get back on the horse," Lanny said, "and that having been through failure, the entrepreneur would be less terrorized by the prospect. Though bruised, the owner of a failed company knows that no one is going to die because a business goes under." Andy Whitman, managing partner at 2x Consumer Products Growth Partners, a Chicago-based investment company, put it this way: "Most of us have failed at something. I look at whether people can articulate what went wrong and what they'd do differently next time. Overcoming adversity can make an entrepreneur stronger and more savvy." Seen through this lens, a second business, unlike a second marriage, is not a triumph of hope over experience, but a triumph of experience, period.

GOOD-BYE TO ALL THAT
Status and reputation go down with the business

"I am in free fall. What felt like solid ground has vanished."

Anyone who has lost a business knows just how Gail Horvath felt when she wrote those words. Gail shared with me her diary entries for 2003, the year her company went bankrupt. For almost three decades, Just Desserts, the San Francisco baked-goods business that Gail started with her husband, Elliot Hoffman, had cranked out high-quality confections for a group of loyal and passionate customers. Then a couple of bad decisions—to go into frozen products and expand to a bigger plant—proved fatal. The failure was especially devastating coming, as it did, after such a long successful run. "Our business felt solid and bigger than life," wrote Gail, "as if it would always be there, with its uncanny ability to claw itself out of any difficulty."

As Gail attests, entrepreneurial companies occupy vast mental, emotional, and physical space in their founders' lives. They define how founders and their families live and—to some extent—who they are. With failure, an entrepreneurial family's identity and position, as well as its security, crumbles. Friends and relatives gingerly avoid the subject, treating loss of a business, as one spouse put it, like a serious medical condition that everyone is aware of but too diplomatic to acknowledge. And this disease is not support-group fodder: rarely do entrepreneurs who've passed through the valley pop up to comfort current sufferers. Business failure is the loss that dare not speak its name.

Discomfort and humiliation on the part of business owners only

deep the chasm. Philip's depression precipitated that couple's isolation. But Eve didn't improve the situation by avoiding conversations
with her brothers—both successful attor-

> "The company formed an integral part of our relationship, defining us as a couple. It's hard to believe that it is now gone from our lives."

neys—and others whose "normal" lives seemed to taunt her.

Making matters worse, knowledge of the loss can't be contained within a small circle of loved ones. Businesses play visible roles within their communities. When they fail, their founders' standing within those communities suffers. That was certainly true for Gail Horvath and Elliot Hoffman. As Gail wrote in her diary: "The company formed an integral part of our relationship, defining us as a couple and giving us our special status in the San Francisco Bay Area community. It's hard to believe that it is now gone from our lives."

It is a contradiction of the entrepreneurial psyche: while founders relish doing what no one expects, they also care quite a bit what people think. In the wake of business failure, the entrepreneur pauses from silently beating himself up only to imagine how others are verbally beating him up. What's the word on the street about what happened? Do people judge him? Has he lost credibility? He wonders about his position on the boards of local philanthropies, his leadership role in business forums and industry organizations, and if he will ever regain his standing. One spouse told me that her husband had so financially overextended the family to keep his business afloat that they were forced to sell their spacious home and move to a less desirable part of town. The husband, once a highly respected member of the community, "was now recognized as a failure who had to move into an apartment to shelter his family," she said. Notability converted to notoriety as his social standing was suddenly ripped away.

To the extent that her business contributed to the local economy, specters of guilt may continue to haunt the entrepreneur. In the supermarket, she encounters a onetime employee, now without a job. A photo of the company's old office appears in the window of a realtor, and she walks swiftly past, aware that last month's rent remains unpaid. The spouse suffers too, cognizant of the whispers at church, the invitations to social events that never arrive. Acquaintances that once were warm become cordial. Those who were cordial become cold. As one entrepreneur put it, success is busy and full of noise. With failure, life falls silent.

Even more wrenching than letting down the community is letting down one's children. In chapter 6, I described the singular joys of involving children in the family business. The flip side is that progeny suffer singular disappointment if that business expires. They must cope not only with their parents' woe and declining quality of life but also with the burden of knowing that their family is responsible for people—people they may consider friends—losing their jobs.

A parent's business failure may also have repercussions on her child's future. Joanna Hoffman, Gail and Elliot's daughter, was 17 when her parents lost Just Desserts. Suddenly finding her parents in financial distress, Joanna was forced to pass up the first-class college that had accepted her and settle for a less prestigious school, which offered more financial aid. Even then, she had to sign up for a work-study program. By contrast, her older brother, pre-bankruptcy, had been able to enroll in the college of his choice.

In the worst cases, the lost business was meant to be a legacy. The entrepreneur spends years building a vessel to carry forward the family name, something his children will one day lead and make their own. Breaking that promise breaks the founder's heart and rattles the thwarted heirs, who see their road forward abruptly washed away. "My future was devastated," said one young woman who was about to join her father's business when it went bankrupt. "I was finishing college, and I had no plan."

The collateral damage from a business's implosion is extensive and deep. The entrepreneur may shoulder full responsibility for the loss, but he cannot stop the suffering from being shared.

LOVE AMONG THE RUINS
Marriages strengthened by failure

Fortunately, many entrepreneurs are like walking juicers: forever prepared to turn lemons into lemonade. When I talked to company founders about illness, for example, several described how personal health crises or the possibility of losing loved ones refocused them on what really mattered. Scary as those experiences were, they had the salubrious effect of redirecting entrepreneurs' noses toward roses and away from grindstones.

The same is sometimes true of company failures. I spoke with one woman whose husband lost his business after four years and several million dollars had swirled down the drain. She told me that in the beginning she had been excited about the enterprise because, for the first time in years, her husband was "on fire." But she soon grew disenchanted with his prolonged absences. Meanwhile, her husband's health declined as he started smoking heavily and stopped exercising. Worse, he grew emotionally unrecognizable to her. At one point, during an argument, he told her that the company was more important to him than anything, including her and the kids. "That's the closest we ever came to divorce," she told me. "What saved our marriage was that the business went belly up."

In the aftermath, her husband spent three months catching up on his sleep and becoming reacquainted with his three children. He went back to his legal practice, and the couple started laughing together again. "It was like he had survived a war," the spouse said. "When it ended, he saw his little world was still intact, and he was so grateful."

Bill Bartmann had his own epiphany after his business failed: an event that reminded him what a crucial ally his wife, Kathy, could be. Commercial Financial Systems, a debt-collection service that was valued as high as $6 billion, collapsed in 1998. The Bartmanns lost everything and wound up as front-page news in Tulsa—their

Kathy and Bill Bartmann.

hometown and their company's. They also faced the disgrace of indictments for fraud (later dropped) and the pain of being shunned by many they'd considered friends. Through this very public and humiliating ordeal, the couple circled the wagons. "You become the only friend that person has left," Bill told me.

Bill goes so far as to say that his marriage probably stayed together *because* his business failed. To use his metaphor, building a business is like climbing a mountain. As you ascend, you shuck extra weight and what you consider nonessentials. But when you reach the top and look down, you see your most important relationships littering the slopes. "Before I lost my business, there were times I wasn't the best husband and father," Bill said. "I put the quest ahead of more important things. When I fell off the mountain, Kathy was there to catch me." Being a billionaire, he concluded, is very expensive. "It may cost you everything you have."

Bill and Kathy are happier now, and his two daughters work with him in a company he launched in 2010. After the dust settled, Bill said, he learned something about the strength of his marriage.

"I feel so appreciative of Kathy for sticking by me. But it also made me feel like a schmuck. Because it was always there, I just didn't see it. The person standing right next to me. I had it all the time."

Although the marriage of Gail Horvath and Elliot Hoffman never faltered, the bankruptcy of Just Desserts rocked everything they thought they knew about their lives. Their daughter gave voice to the couple's dread when, on the heels of the bankruptcy, she asked what they were planning to do now. Get jobs? Gail wrote:

> The unspoken question in her voice struck the chord of fear that grips my gut at unexpected moments. Our last "jobs" were over 30 years ago. What are our marketable skills? What would I write on a résumé? What does it mean to start all over again in our mid-50s? There is no safety net. Is there time left to rebuild a nest egg before it's too late?

Well, they're giving it a try. Dr. Marshack would be pleased to see how the two have assimilated the lessons of their company's failure and learned from them. "You keep hanging on to a story of your life that is secure and safe," Gail told me. "You realize that it's a myth. It's not real. And that once it falls away, you learn that you can pick up and move on."

So that's what the couple has done. "Our crisis," said Gail, "would have been a terrible thing to waste."

Today Gail works with friends in their strategy and branding business. No longer running a company, she now has plenty of time to indulge her passion: nature photography. Elliot, meanwhile, recently started a new venture that advises small and mid-sized companies on sustainability practices. Gail declined to become part of that business. After Just Desserts, she decided never to put her personal guarantee on anything again. But she is happy to see Elliot back in the game. "It's what I love about him," she said. "He thinks big."

Their daughter has also rebounded from the company's loss and the havoc it wreaked on her college plans. Today, Joanna speaks glowingly of the college she ended up at, has a strong relationship with her parents and brother, and feels only renewed gratitude for her own opportunities in life. "The bankruptcy changed all our lives for the better," Joanna told me. "It helped me to see that setbacks can be opportunities to learn."

The week after Just Desserts cashed in its chips, Gail and Elliot went camping in the California park where they'd met, over a campfire, almost 40 years earlier. They sought solace in nature and in each other, reconnecting with their "before-business" selves and remembering the unencumbered joy and anticipation of the future they once felt. So much was gone, but what remained, wrote Gail, were "those things that cannot be destroyed—our love and our experience, our sense of humor and our spirit of adventure." Back home, she wrote in her diary:

> I sit alone in my office, absent in my thoughts as a spoonful of lemon cake and fresh blueberries passes my lips. I forget how good the stuff is, until the rare occasion when I get the spark and bake up a celebration. My black Just Desserts T-shirt carries a quote attributed to Ernestine Ulmer: "Life is uncertain . . . eat dessert first." She's right, you know.

And so is Gail.

Things to Talk About

- What will you do if the business fails? Is there a Plan B?

- Are there circumstances under which you would consider pulling the plug? Should you agree on benchmarks the business must meet to ensure its survival?

- Consider whether the spouse should be working, taking classes, or otherwise keeping his résumé fresh in case he needs to make a speedy return to the workforce.

- Is this company the entrepreneur's only shot? Or will the spouse endorse her trying again in the future?

Things to Do

- The entrepreneur should keep his spouse informed about the state of the business. Don't baby her, but be sensitive to her limits.

- The entrepreneur should develop a peer group—a local business forum or Entrepreneurs' Organization chapter, for example—to share concerns and seek support and advice.

- If the business fails, avoid hashing endlessly over what went wrong.

- Don't isolate yourselves in the event of business failure. Stay social. Banish the elephant in the room by telling family and close friends what happened and then moving past it.

Chapter 10

Passing the Reins

*Handing down the family business is a glorious
and gratifying exit strategy—assuming the founder
can let go, the heir is competent, and siblings
aren't competing for the top spot.*

As I've mentioned, Gary and I have three kids. All are young adults now, and none, to date, has shown any interest in joining the business. Like the offspring of hippies who flee communes for Wall Street, Alex, Ethan, and Danielle will most likely seek lives far from the madness of entrepreneurship. That's fine with us. Stonyfield was never meant to be a legacy.

Perhaps we are unusual in not indulging fantasies that a Hirshberg presence will linger at Stonyfield for another generation. After all, most entrepreneurs spend their lives nurturing two things: their companies and their kids. It's natural to want to pass one down to the other. On the practical side, family companies are ideal vehicles for transferring knowledge and experience to offspring. They also provide employment and leadership opportunities, which are especially welcome graduation presents in a wobbly economy. I read an article recently about parents buying franchises for their adult children who can't find jobs. Wouldn't you rather settle your daughter in an office across the hall from yours than endow her with a Quiznos?

The emotional drivers are just as powerful. As time passes, parents and children tend to lead increasingly separate lives. Family businesses act like domestic magnets, drawing them back together. The generations can derive great satisfaction from toiling side by side to perpetuate the family brand.

Finally, in an age of smaller families and weaker family ties, I find something optimistic about the very idea of a family business. Maybe I'm being romantic, but I wish small firms still used the "& Son" designation—extended to "& Daughter" of course. S. C. Johnson has 12,000 employees. But its famous tagline, "A Family Company," conjures for me the cozy image of a nurturing workplace and a company devoted to its employees and customers.

Still, I suspect Gary and I have dodged a bullet. Paul Karofsky, Founder of Framingham, Massachusetts–based Transition Consulting Group, which has counseled family companies for 20 years, said that a dysfunctional family enterprise is "like no other hell on earth." Kids coming on board—as designated successors or just employees—create a hornet's nest of emotional and financial complications. Which child will ultimately take over? How do you fairly divide the inheritance when one child works in the business and others do not? Can you maintain equitable emotional relationships with the entire brood while working closely with just one or two? With a sale off the table, how do you create some liquidity for retirement? Can children achieve healthy separation from parents when both have, as one entrepreneur put it to me, "an abnormal amount of information about each others' lives and wallets"?

And, perhaps most crucially, how do you prevent the family's accumulated psychic detritus from clogging the gutters of your nice, clean-running company?

"What's wrong with family business? The family."

There ought to be an algorithm to help entrepreneurs calculate just how messy a generational handoff will be. (How about maturity-of-the-business-multiplied-by-maturity-of-the-child-divided-by-expectations-of-the-parents?) John Hughes, a New Hampshire attorney who frequently counsels clients in succession planning, has seen "way more failures" than successes. "What's wrong with family business?" John asks. "The family."

WE ALWAYS HURT THE ONES WE LOVE
How old tensions complicate new roles

I've already talked about the risks of married couples working together. The parent-child relationship is even more vulnerable. With a spouse, there is at least a presumption of equality: you're supposed to be life partners, after all. But the power differential between parents and children—though it lessens as children grow—is ingrained. Parents may have trouble seeing their offspring as competent adults and feel strange consulting with them as equals. Children fret that their bosses during childhood are still their bosses in the workplace. The buffer of professionalism wears thin when old attitudes and arguments resurface. Employees and bosses who are not related may dislike each other, but they are less able to hurt each other.

Nick Horman Jr. is a self-described "third-generation pickler" who works in his family's wholesale business, Allen Pickle Works, in New York. Nick spoke with regret about the terrible screaming fights he used to get into with his father, Nick Horman Sr. "I'm not proud of it. But family can bring that out in people," Nick Jr. told me. "The fact was he was still my father, not just my boss. In every event, in every encounter, that relationship is there, and you can't pretend it's not."

Like many adolescents, Nick Jr. chafed under his father's dominion. College brought him some independence and distance. But

Nick Horman Jr.

> "In a business, there can be only one captain. I had to exert authority, and my son didn't like that."

upon joining Allen Pickle Works right after graduation, Nick once again felt controlled by his dad. "In a business, there can be only one captain," Nick Sr. told me. "I had to exert authority, and my son didn't like that." Nick Jr. doesn't disagree with his dad's assessment. "It regressed back to a childhood power struggle," he told me.

Even relatively healthy parent-child relationships can turn out to be fragile. Jesse Brubaker, an engineer in his 20s, went to work for his mother's occupational medical clinic right after college. "At the time, I felt close to her," he said. Soon after, his mother was in a serious car crash, and Jesse managed the clinic for the six months it took her to recuperate. When she returned, Jesse felt hemmed in and frustrated. "She didn't take my ideas seriously. She thought I wasn't competent enough—I was still her little boy."

Jesse wound up leaving the company. He remains distant from his mother. "I kept thinking we were going to be able to separate the business from our personal lives and get back to being a family," he told me. "But what happened created a gap between us. We're working to resolve it. But it won't be the same. We've got to grow into something new."

TURNING THE SCREWS
When an irresistible force meets a reluctant heir

Tolstoy wrote that "Happy families are all alike. Every unhappy family is unhappy in its own way." The same is true for family businesses. It would be impossible to limn the innumerable pathologies that infect particular clans. But there are two mistakes all entrepreneurs must avoid if they don't want to sabotage their relationships and businesses. The first is bringing in children who don't want to, or are not qualified to, be there in the first place.

Nick Horman Sr. admits pressuring his son to join the pickle business immediately after college. Nick Sr. himself felt pressured by the fact that Ron Horman, his brother and business partner, had recently brought his own son—also in his 20s—into the company. Nick Sr. would have preferred that his son work outside the business for a few years first, but he wanted to make sure Allen Pickle Works would be inherited equally by Nick and his cousin. According to Nick Jr., his father started turning the screws while he was a senior in college.

> Dad would say, "If you don't join us, you'll have nothing. You'll have to work for someone else." At the time, I resented the expectations, but Dad thought this was in my best interest. I became afraid I was going to blow it—lose out on something that could sustain me. People always tell me they wish they had a family business to go into. But this wasn't something I chose. I wanted to do my art and go to grad school in philosophy. I wanted to become my own person.

Nick Jr. might not have fought so furiously with his father if he'd chosen the family dynasty for himself. The older man was reacting to his fear of losing control of the business to his brother and nephew. But bringing your kid into your company should be a gesture of confidence and trust, not a defensive maneuver to cover a vulnerable flank. Ideally, child and business will need each other equally. Things work best when the entrepreneur feels genuinely grateful that his child wants to bless the family business with his talents.

These days, few entrepreneurs overtly pressure their children to join the family business. But just letting your kids know that is your dream can have the same effect. Don't discount how much they want to please you. Peter Kohn is the son of the founder of an automation component manufacturing company. I love his description of the moment when his father, over lunch, asked him to interview with the head of sales at the family business. A senior in college at the time, Peter had already decided not to join the business, but loyalty to his father prevailed. When Peter agreed to the interview, his father removed the Rolex from his own wrist and handed it to him. "At that moment, I felt like Michael Corleone in *The Godfather* when he makes the decision to shoot Captain McCluskey and Solazzo in the restaurant," Peter told me. "By taking that watch, I had symbolically agreed to join the family business. I didn't love the business. But

Peter Kohn, center, with his father Jerry, left, and brother, Andrew.

I loved the man who ran it." Peter stayed with the company for two years; then it was sold. (He now counsels family businesses and runs Birch Hill Marketing, a brand extension licensing business in Richmond, Virginia.)

THE PRINCE CHARLES SYNDROME

Waiting in the wings breeds resentment

It's bad if you can't express confidence in your kid at the beginning, worse if you can't do so after working together for years. Which brings us to the second mistake founders must avoid. If your child expects to become CEO someday, don't chart a route to succession that passes over your dead body.

For a reasonably ambitious adult child, there is nothing so deflating as the Prince Charles Syndrome. Some parents treat succession plans like living wills to be carried out only in the case of death or incapacitation. Their progeny might reasonably interpret the message as: I've seen you work and I'm not impressed. A financial advisor told me about a widow who took over her late husband's business and grew it substantially. Her two sons, now in their 50s, work in the company, but she refuses to retire because she questions their competence to run it. "If she let go they'd be perfectly competent," the advisor said. "Her inability to do so diminishes her sons' abilities to take hold. It's a vicious circle. They do less, so she asserts more."

Not all planted-in-the-corner-office founders doubt their kids' talent. Some may be threatened by their children's achievements. Consultant Paul Karofsky facilitated an intergenerational workshop in which a father admitted that he was discomfited by his son's success in the family business. "Look what it says about what I couldn't do," the father lamented. Founders have to ask themselves whether they derive more gratification from excelling personally or from watching their children succeed. Are their identities bound up more in their own brilliant performances or in the perpetuation of a thriving family brand? I recently met a woman whose two 40-something sons work in the business she started. "I will die at my desk!" she told me defiantly. Such declarations must make her sons cringe.

Sometimes a child genuinely lacks the necessary combination of traits required to make a business venture work. As a friend of mine put it, entrepreneurs possess an unlikely convergence of leadership skills—a mix of wild ambition, tireless energy, smarts, creativity, and toughness—that are difficult to replicate. If that's your situation, you both need to confront the problem before your kid spends years withering in your outsize shadow. You don't want to be the impossible yardstick against which your progeny feels he or she will always fall short. Nor do you want him to worry how he appears in the eyes of others: powerful in his own right or taller merely because he is standing on your shoulders. The business exists because you slew the dragons. Better your child strike out on his own adventures than end up feeling like a hobbit.

In short, family succession only works when offspring are competent leaders who are passionate about the work. Paul Karofsky said entrepreneurs must make a decision: does the family serve the business or does the business serve the family? If parents take the attitude that blood is thicker than ability when choosing a successor, chances are the business won't be around long enough to serve anybody.

SPLITTING HEIRS
The fractious math of dividing up the company

No matter how objective and businesslike everyone pledges to be, you can't prevent family dynamics from playing out in a company. That might be OK if healthy families and healthy companies had the same attributes. They don't. Good business leaders pick winners and losers: one person gets promoted, the other cools her heels in the mailroom. Good parents, by contrast, make their kids believe they share equally in everything: possessions, opportunity, affection, and respect.

That fundamental disconnect is why Steve McDonnell, Founder of the natural meat company Applegate Farms, doesn't want his daughters involved in the business. He worries that making one child the boss of another would erode family unity. "I'm not interested in playing the odds with the relationship among my daughters," Steve said. "After my wife and I are gone, I want our three girls sitting around a table sharing a glass of wine. I don't want them fighting over hot dogs."

Stephen McDonnell.

When more than one child works in the business, you will have to make choices about titles, reporting structures, and division of labor. This demands something not normally required of parents: a cold-hearted assessment of your progeny's relative strengths and weaknesses. Colored by family history, these assessments are not always fair. Ultimately, though, the boss must choose a successor. Trouble arises when the choice is not obvious. If the old-est takes the helm, is it because he is most qualified? Because he got there first? Because he was always the alpha leader in the family? If a younger sibling gets the nod, does she also become the de facto boss of the family? Be aware that your decisions will likely lock in siblings to a lifetime of unequal relationships.

In many families, some children work in the business and others do not. Inheritance issues can fracture relationships quickly when one brother is connected to a company by blood and the other by blood, sweat, and tears. In cases where there are other significant assets (such as a home, property, or stock) to distribute, the pressure eases somewhat. If there aren't, entrepreneurs may choose to buy life insurance payable to the other children. But that can be prohibitively expensive. It's also theoretically possible to arrange for a buyout of the kids who are not inheriting the business. But that can be difficult and unaffordable as well. The parent struggles to show she loves all her babies equally, as those babies grow increasingly resentful of her and of one another.

Quinn Hogan, a financial advisor with Northwestern Mutual, said that most parents are so afraid these issues will create a rift that they never bring them up. "Maybe a quarter of the families I counsel are up front about it," he told me. "Once they do discuss it, the children's reac-tion almost always is 'that doesn't seem fair.' They argue about equaliz-ing an inheritance that's 20 or more years away." Attorney John Hughes said his goal when developing estate plans is not to make inheritance "equal" but to make it "equitable." Still, if the pie is small and the busi-ness is most of it, slicing comparable portions is almost impossible.

John warns family members to prepare for tough going during the estate-planning process and encourages them to recruit an outsider like himself to mediate and advise. For his own part, John tries to remain an impartial Solomon, even when aggrieved family members try to make him "their Rasputin," as he put it. John sympathizes with offspring's frustration and the depth of their anger. "Everything is on the line," he said. "Your livelihood, your business, and your family."

VITAL SCIONS
The joys of successful succession

I could ramble on to the end of this chapter about reasons to keep children and business separate. But for many entrepreneurs, those reasons pale beside the fact that *these are their kids*. Who else do they trust? Who else do they build for? Naturally, they want to bring them up, bring them in, and do everything possible to make it work.

Fortunately, examples abound of families that have done just that. Grant and Jessica Lundberg are first cousins who are both employed by their family's business, Lundberg Family Farms, the largest and oldest brand of organic rice in North America. Grant is the CEO of the company, which is based in Richvale, California. Jessica manages the nursery and is Chairman of the Board. When I asked them how a company like Lundberg survives for four generations with family relationships intact, Grant explained that the earlier generations were wise and careful about their legacy. Grant's parents, aunts, and uncles gifted the farm holdings to the next generation over dozens of years, slowly getting the value out of their estates tax free. That magnanimous act was also smart estate planning. Long-term thinkers, the company's leaders understood that if they waited until retirement, significant value would remain in their estates, subject to onerous taxes that might result in the loss of the farm. But gifting the lion's share of their wealth left them financially vulnerable. Their descendants solved that problem by providing their parents with generous salaries.

Grant's generation also drained some of the emotion from sensitive decisions by subjecting them to formal systems of communication and governance. For example, the compensation committee bases all wages—including those of family members—on industry standards. "It can be tough to tell family members that we won't all get compensated the same," said Jessica. The family also established a "family assembly" whose responsibilities include setting employment standards for the next generation. Currently, the assembly is grappling with whether to require relatives to be qualified for jobs or to hire them no matter what. They will also decide under what conditions a family member can be fired—one of the fraught lose-lose conundrums in any family business. The family strives to keep financial matters fair among the cousins, seven of whom work in the business. (Six sit on the board.) Since the company stock is not liquid, they have decided to award dividends as a way to keep everyone engaged. All these actions are in the interest of avoiding trouble down the road. It's better to "open a can of worms before you have to, instead of waiting until people's emotions are raw," said Jessica.

Nonfamily companies take great pains to foster camaraderie among employees and management. Morale rises when people like their colleagues, and we all know the play-together-stay-together rule. The Lundbergs have always believed that family companies must be just as diligent, even though their leaders, by definition, share ties that extend beyond the business. "Every six months we'd all vacation together," Grant said. "So I really know my cousins. I knew them when we were little, and I know what they're made of. I trust them completely. My parents, aunts, and uncles understood the benefit in keeping the family together socially to build understanding."

As the fourth generation makes its way through school, the older cousins at Lundberg's Richvale headquarters plan social events—attendance at Giants games, family water-ski weekends—that periodically bring everyone together to keep relationships close and comfortable. "You have to have that fabric," said Grant.

Ideally, the company itself will help create that fabric. Working together in the business strengthens bonds between family members, not only by

Lundberg family, third generation.

throwing them constantly together but also by subjecting them to the same pressures and focusing them on the same goals. Nicole Dawes started Late July Organic Snacks with her father, Stephen Bernard, whose Cape Cod Potato Chips had been her own business training ground. Late July became the cask in which the flavor of their relationship deepened and mellowed. Stephen had the chance to grow close to his grandchildren, who were fixtures at the company. He witnessed his youngest grandchild take his first steps in the office. Nicole profited from her father's experience until his untimely death at age 61. She misses Stephen and his wise counsel. "I wish I could have just one more conversation with him," she said. "There were so many questions I never asked."

TAKE A BREAK, FOR SAFETY'S SAKE
The benefits of time spent outside the company

Before the industrial revolution, families begot lots of children to work the fields. Today's entrepreneurs are less calculating about reproduction. Still, children of entrepreneurs—beloved, cherished, and nurtured though they may be—also comprise free labor. Many will spend long hours in the business, starting from their earliest days when they lie gurgling in a baby carrier by their father's desk while he pours over accounts receivable.

It's hard to imagine better preparation for joining a company than growing up in it. As a child, Jessica Lundberg helped out on weekends and during breaks from school, often working alongside a parent. She came to understand the business intimately: to love it, too, and to see a great future in it. As Jessica, who also considered becoming a doctor, said of her decision to join the company, "The family legacy *and* the opportunity were compelling."

> It's hard to imagine better preparation for joining a company than growing up in it.

Working in Lundberg Farms as a child, Jessica became friendly with the employees. But she knew that easy rapport might suffer once she formally came on board. Employing relatives—particularly adult children—can demoralize and spark resentment among other workers, who fear their own career paths will be truncated and crinkle their noses at the real or imagined whiff of nepotism. "There's a barrier when you're coming in as the boss's kid," said Jessica. "It can be intimidating to nonfamily members. Their job is tenuous, and yours is not. Building relationships and trust is challenging."

Determined to earn that trust, Jessica set out after college to make a place for herself in the business. Harboring zero sense of entitlement, she embarked on a series of low-level jobs: filing papers, working sales shows, driving a tractor, and weeding in the plant nursery, which she now runs. That self-imposed apprenticeship gave her credibility and also exposed her to important parts of the business. Now at the top of the company, she brings to her leadership not only the family perspective but also the perspective of employees in every department. (Lundberg Farms has since created an internship program for young family members. Some jobs are informal, such as working a booth at the farmer's market or leading farm tours. But when other employees are affected by interns' work, interns are held to the same performance and attendance standards as regular staff.)

Jessica is fortunate that her absorption straight into the family business went so smoothly. But the straight and easy road isn't always the best, particularly when it detours around the challenges and choices that shape character. It's equivalent to how you might feel if your 18-year-old declared her intention to skip college in order to marry her high school sweetheart. Much as you may like your child's intended, you'd probably urge her to explore other options before she commits.

By spending time outside the family cocoon, adult children can test whether some other career might make them happier. If they decide to return, they will likely bring with them valuable business skills, knowledge, and connections. Perhaps most important, children who work outside the business before joining it experience the independence they need to be seen as adults by both their parents and themselves. The child leaves a child; he returns a high-potential leadership candidate.

Tony Stein's journey is an excellent model. Son of the founder of Camp Echo Lake in Elmsford, New York, Tony knew the business inside out. As a child, he cooked out and canoed with the other campers. As a teenager, he worked summers there. Tony recognized what the camp needed to prosper, and he proceeded to outfit himself with the necessary skills. After college he earned an MBA, then spent the next few years in marketing jobs at outside companies. Tony told me that he wanted to test his mettle in the wider world, "where my reviews, compensation, and feedback wouldn't be colored by family relationships." By the time he returned to the Adirondacks to run the business (his father had passed away), he had the self-assurance and experience he needed. "Much of my confidence derived from the fact that I knew that if something happened to the family business, I could cut it on my own," Tony said.

Nick Horman Jr., the reluctant pickle scion, started slacking off at work and finally quit. "I had an attitude," he admitted. "I shouldn't have joined the business right after college. I felt like my dad had trapped me. I didn't yet understand the pressures, the financial insecurity that most people face. I took my situation for granted." For two years, he took philosophy classes, worked on his art (sculpture, drawing, and painting) in a studio, and ran his own pickle start-up, selling at farmers' markets.

Then, in 2010, Nick Jr. rejoined Allen Pickle Works to help launch its first retail line. He and his dad don't fight anymore. With maturity and perspective gained from the time away, Nick said he's come to understand that "Dad's earned his stripes. I don't feel entitled to come in and control things." As a manager of the retail line, Nick Jr. is excited to be part of something new, where he can use his creativity in a business setting. Still, he and his dad haven't confronted their personal issues directly. Nick Jr. is realistic that tensions are easier to ignore when the business is thriving. "When the water level sinks," he said, "the rocks may show."

Despite the early arguments, Nick Jr. feels closer to his father since they started building something together. Allen Pickle Works isn't just a place and a livelihood, Nick said; it is "a matrix of meaning, with the force of tradition." The business "deepens the understanding of what it is to be a family."

> "The business deepens the understanding of what it is to be a family."

AND BUSINESS MAKES THREE
What the business taketh away from the child,
the business giveth back

When *Inc.* magazine's Editor-in-Chief, Jane Berentson, first proposed creating what became my "Balancing Acts" column, I suggested calling it "And Business Makes Three." Jane nixed that, for a lot of good reasons. But my abandoned title does capture this reality: an entrepreneurial business occupies a space in a family's life similar to that of a child. Both are endlessly demanding of time, attention, and money. Both engender enormous pride and are a joy to watch grow. And both, for better or for worse, are reflections of their creators.

As I discussed earlier, entrepreneurs as a breed are distracted and diverted by their needy businesses, and they often end up missing big chunks of their kids' childhoods. They see their children grow up in fits and starts between business trips and evening meetings. So when a child comes into a family business, the parent gets a second chance to spend time with her, to teach her and watch her evolve. Often the entrepreneur's spouse is grateful to see the people she loves most at last forming the bond she'd always wished for them. Entrepreneurs and their spouses routinely comfort their children—and themselves—with the assertion that "Daddy is doing it all for you." When the child takes over the business, that promise bears fruit.

Things to Talk About

- As much as you want your kids to follow you into the business, you must make sure they feel the same way. Ask them whether they have true passion for the work. Are they forgoing opportunities that they may one day regret? What do they see as their role in the company, now and in the future? What do their spouses think about their joining the family business?

- Business decisions must be based on the best interests of the business. Encourage your children to speak up with their opinions. But make two things very clear: others in the organization will also have your ear, and you will take the best advice no matter who offers it.

- If more than one child is joining the business, explain to all of your children your thoughts on succession. Discuss their roles and responsibilities and how you expect them to relate both to you and to one another.

- You and your spouse should discuss ways to make sure children not working in the business don't feel less a part of the family. You should also decide how you will try to prevent business disagreements from contaminating personal relationships.

Things to Do

- If your children are young and willing, encourage them to work in the company during summers and school breaks. Give them a variety of jobs, just as you would do with any employee pursuing career development. That way they learn every aspect of the business and you can begin to evaluate their strengths.

- If your child already works for you, solicit her ideas for improving the business and let her know you take her seriously. Consult her about more decisions and, increasingly, more important ones.

- Create a board of advisors to help with estate planning. Enlist an estate-planning lawyer, an accountant, and a counselor who is sympathetic to the emotional issues involved in generational transference. Bring these advisors in early. Don't wait until your retirement is imminent and the subject has become red-hot.

- Create systems within the business to dispassionately resolve issues like hiring and compensation that might otherwise pit family members against one another.

Chapter 11

Once More into the Breach

The family's finances are stable at last.
Life is actually approaching normal.
Then the serial entrepreneur announces her
latest brainstorm. Here we go again.

As a resident of New Hampshire, I do not fear earthquakes. But I do live in terror of four little words: "I have an idea." When Gary utters them, the ground beneath me trembles.

About 10 years ago, we were hiking a local mountain when Gary revealed his brainstorm for O'Natural's, a chain of healthy fast-food restaurants. We'd recently returned from a family trip out west, where we'd been appalled to find our quick-stop dining options limited largely to Big Macs and vanilla shakes. Gary saw an opportunity to do what he'd done successfully at Stonyfield: create buzz and loyalty by offering a healthy, high-quality version of what was essentially a commodity product. While Gary acknowledged that the concept wasn't original, he thought its time had come. "This could be a billion-dollar idea," he told me.

My husband sometimes refers to himself as a "pathological optimist." To me, this plan was just pathological.

This was in 2000; by then, Stonyfield had been profitable and stable for a decade. Yet when Gary broached the restaurant idea, I felt like a place setting that's just had the tablecloth yanked out from under it. Even though Gary said he intended to hire a CEO to run the restaurants, I anticipated a return to the grueling hours and constant distractions I thought we had finally put behind us. And the risk! So in my brain: "Gary knows nothing about the restaurant business." In Gary's brain: "I'll bring in smart people and figure out the rest." Here I thought we had reached terra firma, only to find my husband gazing longingly once again at rough seas.

Painful as the prospect of Gary's new business was, I kept my mouth shut. As long as he wasn't jeopardizing the roof over our heads or our children's college funds, I figured he was entitled to his next dream. I comforted myself with the fact that he'd succeeded once before. This time the learning curve should be less steep. Would be less steep. Had to be less steep.

Serial entrepreneurs are like women who suppress the recollection of labor in order to marshal the stamina to give birth again. All the night sweats and near-death experiences recede from memory. What remains is the thrill of signing that initial customer; the pride of watching those first few employees hard at work and thinking, "This is my team." Even if entrepreneurs can't entirely block the awful memories, they mentally incorporate them into a larger heroic narrative. In retrospect, the bad times become character-building obstacles on the road to ultimate triumph. They imagine themselves as Frodo bravely crossing a rickety bridge loan on his way to destroy the ring—or, in their case, to seize it.

For their families, though, such selective memory is not so easy to muster. While the spouse and children don't suffer more than the entrepreneur does, the difference is that families don't experience the highs that compensate—and for most entrepreneurs, more than compensate—for the lows. The second (and third and fourth) time around, spouses know what to expect: most of it not good. And unlike entrepreneurs, they see little in it for themselves.

Gary points out that I knew what I was getting into when I married him. "While you didn't sign on for multiple rounds of pain, you signed on with me," he said. "You were drawn to the upsides of entrepreneurial business—the excitement, the fascination, and the fun."

All true. I just wish it had crossed my mind to request a one-company-only prenup.

ONCE IS NEVER ENOUGH
Why some people keep starting companies

There ought to be an Audubon guide to help laypeople like me distinguish everyday entrepreneurs from the serial variety. If such a guide existed, it would make a great engagement gift. You can be married to an entrepreneur for years without knowing he harbors the insatiability gene. In fact, he may not be aware of it himself.

In my experience, serials aren't notably more extreme than their single-company brethren. They aren't all adrenaline junkies. They don't have ADD or that disorder where people repeatedly injure themselves because they don't register pain. (Well, maybe some of them *do* have ADD. "Most people change jobs seven or eight times in their career," said one serial entrepreneur. "When I get bored, I start another company instead.")

Launching companies, plural, is just what these folks *do*. During my conversations with serial entrepreneurs, I was peppered with analogies to explain their compulsions. They are athletes, and business is their decathlon. They are artists, and business is their canvas. They are alcoholics, and business is their liquor. They are hunters, and business provides the thrill of the chase. To these entrepreneurs, action is eloquence. "This is who we are," one serial entrepreneur told me. "Even if I won the lottery, I would do the same thing."

Perhaps the most distinguishing qualities of serial entrepreneurs are that they are creative and intellectually restless. When you live with one, you are never safe from the siren song of new ideas. As one of their ilk told me: "The personality of a serial entrepreneur is almost like a curse. You see opportunities every day." But it's not enough to see opportunities. Serial entrepreneurs also feel compelled to act on them. The same traits that led them to launch their first business lure them ever so logically to the next one and to the one after that. They identify a niche and yearn to corner it. They spot a hole and want to fill it. Something needs a fix; they step in. They look at the world through a different lens.

And why shouldn't proven entrepreneurs try to corner that niche, fill that hole, or fix that problem when they see it? After all, they've done it before. Serial entrepreneurs possess a different, arguably more dangerous confidence than first-timers possess because they don't just *believe* they can do it: they *know* they can do it. Not only can they do it; they can do it better than they did it the first time because now they are smarter and more experienced. Even if their previous businesses went down in flames, serialists do not become consumed by doubt and insecurity. They are eager to prove they've learned from history and can transmute defeats into valuable lessons for the next launch.

Unnervingly for the spouse, sometimes what the entrepreneur has learned is that he can power his way through on sheer determination. When I asked Gary what made him believe that, with no experience in restaurants, he could start a successful one, he replied that at the time he cofounded Stonyfield, he knew nothing about yogurt, either. "In the calculus of the entrepreneur, knowledge is less significant than confidence," Gary said.

But that confidence is often misplaced, said Noam Wasserman, professor of entrepreneurship at Harvard Business School. "Starting their second business, entrepreneurs think they have it nailed," Noam told me. "But especially if they change sector, geography, or the cofounder, they can make the mistake of using the same hammer to drive in a very different nail." Investors, too, may be complacent, challenging the entrepreneur less because they figure he knows what he is doing.

To be fair, many serial entrepreneurs have more pragmatic motivations than satisfying their need for stimulation and challenge, or the desire to fashion new buckets to contain their overflowing creativity. I spoke with one or two who kept launching new companies in search of the big payday. Others have several companies going at the same time ("simultaneous entrepreneurs"?) in order to create synergies among them. Danny Meyer, for example, said one reason he has populated much of Manhattan with his eclectic restaurants and food businesses—nine stand-alones plus the proliferating Shake Shack chain—is that the new ventures provide development opportunities for his 1,500-plus employees. But that laudable strategy doesn't mean he's not wired for

Danny Meyer.

serial. "I can't stop thinking of ideas that excite me," Danny told me. "I need outlets for the ones I can't shut up in my brain."

A common reason entrepreneurs start new businesses is that running the old one loses its charm. It is conventional wisdom that leading a growth company is a very different experience from leading a mature one, requiring different skills and—often— a different temperament. Charging up the hill while battling long odds creates an

> "I can't stop thinking of ideas that excite me. I need outlets for the ones I can't shut up in my brain."

adrenaline rush the entrepreneur doesn't feel when settled into the corner office with its family photos and plaques. A business owner may reach a point where his company is no longer a good fit, whether that judgment is his own or his investors'. So he decides to sell or hand over management to a professional CEO. Cut loose, he finds the idea of working for someone else even more abhorrent than when he started the original company. What choice does he have but to do it again?

Marc Ostrofsky is a classic serial entrepreneur. A denizen of Houston, Marc has started or invested in so many Internet businesses that a Houston newspaper referred to him as a "technology wildcatter." So far he's sold three to larger acquirers, and he isn't done company hatching. "It's a game, proving that it can be done," he told me. "I do enjoy the start-up phase and getting the company so that it's self-sustaining, then selling it to a bigger player that can add more value."

Some entrepreneurs nurture a cherished cause and start multiple companies in support of it. Gary envisioned O'Natural's (later renamed The Stonyfield Café) as a logical extension of the mission

of our organic yogurt company: to improve the health of people and of the earth by promoting natural and organic food. Likewise, Dennis Cail, of Dallas, has founded two businesses that serve to make "green" companies more efficient: greenjobforce.com matches eco-conscious job seekers with employers, and Alternative Business Solutions is an environmental consulting firm that helps companies set benchmarks for using fewer resources.

Dennis Cail.

At other times, darker forces are at work. Leaders may so revel in their status that they're always hungry for more things and people to lead. Frustrated by stalled growth, some entrepreneurs decide that running multiple small organizations is the only way to gain the scale of power they crave.

In the worst cases, entrepreneurs start company after company because the constant furor gives them an excuse to avoid family problems. One man told me that he kept creating businesses to escape his marital woes. Unfortunately, he didn't have that insight until after his divorce.

GROUNDHOG DAY

The spouse prepares to live through it again

The spouse's reaction to the prospect of another business varies depending on how the family is situated. If they need more money and starting a business is the best way to get it, chances are she will grit her teeth and acquiesce. Or if the entrepreneur made a pile on his first business, expects to spend minimal capital on the second, and has a credible plan for off-loading much of the work, then it may be no big deal.

More often, however, it is not clear how the next business will affect the family's finances. Like the first business, it could make things better. It could make them worse. The nature of the risk hasn't changed, but life stages give it more consequence. Entrepreneurs launching second, third, and fourth companies are by definition older than when they started out. If they fail, there are fewer years to rebound. No wonder that when the adrenaline kicks in for the serial entrepreneur, the cortisol spikes for the spouse.

Risk engenders fear. The prospect of endless risk engenders existential dread. When an entrepreneur launches her first business, she and her spouse may view it as a big adventure. The ride will be wild and full of ups and downs, but at some point they will climb back onto the platform and head to the midway for corndogs. So imagine the spouse's horror when he realizes there is no platform, no corndogs—just an endless track that rises and falls precipitously into the distant future. "Serial entrepreneurship? You mean serial delusions," one embittered spouse said to me. "There's never any problem—until there's a problem. Something always goes wrong."

> "Serial entrepreneurship? You mean serial delusions. Something always goes wrong."

The realization that the entrepreneur plans to make a career founding companies may also provoke jealousy as the spouse anticipates competing with a succession of sparkling new businesses for his passion and attention. The couple's children grow up and move out; she waits for the company to do the same. Every time they're preparing to reorient their lives around each other, something new comes along to dazzle and excite him. The question is implicit: "Now that you know how much time a start-up takes away from *us*, why do you want to do it again?"

Still, if the entrepreneur had the time of his life building the first business and nothing since then has matched that thrill, the spouse may feel churlish to deny him. Indeed, some entrepreneurs consider the spouse's willingness to rally uncomplainingly behind plan after plan as the ultimate sign of devotion. I've asked numerous serial entrepreneurs why they think their spouses are content to live this way. Almost invariably they give the same response: because she knows it makes me happy. Belinda Roberts, of Austin, Texas, exemplifies this response. Her husband, Todd, has launched four companies. When I asked if she'd ever put her foot down, she replied: "He'd be miserable. It would be heartbreaking. He's not ready—he'll never be ready—to give up the dream."

Sometimes the spouse simply has faith. Kalika Yap has started and still runs four companies, three based in Los Angeles and one in Hawaii. Kalika's eclectic interests and talents are reflected in the diversity of her businesses: a design agency; a company selling her patented purse holder; a chain of waxing salons; and a business that powers the online operations of several global brands. With the family juggling so many balls, her husband, Rodney, naturally worries. But he believes that one of Kalika's companies will eventually take off. His wife's constant churn of ideas and the unflagging energy that has

The Yap family.

produced so many businesses serves to bolster his faith in her. "She has the vision," Rodney said admiringly, "and has convinced me that she can pull it off."

Spouses who are entrepreneurs themselves or come from entrepreneurial families tend to be better at taking the serial thing in stride. Kent Lewis is working on his fourth start-up, Formic Media, in Portland, Oregon. His wife, Erica, is simpatico because she had her own vacation-rental start-up before they met. "I've lived the excitement. I've chased the dream," said Erica. "I wouldn't trade what I'm doing now—being home with the kids. But when Kent returns from an interesting event, I do get jealous." Mallary Tytel, a South Dakota entrepreneur married to a serial entrepreneur, tries to be realistic. "You have two choices: fighting it or going along with it," she said. "As an entrepreneur myself, I know there's no percentage in going against the grain."

But for people like me, who can't imagine starting one business, let alone several, the announcement that we're back to the races elicits shock and disbelief. Our negative reactions run up against that pathological optimism I described earlier, which along with boundless energy and creativity is ironically what attracted us to our serialists in the first place. Lloyd Shefsky, Founder and Codirector of the Center for Family Enterprises at Northwestern University's Kellogg School of Management, labels the serial entrepreneur's mind-set as "the proverbial half glass steaming over." Meanwhile, the spouse is frequently just steaming.

Is there a point when the spouse gets to say *enough*? When her desire for calm and security outweighs the entrepreneur's desire to be "who I am"? Is it selfish to discourage a loved one from doing something he desperately wants to do because it makes you uncomfortable? Or is he the selfish one for persisting despite your discomfort?

That's a question every couple must resolve for themselves. But the spouse can become understandably exasperated or resentful if she must answer it again and again.

VOICES OF EXPERIENCE
This time, the family gets a say

Just because it's happening again, doesn't mean it has to happen the same way. Serial entrepreneurs relish the chance to fix what they got wrong in their previous ventures. This time around they vow to bootstrap longer, pay more attention to those early hires, and make sure investors' goals line up with their own. Spouses climbing into the ring for another round should remind the entrepreneur that things went wrong in their personal lives as well and insist they not repeat those mistakes either.

Wes Moore and his fiancée, Kari Gauthier.

Wes Moore is a New Hampshire–based serial entrepreneur who doesn't need reminding. His current business—an online video platform called iPlayerHD—is his ninth. He was running four companies when his marriage failed.

Wes knows what he screwed up. He and his former wife had all the trappings of success. He drove a red Ferrari. She traveled, worked out at a fancy health club, and retained a professional maid. Because each new company enhanced their wealth, Wes thought starting multiple businesses was good for his relationship. He said that he "forgot" about his marriage and that the couple didn't take time to communicate and connect their worlds. "It turned out my wife cared more for the health of our relationship than the health of our balance sheet," he said.

Wes later realized other ways that serial entrepreneurship made him less fit as a mate. "Entrepreneurs feel they have to have all the answers," he told me. "Starting several businesses only reinforced that. The control issues became habit-forming, a way of being. When you apply that trait to your personal life, it doesn't go over very well."

But he has learned from his mistakes. Wes now has a girlfriend whom he keeps involved in and informed about his work life. Had he been equally attentive to his wife, Wes believes they might still be together. He explained:

> I wanted to be a serial entrepreneur, not a serial relationship killer. My marriage became a casualty of my need to work a billion hours on all these businesses. I'm not going to blow it a second time. If you build a few businesses but lose your family in the process, you've had your eye on the wrong ball.

"If you build a few businesses but lose your family in the process, you've had your eye on the wrong ball."

The entrepreneur may argue that with the next company things are bound to go better simply because she is better at the job. In her first company, she learned to delegate and manage her time. With this venture, she will use those skills to make sure her family gets a more substantive end of the stick. Whitney Trujillo, a Denver entrepreneur who has founded three online businesses, compared her first company to an MBA program. She was one of several serialists to list for me the various ways they are now able to keep work manageable. They ask the right questions and find solutions quickly. They avoid burning energy on problems that can resolve themselves. They are comfortable dropping the occasional ball. And they have learned that—post-start-up, anyway—they don't have to work around the clock.

Such personal growth is encouraging—but not sufficient. So, when the serial entrepreneur gets that eye twinkle again, the family must sit down and discuss the ramifications just as thoroughly as they did with the first company. Theoretically, they are in a better position this time around to contest the plan. The argument, "What if this happens?" doesn't carry nearly the weight of "What if this happens *again*?"

These discussions can be painful, particularly for the entrepreneur forced to confront past sins. The spouse pokes with the dull pin of experience at his inflated expectations. In response, the entrepreneur must acknowledge—with humility—his past overestimations and explain how projections for the new business are more conservative and realistic. Family members need to make clear what sacrifices they are and aren't willing to make. They may impose conditions. This time you need a partner. This time you must agree to cut bait if we're still losing money after three years.

Not that those conditions will necessarily be met. "We've set some financial boundaries but have gone beyond them," said the otherwise supportive Rodney Yap, referring to his wife's four companies. "I'm past my comfort zone." A friend whose husband started a second company recounted her no-win position:

> It's a crappy part for the spouse to play. To say no or "have you thought of this or that problem?" You become the editor, not the writer. The way I dealt with it—and I'm not proud of this fact—is, I said, "You want to go through this again? Fine, but I don't want anything to do with it." We agreed on a certain amount of money he'd sink into it. But we passed that number long ago.

In hindsight, Gary and I wish that we'd discussed the Café at greater length before he launched. Our situation was almost identical to the one Harvard's Noam Wasserman described. Much about the turf was unfamiliar. Gary had changed sectors and geography. He was the Founder but not the CEO. In the end, my husband's learning curve was as steep as it had been with Stonyfield.

One thing we both learned from Stonyfield was that Gary has a penchant for underestimating how much money he needs to grow a business. As he worked on O'Natural's, I could have justifiably inquired how he would avoid repeating that mistake. I doubt he would have adhered to some arbitrary limit on our personal financial investment.

But if we'd set a cap, reaching it would have triggered a pause and a chance to reassess.

When laying down ground rules for the next business, many spouses don't know what to ask or to ask for. That makes it tough to press for answers more specific than, "I've got it covered." Gary didn't know very much about restaurants, but I knew less. Still, perhaps my probing would have helped him think the venture through. At the very least, I would have felt better about being consulted and informed. Realistically, though, Gary was going ahead no matter what I said.

"DO NOT GO GENTLE INTO THAT GOOD NIGHT"
Forget about retirement

When it comes to retirement, spouses like me can forget the golf course, the cross-country road trip in an RV, the carpentry projects, and the leisurely postprandial walks. For the serial entrepreneur, all that sounds like one long slide into decrepitude. Start-ups, by contrast, are by definition about the new, the fresh, the unpredictable. I understand the allure. What better way to avoid dwelling on endings than by immersing oneself in beginnings?

For those of a certain age who aren't happy unless they're working, starting companies may be an easier option than getting a job. They don't have to find someone willing to hire them. No one asks questions about outdated skills or whether someone younger might be more qualified. If the entrepreneur has access to capital, getting back into launch mode is something she can simply choose to do. Assuming that the couple's retirement money isn't at stake, golden-year entrepreneurship is often easier on the family than earlier ventures. The

> For those of a certain age who aren't happy unless they're working, starting companies may be an easier option than getting a job.

kids are grown and (hopefully) out of the house. The spouse's own career may have wound down. For the first time in their lives, the couple faces long stretches of free time. Why not fill it with something meaningful?

Dennis Pushkin, who ran and sold a couple of businesses over his 30-year career, tried to retire—three times. But he quickly grew bored. At 51, he cofounded MoreVisibility, an Internet marketing agency, in Boca Raton, Florida. Now in his early 60s, Dennis told me he'd consider launching yet another start-up, solely to provide a vehicle

Dennis Pushkin with daughters Hilary Pushkin, left, and Pamela Freeman, right.

for working with his two grown daughters. "In retirement, I grew itchy and mentally lazy," he told me. "I missed the action. My wife was supportive and knew that I needed to get back into the game." I asked Dennis at what point a serial entrepreneur stops incubating businesses. "I think you age out of it," he said. "But we never say never."

"Never" certainly doesn't figure in George Naddaff's vocabulary. Best known for the rotisserie chicken behemoth Boston Market, George launched his fourth company, the Newton, Massachusetts–based UFood Grill, when he was 75. Now 82, he has plenty of friends who "retired to Boca, got on the golf course, smelled the pesticide, and died," he told me. "If you love what you do, it's not work. This week we got a contract to put a UFood on two military bases!"

After 35 years of marriage, George's wife, Marti, is happy to see her husband enjoying himself and couldn't imagine things any other way. "Business is his hobby," she said. "Without it he'd wake up in the morning . . . and do what?" George's creative engagement with his work not only energizes him, it also distracts him. He lost his two brothers in 2010 and has outlived many friends. If George greeted the day with nothing planned, "he might have to deal with what used to be and the emptiness now that so much is gone," Marti said.

Sometimes, though, a couple's financial security is imperiled by a new business, or the spouse simply cannot bear to go through it all again. In those situations, there are less risky ways for an entrepreneur in later life to flex those creative muscles. Passive or active investing and mentoring can be like methadone for the business owner, providing some of the thrill without all of the risk. Gary loves to mentor. "What I remember most about Stonyfield's dark days was the loneliness," he recalled. "I'm rewarded by the idea that with a little of my extra time and money, I might be able to help others avoid some pain."

> Passive or active investing and mentoring can be like methadone for the business owner, providing some of the thrill without all of the risk.

Jeff Furman, too, has found satisfaction in working with younger people. Jeff is Chairman of the Board of Ben & Jerry's and a serial nonprofit entrepreneur. Almost 70, he counsels young environmental and social activists and embraces their youthful enthusiasm. (Jeff recognizes that one reason Ben & Jerry's succeeded was that the founders didn't listen to advisors who told them their enterprise made no business sense—which, in the beginning, it didn't.) His wife, Sara, has retired from her job as an administrator and thrown herself into environmental causes. The two have "retired" into a life of social mission, which is quite similar to what they did before.

As for Gary and me, we are fortunate that he still gets a charge out of running the mature yogurt company. "In my work at Stonyfield, I'm inventing new enterprises all the time," he said. "I take huge risks every day." Still, it was with some trepidation that I asked him about his vision of what is next for us. Fortunately, it corresponded—at least somewhat—with mine. My husband painted a lovely picture of the two of us reclaiming a piece of property by creating gardens and planting trees: healing the world, one organic acre at a time. For me there's a satisfying completeness to that. After all, it's where I started, on my New Jersey farm.

Maybe in "retirement," Gary and I will be able to align not only our visions but also how we spend our days. Well, parts of them. "You don't want to be with me all day long anyway," Gary told me. "I'll always do walkabouts—to help other entrepreneurs, to make a difference, to have an impact. I relate to Bilbo Baggins. He needed to leave the Shire. We both have that gene."

As for the Stonyfield Café, it has predictably consumed a considerable amount of my husband's time and energy. Also cash: Gary has put in much more than either of us expected. The Café's prospects look better now, but it's not soup yet. I avoid discussing it with Gary and try not to think about it too much.

Gary has assured me that he won't start another company unless I am fully behind it. If this is true, he won't be starting another company anytime soon. Or, actually, ever. Still, I know for us there will be no calm after the storm. "The image of being mellow all day every day is a fiction for me," Gary said. "It's not real for an entrepreneur. I can't even imagine it."

Things to Talk About

- Why does the entrepreneur want to start another company? Does she have a truly great new idea, or is she just bored?

- How will the experience be different this time? Can the burden on the family be made lighter?

- If the spouse has put his own career on hold for the first business, has he had the opportunity to accomplish some of his own goals before subsequent ventures?

- Realistically, will there ever be an end game? Or will the entrepreneur be raising seed capital in the afterlife?

Things to Do

- If the couple is not young, put the retirement fund off-limits.

- If the entrepreneur is still running her first company, look into whether the new venture can be incubated within it, to reduce the risk.

- Set caps on what the entrepreneur can spend; then, as she approaches those caps, take the opportunity to pause and reassess.

- Look into other activities—such as mentoring or investing—as alternative ways for the entrepreneur to scratch that itch.

Chapter 12

Sick Happens

Entrepreneurs strive to design their lives and
control their fortunes. But when illness strikes,
all semblance of control flies out the window.

My mother always says that there are problems and then there
are troubles. Problems are hard, but most of them, ultimately,
can be solved. Most business complications, even those that
make you want to lay your head on your desk and moan, fall into that
category. But troubles take you down. Sometimes they take you out.
And no matter how smart or rich or prepared you are, you can't solve
them, only (hopefully) survive them. Gary and I launched the millen-
nium flush with troubles.

In 2001, I was diagnosed
with advanced breast cancer.
Six months of "the killing cure"
ensued: surgery, chemo, and
radiation. Just as I was finishing
my treatment, Gary's two brothers were admitted to the hospital. The twins, then 39 years old,

Bill, Gary, and Jim Hirshberg.

had been born with a rare form of muscular dystrophy that allowed them to live somewhat normally until their heart muscles became irreparably damaged.

I made it through fine. Gary's brothers both died, in early 2002.

At the same time that he was coping with my illness and his brothers' deaths, Gary had a company to run. Even after 18 years, Stonyfield still commanded his attention. During our year of woe, Gary was in the midst of protracted negotiations with Groupe Danone to sell off part of our business. Stonyfield relied on Gary's energy and ideas to move forward, and the Danone deal, in particular, required his unwavering concentration and attention to detail. But running back and forth to hospitals invariably scrambled Gary's schedule and affected his ability to focus.

Business is lonely in the best of circumstances. In these worst of circumstances, Gary's normal source of support—his immediate family—was largely distracted or out of commission. To get through, he relied on lessons gained from his years at the helm of a company in a precarious state; lessons that helped him cope with unpredictable changes and constant crises. For one thing, he learned to breathe deeply and avoid panicking. "Because of the business, I had already become good at triaging," he remembered. "Medically, the big picture was daunting. So I focused on what was most critical and forced myself to take it all day by day."

A loved one's serious illness destroys the entrepreneur's resilience. And entrepreneurs are just as vulnerable to illness as anyone else, their archetypal superman complexes notwithstanding. Recently, an article on a resource site for businesspeople caught my eye. The writer interviewed company owners about characteristics they felt were essential to success. Good health was right up there; many of the respondents described themselves as people who "refuse to get sick." It's the same failure-is-not-an-option mind-set that leaves both businesses and families without contingency plans—and causes spousal hands to shake as they insert the thermometer.

Illness can absorb considerable energy and concentration for months or years. Company owners who back-burner their businesses for that long risk losing them, even as the medical bills mount. Entrepreneurs can say what they will about the limitations of traditional employment. At least such jobs usually provide medical leave, paid vacations, predictable hours, a reliable paycheck, and—most critically—health insurance. Business owners create family-friendly leave policies for their employees. But if they try to take advantage of those policies themselves, often there is no one to take up the slack.

Illness is the rudest awakening to the dream of entrepreneurial control. The family's carefully calibrated life reels off into chaos as all those mechanisms meant to balance the business and the personal seize up, then collapse. Priorities are shuffled, then shuffled again, when instinct (must care for self/loved one!) rams into expediency (must preserve paramount financial and psychological investment!). The fear of losing everything is compounded by the fear of losing everything.

THE CAREGIVER IN THE CORNER OFFICE
Cutting back when family members get sick

Gary had little choice but to work a full load during my cancer treatment and his brothers' illnesses. But, in a way, the 12-hour days offered the solace of escape from sickness and sorrow. Work became a refuge from Gary's sense of helplessness, a place to exert dominion when the rest of his world was spinning out of control. Trotting down hospital corridors, arms loaded with flowers, or sitting by bedsides chatting about trivia in an effort to lift our spirits couldn't stitch me or his brothers back together again. And Gary, like most entrepreneurs, fares poorly when there's nothing he can *do*. At work, at least, his actions still had consequences. His decisions made a measurable difference.

Maybe if the timing had been different Gary would have cut back more. Others have. When you own a company, you never stop working, but—depending on the stage the business has reached—you can often change how and when you work. Entrepreneurship confers options: to travel less, to cancel meetings, to rearrange work appointments around medical ones. Often those options come at a cost to growth, which is why in normal times entrepreneurs shun them. But in times of crisis, they are a blessing, as are the kindness and support of many employees and customers.

A few entrepreneurs I spoke with chose to sell their companies or at least a significant share when family members got sick, thereby easing the pressure by providing a cash cushion. But most decided to hang in there, with modifications. One company owner, "Mark," described how he has changed his work habits in response to his young daughter's autoimmune disease. Mark lost his wife to cancer when the girl was just eight. As the single parent of a sick child, he has cut back significantly on his work hours and travel. Software training sessions Mark used to lead off-site are now conducted over the Web. At present, his daughter is stable, but Mark remains focused primarily on her well-being. "My business would have grown more had it not been for her illness, but I make enough to pay the bills," Mark told me. "I'm very content taking on the role of homemaker."

Nioma and Drake Sadler, with son, Kai.

Sometimes, simply modifying your work habits is not enough. Drake Sadler is Founder of the tea company Traditional Medicinals, based in Sebastopol, California. When his 13-year-old son, Kai, was rushed to the hospital with a life-threatening strep infection, Drake and his wife, Nioma, planted themselves at the boy's bedside. Kai went into septic shock and was hospitalized for a year. The boy endured more than 50 surgeries. (Kai is well now and back to being a normal teenager.)

Fortuitously, all this happened shortly after Drake had hired a CEO to succeed him. But the smooth, yearlong transition he had anticipated never happened. Instead, Drake made a clean break with day-to-day operations, not returning to the office for 7 months. (He is now the company's Chief Visionary Officer and Chairman of the Board.) "I'm right up there with other entrepreneurs in terms of being a control freak," Drake told me. "With Kai's illness, everything was out of my hands. It was an exercise in letting go."

> "I'm right up there with other entrepreneurs in terms of being a control freak. With Kai's illness, everything was out of my hands. It was an exercise in letting go."

Interestingly, Drake—like Gary—found help navigating this terrifying experience from the skills he'd cultivated as CEO: focus, critical listening, collaboration (in this case, with Kai's many caregivers), and the ability to make tough decisions quickly, without panicking. Drake also credited his natural optimism with helping him get through it. Entrepreneurs tend to believe that things will work out if they just keep showing up and doing their best. Of course, that is less true in matters of health than in matters of business. But when shadows mass, faith that life rewards a positive mind-set is something to cling to.

THE PATIENT IN THE CORNER OFFICE
Soldiering on when the entrepreneur gets sick

The entrepreneur's view of illness as a surmountable obstacle is most apparent when she, herself, becomes ill. Nobody wants to be defined by disease—company founders least of all. Illness equates to weakness, and weakness is antithetical to the entrepreneur's self-image. People say doctors make bad patients, but I would argue that entrepreneurs are worse because they believe they can return to health the same way they accomplish everything else: by sheer force of will.

Mentally, entrepreneurs reframe their conditions as another set of numbers to beat or an unexpected downturn that requires an aggressive response. Medical professionals are like suppliers, expected to do what it takes to keep these CEOs on track with their demanding schedules. Family members and employees are clients who must be reassured that the business owner will—as always—come through in the end.

So entrepreneurs square their shoulders and trudge ahead, making demands on themselves they would never expect relatives, employees, or even business partners to make in comparable circumstances. One business owner diagnosed with cancer told me that the strain would have been much worse if it had been his wife instead. "You learn to soldier on in a business, and that applies to your personal life too," he said. "You develop the ability to adapt your emotions to what is most convenient."

Dan and Krissi Barr.

Krissi Barr, Founder of Cincinnati-based Barr Corporate Success, has taken this determined approach to coping with her recently diagnosed early-stage breast cancer. "I am quarterbacking my treatment the way I would a project at work," Krissi told me. Her company, which helps individuals and businesses with strategic planning and execution, is growing, and her calendar is full. But Krissi *is* her shop. When she's not working, there's no revenue stream. So she found an oncologist who let her schedule chemo treatments around client meetings and speaking engagements. When Krissi's oncologist told her to cut back, she did—on volunteer commitments, not on her business. She explained:

> This is how the entrepreneur maintains control: by adapting to new realities, prioritizing what to do, and being in charge, not a victim. I don't want to compromise anything.

I'm approaching cancer with the same winning mind-set
with which I approach my business. The mental aspect is
so important in getting through a serious illness.

Of course, Krissi isn't the only one affected by her illness. When
entrepreneurs get sick, their families, like all families, ache and fear for
them. While their concern is no greater than in families not tethered
to a business, these situations can be more complicated. All those grueling negotiations over how the family will live, what they will sacrifice
for the business, the trade-offs between the long and the short term
are suddenly moot. The spouse who grudgingly accepted his wife's
long hours now wonders whether they threaten her health. Yet if he
insists that she put her dreams on hold, does he risk crushing her spirit
and breeding resentment? If he begs her to step away from the family's sole hope for financial security, does he court greater calamity? In
chapter 1, I discussed the spouse's decision to opt "in" for the entrepreneur's risk. But does that mean he must also opt "in" for what may be
the greatest risk of all?

Fortunately, such agonizing choices do not haunt Krissi's husband.
His wife's cancer is gone now, and Dan, an executive at a large company, trusts her to remain vigilant and to respond appropriately to
changes in her health. "She's already beaten the cancer physically, but
also mentally," Dan said. "It's good for her to stay determined. She's
not a victim."

Dan thinks Krissi was working too hard before her diagnosis. If
the recent scare prompts her to take things a little easier, in his mind
that's all to the good. He's not pressuring her to cut back, though,
since he has no reason to worry that work stress will cause the disease
to return. He hasn't had to beg or threaten or make desperate bargains
with Krissi to prevent her from risking her life for what is, at the end
of the day, just a business. Like the spouse of many an entrepreneur,
Dan has acceded to his wife's will. He is lucky there has been little cost
to doing so.

For others, however, the cost is enormous. Karen Gonzalez and her

husband, Jerry, live in Los Angeles, where Jerry is Founder of Maria
Elena's Authentic Latino, a manufacturer of certified organic Hispanic
foods. In 2007, Jerry was diagnosed with stage-four colon cancer. His
oncologist gave him a choice: become a professional patient or try to
incorporate the illness and its treatment into his life. Because the business was in start-up mode, Jerry believed he had to stick with it or all
his work would be for nothing. He scheduled meetings around chemo
and continued to attend trade shows. As the treatments progressed, he
grew increasingly fatigued but still dragged himself to the office.

Cancer didn't compel Jerry to slow down. In fact, it made him work
harder. Although he has been free of the disease for several years, "the
chance of cancer recurring is great, and that scares me," he said. "I feel
as though I'm in a race. I'm driven by the need to prove that what I've
set out to do is going to work. And I need to get my family on sound
financial footing. I can't stop to smell the roses."

Karen took away a different lesson from her husband's illness. "My
thought is, are we wasting time?" she said. "Should we give up everything: have a slower pace of life away from L.A. and spend quality

Jerry and Karen Gonzalez.

time together? We've put everything into this business. At what
point do you say *enough*?" Karen
sees the disease suspended, like the
Sword of Damocles, above her husband. She is terrified that the stress
and long hours required by a start-
up will make that sword drop. Perhaps Jerry's preoccupation with the
business will cause him to ignore
symptoms. Or he may choose to defer medical tests because of the
expense. Yet she understands that what threatens her husband's life is
also what gives that life meaning. "I don't want to burst his bubble and
hurt him by saying I think he should stop," Karen said.

Like most entrepreneurs, Jerry is forever imagining ways to

expand his business. The potential to create products and meet with key companies fans the flames of his aspirations. Recently he told Karen his plan to add a new flavor to his line of drinks. "I was stunned," Karen said. "Why isn't he happy with what he has? I'm rendered speechless sometimes."

> Biological realities can corrode even a will of steel.

Krissi and Jerry are strong people, and I sincerely hope that both will prevail over their conditions. If optimism and confidence cured disease then I wouldn't be writing this. But the body gives the spirit only so much autonomy. Biological realities can corrode even a will of steel.

NOT IN FRONT OF THE WORKERS
The strain of secret sickness

An entrepreneur's illness concerns others beyond friends and family. The more the owner's identity is conflated with his business, the more employees, investors, and customers worry. Aside from heads of state, it is hard to imagine a physical decline more public than that of Steve Jobs, who was among the most admired entrepreneurs on the planet. Many inside and outside of Apple expected that company's golden age of innovation to end when Jobs was first sidelined by pancreatic cancer. His illness led to calls for greater transparency about health issues by the CEOs of public companies. But CEOs of private companies should also expect anxious scrutiny when they or a close relative become ill. While grappling with disease, they must rally the strength to reassure stakeholders that, although circumstances have changed, business will go on as usual. "Thirty-five families depend on me," said one business owner, whose son is gravely ill. "I'm a leader. They can't see me fall apart."

Jerry Gonzalez, not a man to employ euphemisms when discussing

his condition, was unusually open about his cancer. After chemo-
therapy, he would visit the office to do email and other light work.
Sometimes he would go down to the warehouse "and show the young
ladies manufacturing the *horchata* the lines in my chest leading to the
pump," Jerry said. "They were speechless." Jerry believes his presence at
Maria Elena's prevented employees from worrying about a worst-case
scenario. "In retrospect, I think it benefited them, because they knew I
wasn't OK but I was working toward it," he said.

Sometimes, for good reasons or bad, entrepreneurs choose to remain
mum about their conditions. This may be most common when their
illness is not of the body, but of the mind. According to the National
Institutes of Mental Health, about a quarter of American adults suffer
from a diagnosable mental disorder in a given year. Company owners
are not immune. But while entrepreneurs struggling with cancer or
recovering from a bad accident can usually rally employees and win
patience from suppliers and customers, those with mental illness may
suffer in silent shame.

I spoke with "Sue," who runs a business-to-business company with
her husband. "Jay" suffers from severe, debilitating depression. Despite
his use of medication, those bouts can last for months. Sue is sensitive
to the stigma surrounding mental illness and doesn't feel she can level
with the couple's 12-year-old daughter or with their employees. But
she wonders if they know anyway. Sometimes the affliction is so obvious that Sue assumes everyone *must* be aware of it. At the company's
holiday party, for example, Jay couldn't function. "He just sat quietly,
expressionless, and looked like he was about to cry," Sue told me.

When Jay descends into his private hell, Sue covers for him: doing
most of his job, in addition to her own. Jay often sleeps until noon and
arrives at the office after lunch. Employees wonder aloud where he is
and when he'll return. Sue fudges her replies. During these periods,
Jay makes poor decisions, so Sue insists on reviewing them all. "He's
lost the privilege of being in charge," she said. Even when her husband
is well, Sue is selective about the information she shares with him.

She buffers bad news, fearful that some small setback may trigger six months of incapacitation.

As the spouse of a sick entrepreneur who is an entrepreneur herself, Sue suffers the double strain of sustaining both the company and her family. The need to keep Jay's condition secret means there are few people she can confide in or from whom she can seek help. And, of course, the person with whom she would naturally share the heaviest burdens—in business and in life—is lost to her. So is the singular joy of creating a business with the person she loves.

> "I try not to think about it. What's my alternative?"

When Jay crashes, "the weight of my world falls on me," said Sue. Her daughter, who sees without understanding, simply says, "I just want my daddy back." Sue is always exhausted and knows she can't go on like this indefinitely. "So I try not to think about it," she said. "That can be more dangerous than just getting up every day and doing it. What's my alternative?"

RELUCTANT ENTREPRENEURS
Launching companies in response to crisis

In conversations with founders and their families about illness, I assumed I would hear tales of people ratcheting back their ambitions or chugging along because they have no choice. When storms break, even the most intrepid entrepreneurs may regret having sailed so far from shore and try to head back. The dream of building a business can seem inconsequential or self-indulgent when—to borrow a term from Jim Collins—your Big Hairy Audacious Goal is to stay alive.

But occasionally entrepreneurs are born from such trials. I was surprised by several stories about people who never seriously considered starting companies until *after* a loved one got sick. These reluctant entrepreneurs believed they could make more owning their own businesses than working in the professions for which they had trained. Facing the prospect of enormous, endless medical expenses, they counterintuitively viewed entrepreneurship as the less risky option.

For 30 years, Holly DiMauro has watched her husband's progressive decline from multiple sclerosis. Richard, an engineer, has always been the family's main breadwinner; but Holly has accepted that soon that role will fall to her. As Richard's earning power grows less reliable, the family's financial needs are rising. (In addition to medical costs, they have a son in college.) And Holly is determined that her husband will not be consigned to a nursing facility because they can't afford to care for him at home.

Trained as a medical lab technician, Holly thought she could earn more by starting and selling a business. She knew she'd have to work hard no matter what and figured she might as well enjoy and find fulfillment in it. So she launched Holly's Oatmeal in Torrington, Connecticut. Holly has been laboring to grow the company while the family can still live on Richard's wages. She hopes that by the time he becomes incapacitated the company will be able to support them.

Richard encourages Holly and said he feels guilty when his wife takes time from the business to ferry him to doctors' appointments. Still in the throes of start-up woes, Holly is inspired by her husband's endurance. "It's horrifying to watch sometimes," she said. "If he can do what he does, I can run this business."

Kenny Kramm's conversion to entrepreneurship was more sudden and wrenching. Kenny was 29 years old, perfectly content working behind the counter at his father's pharmacy. Then his daughter Hadley was born 12 weeks prematurely. While she was in the hospital, a medical error caused catastrophic and irreparable damage, including continual seizures, a blood-clotting disorder, and cerebral palsy. With treatments, therapists, and special equipment, her ongoing care would cost as much as $100,000 a year.

Back home from the hospital, Hadley refused to swallow the medicines preventing grand mal seizures, so Kenny began mixing them with flavorings used by candy manufacturers. When she finally accepted banana-flavored Phenobarbital, her father conceived the idea of making safe flavorings that pharmacists could combine with pediatric medicines. With his job at the pharmacy paying only $70,000, Kenny launched FlavorX in order to create a financial lifeline for his daughter. "It was a risky thing to do because we had such large expenses at the time," Kenny said. "But those expenses were only going to get larger. We had to make it work."

Kenny did make it work, growing FlavorX to more than $5 million before selling it to an investment group. He returned to his job at the pharmacy, only to see his daughter's needs mount. Now that Hadley is 18, Kenny said,

> We had to completely redo the house, put in a new wing so she could have her own bedroom on the first floor because we couldn't carry her upstairs anymore. She needed a specially designed shower. She needed visual stimulus, so we built her a pond with fish in it and a deck so she could look at the pond. The cost is up and up and up.

Kenny, unexpectedly, found himself in company-building mode once more. His new business, Center Pet, applies the flavoring technique he used for children to veterinary medicines. "The money we got from FlavorX was supposed to make me comfortable that after we are gone she'll have enough to live the way I want her to live," said Kenny. "But I didn't feel comfortable. Now I have to make this business just as successful."

SILVER LININGS
The boss gets sick; the business gets well

When entrepreneurs themselves get sick, they understandably don't run out and start new companies. In most cases, their only choice is to ratchet back their activities and, often, their ambitions. Adjusting down the numbers on the five-year plan piles psychological on top of physical pain. For entrepreneurs more than most, retreat can feel like defeat. But sometimes retreat leads to surprising wins.

That's because accommodating an illness is different from succumbing to one. And sometimes the adjustments company leaders make have a salutary effect on both their businesses and their families. Most often this occurs when a common entrepreneurial lifestyle— high stress, no rest, business meetings while feasting on big honking slabs of beef—most likely contributed to the ailment in the first place.

This was the case for Bill Roark, Founder of Torch Technologies, an engineering company in Huntsville, Alabama. In 2010, Bill's life was shaken. "I was a poster child for heart attack, and I had one," he told me. "I'd gained 100 pounds since I started the company, from all the work and stress. I never took time off. That wasn't a conscious decision on my part. You just get so focused." After Bill got out of the hospital, he cut his workweek from 60 or 70 hours to about 40. Bill golfs more now and comes home in time for supper. He and his wife, Brenda, enjoy long vacations and spontaneous getaways. "We've gone on more

Brenda and Bill Roark.

trips in the last year than we have in 30 years of marriage," Brenda said. "We've drawn closer together and have a better quality of life."

Brenda used to urge Bill to scale back, but he'd tell her no one else could do his job. During his absence, he received welcome proof that wasn't so. His managers performed flawlessly. "Before Bill's heart attack, his team wouldn't step up because he was always there," said Brenda. "It took a health scare to get him to slow down and delegate."

Bill's crisis had a maturing effect on the company, according to Joe Hill, Torch's Chief Technical Officer. Senior managers—most of them engineers—became more accountable for business operations, which had previously defaulted to Bill. In addition, Joe said, "each manager started thinking, 'What would happen to my business unit if something happened to me?'" Bill had always encouraged his staff to delegate more, but "we engineer types are not very comfortable with relinquishing control," Joe said. After Bill's crisis, management started aggressively recruiting and hiring staff who could assume more technical responsibility. That enabled the managers to focus more on business development. In the year after Bill's heart attack, Torch Technologies grew 30 percent.

Bill's crisis had another unexpected and advantageous effect. Many employees began paying more attention to their own health, getting long-deferred medical tests.

Similarly, Tim Barrett was surprised at how well his business fared on its own. In the fall of 2010, Tim went to the hospital with back pain and a fever. He was diagnosed with a severe staph infection. Barrett Distribution, his logistics-services company based in Franklin, Massachusetts, was without its CEO for two-plus months. During that time, the business prospered, opening two new distribution centers.

When Tim saw what his management team could do, he started thinking about what he didn't have to do—and about what he could be doing instead. "I saw clearly that we have a high-performing team and that I have the freedom to let them run with decisions," Tim said. "I felt freed up to provide more leadership and overall direction to the company. I became focused on working on the business, not in it."

Tim still works as much as ever, and his wife, Lauren, worries that he threw himself back into the business too soon. Still, like Bill Roark, Tim interpreted his brush with mortality as a message to spend more time with his family, which includes three young children. "A gravestone near my parents' has the guy's company name and logo on it," Tim said. "That's the last thing in the world I'd want to be remembered for."

An entrepreneur's priorities can also be reordered by the illness of a family member. The ordeal causes the entrepreneur to "get real," as one business owner put it. After his child developed a serious neurological disorder, he began applying a don't-sweat-the-small-stuff philosophy at work. "So many business owners freak out about their companies," he told me. "My son's alive. What else really matters?"

Our own annus horribilis had a similarly powerful effect on Gary. He, too, viewed business complications as insignificant compared to our life-shattering challenges. "Our troubles made me more appreciative of the fact that life is a temporary condition," Gary said. We both put more focus on our marriage and ways we could be closer and more cooperative. The experience also gave Gary some emotional distance from Stonyfield, which sharpened his observations about its internal dynamics. He grew less tolerant of negativity, intensified his management reviews, and made several overdue personnel changes.

> "Crisis can make you clear. And steely."

The multiple traumas also affected Gary's negotiation with Danone. With mortality darkening our door, he focused on liquidity and a future exit route. "Our kids were young," he explained when I asked him to recall that time. "If you were going to be gone, I wouldn't want to be working 80 hours a week anymore." The devastation confronting Gary drained him, but it also armed him with a what-the-hell courage that helped him stick to his guns when the Danone deliberations reached periodic impasses. "Crisis can make you clear," he said. "And steely." Gary closed his deal with Danone in December 2001. Four months later, his brothers were gone.

IF BAD THINGS HAPPEN
Endure them. Learn from them.

Entrepreneurs are creators. Illness and injury are destroyers. They make a mockery of what has been willfully and lovingly fashioned—a marriage, a family, a business—and threaten to take it apart.

Illness never strikes at a "good" time. It strikes when and whom it wants. And entrepreneurial families—their eggs piled precariously in one basket—don't see it coming. Well, no one ever does, of course. But entrepreneurs, with all their wonderful optimism and confidence, are especially blind. They worry that external forces may batter their fortunes, but they rarely fret about more intimate vulnerabilities.

Business owners and their families can prepare, but only so much. They can buy insurance and try to maintain a financial cushion. The entrepreneur can—and should—create contingency plans within the company so that if the chief visionary, salesperson, strategizer, and motivator is suddenly gone, other visionaries, salespeople, strategizers, and motivators can take her place, for a time at least. The company leader's ultimate job is to make herself replaceable. A truly mature company no longer relies on its founder, just as a grown child no longer relies on her parents. Such independence is a sign of the organization's strength, not the entrepreneur's weakness.

If illness can be said to have an upside, it is the opportunity to become reacquainted with our true values. As one business owner put it, serious illness focuses the mind and strips us down to our essence. There's nothing like a health crisis to add weight to the "Life" side of the "Work-Life" scale. It's preferable, though, to simply reorder your priorities now and give the pain and suffering a pass.

> If illness can be said to have an upside, it is the opportunity to become reacquainted with our true values.

Ten years ago, Gary and I despaired that our life together could be nearing its end. These days we rarely dwell on the possibility of losing each other. But last year a deadly earthquake struck Christchurch, New Zealand, where Gary was giving a speech. Even before I heard the news on television he had called to let me know he was OK. He and his group were airlifted out by a C-130. The hotel he had stayed in was destroyed. His clothes and money went with it.

Gary came home that same week. So, no real suffering on either of our parts. Still: a close call. And another reminder that fate can take it all away from anyone at any time. All we can do is keep building. Our businesses, we hope. Our lives, absolutely.

Things to Talk About

- What the family plans to do for health and life insurance should be among the very first topics of discussion for aspiring entrepreneurs and their spouses. You need a good answer for this.

- Spouses who start a company together should determine how their roles will shift if one gets sick. Do both have access to all the information needed to run the business?

- Is the entrepreneur willing to comply with medical advice to cut back if necessary? Spouses battling over how much an ailing entrepreneur should work will only make matters worse.

- How much about the entrepreneur's condition should be revealed to employees, customers, and other stakeholders?

Things to Do

- Both entrepreneurs and their families should follow all sensible precautions for maintaining healthy lifestyles. Diet, exercise, regular checkups—you know the drill.

- Create contingency plans for the company. Entrepreneurs should build strong management teams and make themselves dispensable as soon as they reasonably can.

- Buy "key man" insurance, if you can afford it. These policies are designed to protect a business from loss of income resulting from the death or disability of a principal.

- If the entrepreneur or a family member gets sick, the caregiver should remember to take care of him- or herself as well. Try to find some joy in life.

Chapter 13

If Not Now, When?

For company builders, there is never a good time
to do things other families take for granted,
such as buying a house, taking a vacation, or
even having a child. Should you postpone—
perhaps forever? Or just do it?

I n the early years of Stonyfield, our family took vacations we
couldn't afford and paid off the Visa bills for six months afterward.
I remember making copies of the credit card statements for Gary
and writing "HELP" across the top in big letters, as if he could magi-
cally convert 50-cent yogurt coupons into cash to cover minimum
monthly payments. With our economic future bleak, spending money
on leisure travel was arguably not a responsible decision. But, as I've
mentioned, we worked long hours and shared a freezing, dilapidated
farmhouse with two small children (our third came later), out in the
country with very few friends around. Our lives were chaotic and more
than a little pathetic. So we chose to extract as much joy as possible
under the circumstances.

The role models for our personal lives were Gary's business partners, Samuel and Louisa Kaymen. I will always be grateful for the
courageous example they set by refusing to postpone life's milestones
until they'd achieved financial security. Specifically, I was impressed

by their decision not to let lean times dissuade them from having the large family they wanted while they were still young enough to enjoy it. Before Stonyfield, Samuel taught at a Waldorf school. He and

The Kaymen family, 1984.

Louisa resided with their six kids in a wood-heated barn; the children nestled together in sleeping bags in the loft. During the years we lived with the Kaymens—and the business—we would often hear howls of laughter through the thin wall separating our apartments. Observing the love in that family made our own decision to not wait for children seem sane—even sensible.

Inspired by the Kaymens, Gary and I managed to separate our reactions to our business situation (depressed) from our feelings about our personal future (optimistic). Gary may have had all his fingers in the dike, but intuitively I knew that I shouldn't spend my time piling sandbags. We never fooled ourselves that "someday" would come: that the business would reach a definitive benchmark that allowed us to progress with our lives. Maybe our attitudes were influenced by our backgrounds. Neither of us had experienced deprivation growing up, so even in the darkest times we couldn't imagine a change-of-clothes-in-a-shopping-cart future. We were never profligate. It's just that self-denial was not our default position.

Among company builders, this damn-the-torpedoes philosophy is uncommon. Few start-up entrepreneurs take regular vacations like Gary and I did, unless they've safely banked or expensed the costs. Some would think twice about having children during such a tenuous period. Starting a business is so risky that compounding that risk with large personal expenditures or additional dependents seems reckless. Good things come to those who wait, right? So wait is what many entrepreneurs do in the expectation that life, in the long run, will be easier.

More typical than Gary and I or the Kaymens is a couple I'm friendly with. He is 34, with a six-year-old business that, though growing well, remains a risky enterprise. She is 38 but plans to wait to have kids until he's home more. (The pair chose to live near the nexus of two interstates—a grim nod to his life on the road.) I understand her fear of being widowed by the business and of raising a child with no money and no security. But if she waits for the "right" time to bring a baby into the world, she will likely welcome Junior along with her first AARP card.

The fact is, when you are building a business, there is never a right time—for anything. There's no *right* time, because there's *no* time, and usually no money either. For having kids, buying a house, saving for retirement, taking a vacation—even getting a dog. Planning becomes difficult when income, if it exists at all, is insecure and savings are usually (to put it gently) unsubstantial. So an entrepreneurial life becomes all about postponing—"When we break even …"; "When we get that contract …"; "When we hire that salesperson …"— ah yes, *that's* when our lives can move ahead.

Only that day doesn't come, because the business never grows up. It may reach a point where it no longer needs constant coddling. But a company is an evolving organism that constantly challenges its founder, sucking up attention and resources at every stage. If you allow a business, even a successful one, to dictate your life, you will always find reasons to delay making the big personal investments. Sure we *could* take out a mortgage. But if we use that money to open a new branch, it will mean more money down the pike to buy a larger house, by which point it will be time to expand overseas … and what's so bad about renting?

The inescapable fact is that while you are building (and building and sometimes rebuilding) a business, you are also composing a life. There are personal opportunity costs if the former activity causes you to postpone important events in the latter. That is especially true if family and business are young at the same time. Put off having kids too long and you may end up with fewer than you wanted or none at all. Put off taking vacations and you won't create those memories and points of connection that glue a family together. Put off starting a college fund and risk informing your valedictorian that the Ivy League, alas, is not in the cards. Starving yourself in anticipation of a future opportunity to gorge is not necessarily a good strategy.

> With apologies to John Lennon, life is what happens while you are busy making a five-year business plan.

With apologies to John Lennon, life is what happens while you are busy making a five-year business plan.

LOVE CAN WAIT
Saying "I do" to a business

Many entrepreneurs don't so much put off marriage as neglect to get around to it. They are simply too busy and distracted to sustain a social life. Such people generally take the long view of work-life balance. They don't try to mix the professional and the personal on a daily or weekly basis. Instead, they figure they'll knock themselves out for 10 years and then settle down and get a life.

That decision can be construed as admirable and unselfish. Sure, these entrepreneurs may be lonely for a while—a long while. But think how much more attention and material wealth they can bestow on that flickering-in-the-future family. And by driving solo, they avoid subjecting innocent passengers to a treacherous and terrifying ride.

At 40, Shawn Thomas is ready to get married and have kids. Still, he does not regret deferring family life until he'd achieved financial security. Shawn has had a few serious girlfriends since 2002, when he launched Nashville-based Uniguest, which sells products and services to hotels. (He recently resigned as CEO.) But those relationships fizzled as Shawn pushed himself to succeed. He is not persuaded that a wife would have fared better than his girlfriends. "I am unsure if a marriage would have survived my last decade," Shawn said. His doubt deepened as he observed crumbling marriages among his entrepreneurial peers. "By the time they've gotten past the craziness of the start-up years, my peers—both men and women—have become alienated from their spouses and wind up leaving them for a new model," said Shawn. "As for me, I want just one wife."

Shawn Thomas.

It's hard to argue with do-it-once-and-get-it-right. And entrepreneurs, being optimists, assume that when the time is ripe domestic possibilities will be waiting for them—one more opportunity to be seized. It is the entrepreneur's creed: give me a great product, and I can find a customer. And what better product than an accomplished, financially successful business owner?

What these entrepreneurs don't anticipate is that some customers—that is, potential spouses—may question the decision to spend years focused fully on the company. They reasonably doubt the entrepreneur's willingness to make room in his life for them and fear entering a polygamous relationship with a $10-million, 35-employee sister-wife.

The decision to postpone marriage is, unfortunately, especially suspect for a woman. Sara Gragnolati is Founder of Boston-based Cocomama Foods, whose products are made from grains like quinoa.

To save money while building her business, Sara moved in with her parents and put her social relationships on the back burner. She is excited about her company's prospects, but at 33, she is also ready to follow the domestic path well trodden by many of her peers. The fact that she has her own start-up, however, makes some men uncomfortable. As Sara explained:

Sara Gragnolati.

> Some guys are intimidated by a woman business owner
> and make the assumption that I don't want to date or get
> married or have kids. Even friends assume I'm too busy
> or professionally involved for a relationship—which isn't
> the case. For a man, owning a business gives him a sort of
> cachet. For a woman, it can be seen as being in conflict
> with family and commitment.

Sara is right about the gender imbalance. Still, plenty of women look askance at a man who buries himself away in a business. It's a bit like meeting a 45-year-old who still lives with his mother. We admire his loyalty but can't help wondering, "What's up with that?"

Even if an entrepreneur already knows who her life partner will be, the business can prevent the couple from settling into formal domesticity. Ellen Smoak, her longtime fiancé, Jonathan, and Jonathan's brother run Cityscape Real Estate, a Tampa-based company that fixes up foreclosed properties for banks. As the years pass, Ellen is getting impatient to move ahead with her life. She told me:

> I am quickly approaching 33, and Jonathan is almost 38.
> We don't have kids, have been engaged for three years
> without a wedding, and seem to put off almost everything
> because of this business. Instead of planning a wedding,
> we plan operational strategies for the company. Instead of
> saving money for a vacation, we spend everything we have
> on keeping the doors open. And instead of making time
> for the things we love, we make time to deal with all our
> employees' wants and needs.

If entrepreneurship causes some people to postpone marriage, it can also keep relationships on life support that should be unplugged. Putting off the end of something can be just as damaging as not starting it in the first place. Kirsten Bradford, CEO of Spohn Ranch, a Los Angeles company that builds skate parks, was in a long-term relationship with one of her cofounders until a few years ago. She wanted out, but a third partner argued that a breakup could destroy their business. "My former boyfriend and I stayed together an extra four or five years longer than we should have," said Kirsten. "That's something I put in the regret column."

Kirsten Bradford and her boyfriend, Jeff Dermer.

SLOW BROOD
The cost of waiting for kids

Of course, people in many walks of life defer starting families until they are professionally established and financially stable. But a job—even a very demanding one—doesn't require the same commitment as owning a business. Both young families and young companies require their "founders" to be all in all to them, at least until they are self-sufficient. (For kids, that can take two decades. For companies, it can take forever.) That commitment means that if things go wrong, you can't just move out or start shopping your résumé around.

For obvious reasons, the question of when to have kids is most harrowing for female entrepreneurs. If they prioritize the business, they risk feeling ripped off and penalized because of their sex. If they opt for family—abandoning their dreams of ambitious, fast-growth ventures in favor of "lifestyle-adjusted" businesses—they may feel they've copped out or bowed to outmoded gender roles. One reason why average revenues of female-owned companies

For a woman, the choice may be: "Do I have a baby and offer my PR services to local merchants only, or put off the baby and try to build a global marketing firm?"

are just 27 percent of male-owned businesses is that women are more likely to tamp down their ambitions to accommodate family life. So for a woman the choice may not be, "Do I have a baby or start a business?" It may be, "Do I have a baby and offer my PR services to local merchants only, or put off the baby and try to build a global marketing firm?"

In 2002, Jen Sterling had big ambitions for her young company, Red Thinking, a brand strategy and design firm in South Riding, Virginia. But she and her husband also wanted children. At 34, Jen was painfully aware of time slipping through her fingers. One night, in a "2:00 AM desperation kind of moment," she searched the Internet and found 25 other women-owned design firms and emailed their leaders what she called a "You don't know me but . . ." note, asking for advice. Every one of them replied. Jen recalled:

> Two said, "Don't do it. It will have a negative impact on your business and marriage." Half a dozen said, "Do it, but understand that you won't be fully effective at either one." The rest were very positive. One of them said that her child was her best design ever. Eighteen months later, I emailed all of them with a photo of my new baby daughter, Rachel.

Jen's decision was not without consequences for her business. As a parent, "I can't be the rock star designer, featured in magazines, living

Jen Sterling and her daughter, Rachel Harris.

and breathing the business and focusing all my energy on it," she told me. "I do want to be that someday. While I don't regret setting that dream aside, it was a hard decision to make."

Careers like Jen's are entrepreneurship's version of the mommy track. Employed women put their jobs on hold to have children; entrepreneurs regretfully put the brakes on their companies' growth. When their kids reach school age, employees often return to reduced status and responsibilities. Similarly, entrepreneurs restart, rejoin, or ramp up their companies only to sometimes find that, in their absence, other firms have filled the gap and they have lost their marketplace edge.

For entrepreneurs who hope to start companies and families at roughly the same time, having trusted, able partners is a huge advantage. Su Midghall feared that she'd shortchange her children if she maintained her workload and the galloping pace of her business, DHM Research, a public-opinion research firm in Portland, Oregon. That was a nonstarter. "I figured I had only one chance to parent, and I wasn't going to screw it up," Su told me. So she was grateful that her colleagues were willing to step up when she scaled back to have a child. "We look out for each other," Su said.

But Su didn't step out of the picture entirely. Instead, the partners limited the number of jobs they took on, keeping the firm on an even keel. Reducing her salary to help compensate for the limited growth, Su also changed her role to finance and other administrative tasks, which she could work on at home in the evenings. "I felt it was important to have the conversation about salary and work expectations up front instead of allowing people to assume the worst—that I'm not pulling my weight," Su said. When her children were six and nine, Su came back to DHM full throttle. In the years following her full-time return, the firm doubled in revenue several times.

Other entrepreneurs are unwilling to starve young businesses of their personal attention. They concentrate on seizing a market opportunity only to realize—perhaps too late—that the window of biological opportunity is smaller. Lisa Spahr's mother and siblings all work in factories, and Lisa was the first in her family to attend college. Hungry for success, she threw her youth into building a business-coaching company in Pittsburgh. After marrying at 35, she decided she was finally ready for children—only to reconsider a month later. Do we have enough money? she wondered. Am I in the right stage of my business? "I got cold feet," Lisa said. "I negotiated with my husband for six more months. Maybe 12."

Soon thereafter Lisa was diagnosed with a medical condition that might have prevented her from having children at all. She marinated in regret. "All these years I put myself first, my education and success," she told me. "I thought this would be a cross I'd have to bear as a result of being selfish." (Fortunately, instead of a cross, Lisa now carries around her baby daughter.)

Couples often postpone children even when the husband is the entrepreneur. Their intentions are irreproachable: to ensure security for

the child and avoid additional disorder in already jumbled lives. But biology doesn't give a fig for smart planning. Erin James Scannell founded a financial-planning business in Bellevue, Washington, with his girlfriend. They delayed marriage for six years and children for another four, until the business was humming along smoothly. "We thought it was such a good plan," Erin told me. "We'd get financially and emotionally stable, and then have kids." Unfortunately, Erin's wife, Tanis,

The Scannell family.

suffered several miscarriages, and they wound up resorting to in vitro for their first child. (The couple now has two sons.) "The family stuff we put off for business reasons ended up causing us a lot of anxiety later on," Erin said.

LET'S GIVE IT UP FOR . . .

The company's needs come first

Starting a family is only the biggest boulder that gets pushed down the road by entrepreneurship. Anything that requires a significant investment of money or time by the couple, or by the founder or spouse individually, is subject to delay. Everyone in the family should expect to sacrifice something—career or education opportunities, sleep-away camp, new kitchen appliances, restaurant meals that don't come wrapped in foil. All such doing-without is an investment in the future, and can even be character building. But entrepreneurs' families travel different timelines than do their conventionally employed counter-parts: timelines demarcated not by dates but by question marks.

Professional advancement is one common victim. Spouses may turn down promotions, new jobs, or advantageous relocations so as not to uproot the business or shift more child care onto the entrepreneur. I spoke with one business owner, "Elaine," whose husband, "James," is in the military. James wants to continue scaling the career ladder, but he knows that a promotion would likely require transferring to another city or country, which would cripple his wife's consulting busi-ness. That happened once before when James was sent to London, and he doesn't want to put Elaine through it again. So he has intentionally stunted his career by staying "under the radar," as Elaine put it, and not testing for a higher rank. "When your spouse gives up something important so that you can grow your business, it's twice the pressure," said Elaine.

Entrepreneurs don't pass up professional advancement; by defi-nition, they are constantly advancing themselves. But their packed schedules can prevent other kinds of personal and professional devel-opment. CEOs love to dispatch high-potential employees to execu-tive education programs or to get the MBAs they themselves never had time for. College entrepreneurs drop out, swearing they'll return to finish their degrees after launching their dorm-room dreams. They rarely find the time. Kirsten Bradford, the woman who stayed too long in a relationship with a business partner, started her skate-park firm while in college. She is just five courses shy of completing her bach-elor's degree requirements, which is a manageable number to someone who isn't consumed by company building. But Kirsten, unable to turn her attention from work, keeps deferring that goal.

While spouses slow-boat their careers and entrepreneurs their educations, the family as a whole most commonly forgoes "things." Specifically, they forgo "nice things." As I discuss in chapter 8, an already resentful spouse may view as perfidy an entrepreneur's decision to buy an office copier instead of a home dishwasher. Less rancorous couples, however, agree that business needs are often more urgent; they choose to make do for another few years with the flaking house paint and washing machine that regularly swamps the towels. Such sacrifices are reasonable and to be expected. Still, living shabbily is depressing, and coping with obsolescent cars and temperamental appliances stressful. If the business stumbles along for years, then prolonged exposure to the slow, the threadbare, and the creaky degrades a family's quality of life like a low-grade headache.

> If the business stumbles along for years, then prolonged exposure to the slow, the threadbare, and the creaky degrades a family's quality of life like a low-grade headache.

Living without creature comforts is especially painful when you're not accustomed to it. "Angie" and her husband, "Dave," live in Wisconsin with their three teenage children. Dave was earning a six-figure salary in his corporate job when he quit to start a real-estate development business. His company's prospects are improving after what Angie said were a "brutal" couple of years, but the family is still very careful with cash. They have forsaken vacations and new cars; they even got rid of their landlines. Angie got a job to shore up the family's income. Still, the kids can't buy the relative luxuries that fill the lives and homes of their friends. The couple encouraged their son to attend a less expensive college. And all the money they'd been saving for retirement is now sunk into the business. Angie is gratified to see her husband fulfilled in his work. Yet, she said, "This is hard because you want things."

On the flip side, it's easy to fall into the habit of sacrifice, so that even when postponement isn't necessary, spending on oneself can seem indulgent and unwise. For more than a decade, Kirsten Bradford reinvested every penny in Spohn Ranch. Finally, she and her three partners decided to distribute some corporate profits so they could all buy homes. While Kirsten has no regrets, "extracting that money from the business made us all lose a lot of sleep," she said.

COME FLY WITH ME
An exception for travel

I started off this chapter talking about vacations. I'd like to return to them now. As you've probably gleaned, I feel strongly that experiences—the kind that forge memories or expand horizons or provide fleeting epiphanies—should not be postponed, no matter how demanding the company. Certainly there are small, inexpensive ways to share meaningful moments, and I encourage everyone to periodically leave the office before the sun goes down and spend an hour taking a walk with your spouse or teaching your daughter to ride a bike. But when families discuss what to sacrifice due to limitations on time and/or money, I think vacations should be off the table. Getting away from it all—or, even better, getting away *to* someplace new and exciting—is not only refreshing; it can be life altering.

Vacations are hard on business owners because they require days or even weeks away from the office. And while entrepreneurs may believe their families can do without private schools and iPads, they don't believe their companies can do without *them*. So they urge their spouses, "Let's wait a while, and then we can really *do* Europe." But Paris when you're 50 is not the same as Paris when you're 30. Or maybe Paris will be the same, but you will have changed.

> Paris when you're 50 is not the same as Paris when you're 30.

So a tip of my hat to Seth Weinroth, who was brave enough to take an extended vacation during start-up, a period when many entrepreneurs spend nights sprawled on their office couches. A year after Seth and his wife started their Massachusetts-based recruiting firm, they enjoyed an entire month on Cape Cod. Years later the couple launched a second company and took off again—this time to Italy. Since then, they have taken other long trips with their two children. And while the expenditure of time and money on each jaunt made them anxious, the financial-cost-to-emotional-benefit analysis justified their decision. Their employees always stepped up while they were gone, and the family returned with a wealth of wonderful memories to sustain them during tough times. As Seth explained:

> On every level, it was not the right time to do these things. You always feel you'll be giving up a ton—business goals, or cash out of your pocket. We always ask ourselves, what's the worst that could happen, and just how bad would that be? Fifteen years later, will that lost revenue matter as much as this precious time together does now?

Those sentiments are shared by my friend Jay W. Vogt, a Boston-based organizational consultant. Jay is my true vacation poster boy. It's not just the duration of his trips that impresses me—although they do verge on the epic. It's also how hard he works to make them happen and the importance he invests in them.

The Vogt family.

In 1987, when Jay's business was just five years old, he and his new wife, Stephanie, traveled around the world. The trip took Jay away from his young company for almost half a year. And this was before the Internet. "We fast-forwarded our marriage," Jay said. "We lived five years in five months. It was an unbelievable gift to ourselves. I still get teary thinking about it."

Then in 2004, the couple took their teenage daughter, Camilla, to Mexico for six months. Jay wound up buying a house there, and the couple plans to make it their retirement home. Camilla, now in college, is minoring in Spanish and has become so enamored of travel that she spent last summer in Senegal and will study in France her junior year. None of those things would have happened if Jay had waited to travel until the business could spare him. "I look at how transformative these trips were for our family," Jay told me, "and ask myself not how did we do this twice, but why we didn't do this more often."

Jay is a meticulous planner—a spreadsheet kind of guy. Needless to say, he carefully strategized the family's excursions. "Stephanie and I had an austerity budget for over a year before these trips," Jay said. "We did a per-day budget for the six months." The couple managed to save what they thought the vacations would cost and also accounted for the shoulder times, before and after, when Jay would be winding down and then later rebuilding his business. The trips "cast a big shadow financially," Jay said.

Jump-starting his practice again after each sabbatical was easier than Jay imagined. Before he and Stephanie embarked on their world tour, a respected associate had warned Jay that he was committing professional suicide. Instead, "my clients' actual reactions shocked me," said Jay. "There was an almost universal respect and a wistful envy: a sense of 'Gosh, I wish I could do that.'" Today, Jay promotes those sojourns and others the family has taken on his website as a way to distinguish himself from the competition. If one of his entrepreneur clients has a similar dream, he works with her on "packaging" it for her management team ("an opportunity for them to develop in the leader's absence") and her investors ("the visionary needs to charge her batteries").

PLAN IF YOU CAN

Scheduling milestones is hard, not impossible

Earlier I described how, in the start-up years, Gary and I learned to relinquish control of our lives. We had forsaken any traditional sense of normalcy and utterly abandoned any notion of security. We couldn't afford to furnish the baby's room; how on earth could we think about saving for college? And so we planned nothing at all. Instead, we spent money on things that made life bearable and crossed our fingers we'd find a way to pay for it. I've since met other entrepreneurs who are comparably undisciplined, and none expressed any regrets. So while I can't in good conscience urge everyone—or anyone—to behave cavalierly, there's a lot to be said for not adopting deprivation as a lifestyle.

But just because we, and others like us, don't make personal plans, that doesn't mean personal plans aren't possible. Entrepreneurs start out with less solid information than almost anyone, yet they still cobble together detailed, if often optimistic, projections for company milestones. And so what if the family's goals are optimistic? Better to plan to redo the kitchen in two years and have it take four than to throw up your hands and declare home-cooked meals vastly overrated. If all you do is push personal goals further down the spreadsheet until they fall off the bottom and roll under your desk with the pen caps and paper clips, then you're better off just taking the plunge, like Gary and me.

Shajahan Merchant and his wife, Salima, use a homegrown planning tool to ensure that their personal goals don't disappear into the maw of his business. Shajahan is CEO of Manhattan-based Intellectual Capital Services, which provides technology consulting. He and Salima have two children in grade school. Together, the couple has constructed an elaborate "lifestyle exercise" that covers the most important aspects of family members' separate and shared lives.

Annually, Shajahan and Salima schedule a weekend away to take stock of where they've been and where they're going. They tote along a whiteboard. At their destination, they take it out and draw a line down the center—one side for him, one for her. Then they start asking each other questions. What are your three main goals for the next five years? Which of your desires—material, financial, personal, and spiritual—are negotiable and which are not? What would you like me to start doing, stop doing, and continue doing? What activities do you love to do with me? What do you wish for our children? Every few months the couple pulls out the board to monitor how they're pro-gressing. "The exercise of thinking ahead has been extremely helpful," said Shajahan. "Without it, we wouldn't take the opportunity to step back and see if we are headed in the right direction."

This year Shajahan and Salima set two big goals: to take an exotic vacation on their tenth anniversary and to buy a house. Last year they planned four long-weekend getaways and a one-week family vaca-tion—all of which they took. In addition, Shajahan announced that he wanted more education in business. He was recently accepted into the MBA program at MIT Sloan. "There was so much going on that had we not planned for these things, we never would have accomplished them," said Shajahan. "Together we mentally embraced and prepared for the rigors of my MBA program."

I am tempted to drive to Staples and pick up a whiteboard like Shajahan's. True, Gary and I are now in a position to enjoy the fruits of financial security. But even when we were short on cash, postponing for us was always more about lack of time than lack of money. And the time squeeze is as tight as ever. After Stonyfield took off, Gary got into more mischief. In addition to launching the healthy fast-food chain, Stonyfield Café, he began producing organic yogurt in Europe and has joined several international boards. He travels frequently and is more overcommitted than ever.

If I had a whiteboard, here is what I'd write on my half: "Now that the kids are out of the nest, I'd like to take more trips with you for pleasure, not for work. I'd like us to garden together, take a class together, and get really good at swing dancing. I'd like you to scratch a few commitments off your list." Gary would probably agree with me about all those goals (except the last one). On his side, he'd add something about wanting me to pick up a sport we can do together, like cross-country skiing or tennis.

But we're both very busy now, so all this will have to wait. Until when, I'm not exactly sure. Now is not the right time.

Things to Talk About

- What personal sacrifices are you, as an entrepreneur, willing to make for the sake of growing the business? What about your spouse?

- What business goals are you willing to sacrifice to fulfill personal desires?

- In the face of competing business and personal demands, how will you decide where to spend the money?

- If you are a woman starting (or helping to run) a business and debating having a child, how much of the child-care burden will your husband assume? Will his time commitment be enough that neither child nor company will suffer?

Things to Do

- Construct a life plan with your spouse. What are your personal goals for the next three to five years? Which of these are negotiable, and which are not?

- If you have an overarching goal that matters more than all the others, create an austerity budget to work toward it.

- Work with your business partners on a plan that allows you to step back from the company to realize a personal dream. Offer to take less salary, if appropriate, and try to ensure that your absence does not overburden them.

- If you can't make headway on big life goals, find ways to bootstrap your personal life. Buy a condo instead of a house. Travel to a less exotic location or—better yet—swap houses with someone to make the exotic vacation more affordable.

Chapter 14

20 Simple Rules

Nuts-and-bolts advice for
maintaining domestic harmony when
one spouse owns a company.

How does someone who is obsessed live peacefully with someone who isn't? That question—posed to me by an entrepreneur—elegantly summarizes the quandary faced by company founders and their spouses. The short answer is: empathize, compromise, and find ways to show your spouse that the relationship is what matters most. Building on that foundation, I (with some help from Gary) assembled 20 simple rules for maintaining domestic harmony when one spouse owns a business. **(Please note that I have alternated male and female pronouns with each "rule".)**

RULES FOR THE ENTREPRENEUR

Don't act like the boss at home. At work you're accustomed to running things and being in charge. But when you walk through the front door of your house or emerge from your home office, you emigrate from an autocracy into a messy democracy with all its attendant chaos, conflict, and need for compromise. Suppress the instinct to issue commands and instead consult with your spouse and (when appropriate) your children. Decide with your spouse who makes which decisions and don't intrude on her turf.

Give your spouse a voice. Big business decisions affect your family. Acquiring another company, going public, or expanding into new territories will require more travel, increasing the pressure on everyone at home. Thinking about signing a business loan using the house as collateral? Hello—your spouse lives there too! And why restrict your consultations to issues that affect the family? Your spouse may provide fresh perspectives on work matters as well.

Don't squeeze your spouse in. Emergencies or changes of plans aside, avoid those rushed phone calls from the airport or in the five minutes before your next meeting. Your spouse will feel frustrated when the conversation is drowned out by loudspeaker warnings not to accept packages from strangers or cut short because your row is called to board. Much as he misses you during your travels, he won't enjoy conversing while braced for his three least favorite words: "I gotta go."

Visit your spouse's universe. In many ways, you are fused with your business, your identity bound up in its fate. Your spouse, too, cares deeply about the company. But it does not define her as it does you. She spends her days in other worlds, consumed by other matters. Talk to her about them. Better yet, join her at a conference; read one of her students' papers; play audience while she rehearses a presentation; accompany her to the kitchen showroom and weigh in on tile-grout color. You'll understand her better. Her busyness is your business too.

Resist dumping your worries. Consider carefully what and how much bad news to share with your spouse. Don't keep him in the dark, but be sensitive to his limits. You don't want to lighten your own heart at the expense of weighing down his. If your spouse has a low tolerance for the perpetual crises that are part of building companies, find a different pair of ears. Another entrepreneur, a business advisor, or a mentor can provide practical advice and won't be left trembling when the conversation is over.

Turn off the smartphone. OK, you can leave it to buzz and bleep sometimes, or even *most* of the time. But be disciplined about carving out technology-free stretches. Even if you don't respond to the device's whining, its presence at the restaurant, on the dining room table, or by the bed affects the quality of your family's shared space. And a holiday with an omnipresent smartphone is less a vacation than a change in venue. In any case, your BlackBerry looks great in black leather. Slide her into that holster, and everyone will be happier.

Treat your spouse like your most important client. You win customers by offering not simple attention but true attentiveness. As a businessperson, you are solicitous, observant, mindful, and aware— eager both to anticipate and to fulfill their needs. Remember that your spouse is your number-one life client and most important connection. Court him—with a thoughtful gift, a just-because hug, morning coffee in bed. Make it clear you want to keep his business too.

Acknowledge your spouse's role. By keeping the domestic machine running, your spouse lets you enjoy family life while reserving your energy for the business. She saves you money by working inside the company and makes the family money by working outside of it. So go on! Crow about her! To employees, coworkers, suppliers, family, and friends. Post an accolade on the website. Name a product after her. (Note to Gary: Yo My Baby? Apricot Meggo? Get the marketing department on it.) Most importantly, tell *her* that you value her contribution. Some things go without saying . . . but not that.

RULES FOR THE SPOUSE

Give the entrepreneur some space. You've both had exhausting days. But the pressure is usually greater on the entrepreneur, who bears responsibility for his employees' jobs and his family's financial security. Even if he's been sequestered in his home office, there's a reason that door is always closed. So give him a half hour to decompress before handing over the Visa bill and the squalling baby. Let him make the mental shift between the worlds of work and home. Later, when his head has cleared, take your well-deserved break.

Cultivate self-reliance. The entrepreneur, particularly during the start-up years, must devote great swaths of time to her business. You can't count on her being home evenings or weekends or when your boss is giving you hell and you need someone to vent to. Loneliness and dead time are your enemies. So cultivate warm relationships with friends and other relatives and indulge in activities you find personally fulfilling that don't require her presence.

Be a sounding board. You are not obligated to sit through a constant terrifying litany of business woes. But the entrepreneur needs someone to talk to. He will appreciate a sympathetic ear and—even better—advice from a person who is intimately familiar with his personality, strengths, and weaknesses. Know enough about the company to offer informed opinions. And don't be afraid to push back; he gets enough automatic agreement from employees eager to please the boss.

Establish systems. The entrepreneur uses systems and processes to run her company efficiently. Do the same thing at home to prevent her frequent absences and the company's erratic needs from pushing you into chaos. By creating shared calendars, holding regular family meetings, and tracking everyone's priorities so that—with time and money tight—the most important needs are met first, you can establish an island of relative stability in choppy seas.

Give the entrepreneur the benefit of the doubt. You will not agree with every decision the entrepreneur makes. How can he consider buying another business when this one is still wobbly? Why doesn't he fire that employee who went against his wishes? Say what you think, but then defer to his greater expertise and knowledge of the situation. You demonstrated confidence in him when he started the company. Sustain that confidence as he builds it.

Act like an owner. As the spouse, you have a financial stake in the business. But you can expand your ownership role in more creative and fulfilling directions. Look for opportunities where your interests and talents intersect with the company's needs. (For example, I published a Stonyfield Yogurt cookbook.) Even if you don't routinely work in the company, you can run the booth at a trade show, sit in on board meetings, or go along on a sales call. You'll feel closer to the business and to the entrepreneur. And you'll earn the good will of employees, who like to see family members get involved.

RULES FOR THE COUPLE

Set the bar low, but set it somewhere. It's difficult to make time for each other, much less take that desperately needed vacation. But you can sit down for a cup of coffee or take a walk around the block. Every couple needs uninterrupted time to share those grace notes and headaches that comprise lives. Being together reminds you that you enjoy being together. And that reminds both of you why this enormous undertaking is worthwhile.

Prioritize each other's communications. Both of you are busy and can be hard to reach. You respect each other's time too much to phone or email about trivial matters. (When I call Gary at the office, he knows I'm not just curious about how the yogurt is coming out today.) You'll both be more relaxed if it's easier to get in touch, and if you know that each other's missives will move to the top of the queue.

Befriend other company-building families. Couples who have been on the entrepreneurial ride longer than you will empathize and can offer advice from their own experiences. Does the entrepreneur have a business mentor? Ask the mentor's spouse to join the conversation.

Take the long view. The crisis of the moment is probably just a speed bump. Don't feed each other's panic or swerve from fretting over a discrete setback to questioning whether the business was worth starting in the first place. Accept that you are both in for a long series of disappointments mixed with the occasional triumph, and pace yourselves emotionally. A therapist can help you work through the gnarly issues that inevitably arise.

Work together for a cause. Just because you're not business partners doesn't mean you can't collaborate on a venture that matters to you both. Organize a fundraiser, launch a nonprofit, identify opportunities for the company to help in the community. You'll come to appreciate each other's talents afresh. And that passion for giving back can translate into greater passion for each other.

Take frequent inventory. Recall all you've created together, all you've managed to survive. Maintaining a marriage through years of strain, sacrifice, and uncertainty requires grace and grit. You have so many wonderful, horrible, heartbreaking, and hilarious stories—about the company, about the kids, about the rich history you share. To paraphrase Neil Young, you've had your ups and downs, but you're still playing together. The music might not always be in tune, but take a moment to rejoice that you're still making it.

Chapter 15

Those Magic Moments

When owning a company makes possible
a family's most remarkable experiences.

Gary's sister, Nancy Hirshberg, is Vice President of strategic ini-
tiatives at Stonyfield. Before that, she managed the company's
environmental sustainability programs for 20 years. Gary's name
doesn't appear in the company voice-mail directory, so after-hours
calls often find their way back to Nancy, the only other Hirshberg in
the office. One morning, back in the '90s, Nancy came in, retrieved
her voice mail as usual . . . and then nearly fell over. Bob Weir of The
Grateful Dead had left a message soliciting Gary's participation on
the board of a farm group headed by one of the guitarist's friends.

"He was one of my biggest crushes of all time!" recalled Nancy, who
still flushes at the memory. "I kept the call on my voice mail for *years*. I
never wrote down his home number, as I wanted to respect his privacy.
But it put a smile on my face every time I heard him say, 'Hi. This is Bob
Weir.' Bobby saying 'hi' to me each morning! How lucky could I be?"

Nancy's quirky connection with a musical idol would never
have happened without Stonyfield. Her story reminds me that

entrepreneurship—for all its challenges—can bestow on families unexpected benefits beyond the obvious financial ones. The spouses, children, parents, and siblings of company founders sometimes get to see and do things that relatives of the conventionally employed can only dream of.

I asked readers of my column and others to tell me about wonderful experiences made possible by having a business in the family. Not surprisingly, many of their stories involved travel: children tagging along to visit suppliers or clients everywhere from China to Botswana to the Cloud Forest of Ecuador; seeing monkeys in India and a leopard in the Serengeti. Others talked about young kids having fun with grown-up jobs: acting as host and hostess in their parents' restaurant, for example; or learning to take credit card orders over the phone. Many offspring were proud to have products or entire companies named after them.

Entrepreneurs are the first to advise that, in business, it's important to go out on a high note. In that spirit, I conclude with a selection of perks, opportunities, and adventures enjoyed by the lucky families of company founders.

Our company takes entrepreneurs on extraordinary excursions, which are combined with business-building sessions and philanthropy. I was able to take my wife, Missy, and two kids, Zack and Zoe, aged six and four, to Necker Island, Richard Branson's private retreat in the British Virgin Islands. The island holds a maximum of 28 guests, catered to by a staff of 60. At one point, I walked up to the pool after a business session and saw my children sitting in the hot tub with Richard, who was chatting with Missy. After we came home, Missy commented that it was going to be hard to have a "regular" beach vacation after that.

—Yanik Silver, CEO, Maverick Business Adventures

We had been sending Peeled Snacks to the cast and writers of *Saturday Night Live* for a couple of seasons through a connection with one of our investors. As a thank you, SNL gave my husband and me tickets to see the show. Afterward, we got a backstage tour where the likes of Will Forte, John Lutz, and Bill Hader weighed in on our products. My husband is a big Andy Samberg fan, so he was utterly star-struck listening to Andy expound on the virtues of dried mango at 2:00 AM.

—**Noha Waibsnaider, CEO, Peeled Snacks**

My mother is a retired schoolteacher who lives in metro Detroit. She and about a half dozen friends have a stock club. Each month they pool their money—around $30 or $40 each—to cover the cost of the trade. Through a trader I met when I ran a company that bought and sold bankrupt assets, I was able to get my mother's group onto the floor of the New York Stock Exchange. It was the highlight of their trip to New York.

—**Chris Rugh, CEO, 1800AWESOME.com**

My family and I were featured in a story that appeared in *Woman's World* magazine about a professional organizing service, which was a client of my marketing firm. A team of organizers went to town on our town house. For the first time (and probably the last!) everything in our home had "a place" and looked stellar. Even more fun, we all had our hair and makeup done for a big, professional photo shoot right in our living room.

—**Julianne Weiner, COO, Sonic Promos**

In addition to my main business running websites on stock and deferred compensation, my wife and I have a consulting business that works with companies wanting to start or improve their factory tours. As part of that, we've traveled around the country with our kids showing them how fire trucks, airplanes, teddy bears, tea—and, of course, yogurt—are made.

—**Bruce Brumberg, Editor-in-Chief, myStockOptions.com and myNQDC.com**

When I was CEO of The Natural Dentist, an oral care company, I had a lot of connections in the cosmetic dentistry industry. I was able to get my partner, Lori, a place as a subject in a master class at New York University for dentists from around the world learning how to do veneers. So although it involved several two-hour trips to New York, Lori got beautiful new teeth!

—Nancy Rosenzweig, social enterprise CEO and strategist

I run a game company. My kids Allison, 16, and Nick, 14, loved my idea for a giant ball into which you could strap yourself, then roll down hills, run, bounce, and flip. They were the human guinea pigs who tested the prototype. They gave me some great ideas for marketing and promotion and helped come up with the name, Bodi Bouncer. Nick suggested we do a demonstration video, so we spent an afternoon filming the kids' friends using it. My son edited the video on his laptop.

—Stephen Yennaco, CEO, The Giant Game Company

My son Benjamin and I appeared twice on *The Martha Stewart Show* to talk about the family company, Divvies. We make allergen-free food, including Benjamint Crunch, a chocolate bar named for and inspired by Benjamin. The second time we appeared, when Benjamin was 12, we met Joan and Melissa Rivers, who couldn't have been kinder and more gracious (and hysterically funny). Two days after meeting them, Benjamin explained to his friend who they are: "Joan is the Megan Fox of the '70s and her daughter Melissa is beautiful."

—Lori Sandler, Founder, Divvies

Not many kids have their dads pilot them to summer camp or get to watch fireworks from the air. My former company, Rokop Corporation, which supplied continuous casting machines to steel makers, owned a couple of airplanes. I learned how to fly them and was able to take my kids on flights all around the region. One trip was to Luray Caverns, where we saw the "stalacpipe" organ.

—Nik Rokop, Managing Director, Knapp Entrepreneurship Center, Illinois Institute of Technology

When my son, Steven, was nine, he invented a shampoo by combining products like shaving cream, bubble bath, and face cream to sell in my salon, which helps women coping with hair loss. I and several family members have Crohn's disease, and Steven wanted to help. He donated the $500 he made in sales toward research into a cure. I think he's proud to have made a difference in my life as well as in the lives of other families.

—Nikki Walsh, CEO, PK Walsh

My company's success enabled me to join the Entrepreneurs' Organization. Our chapter in Los Angeles threw a party at the Playboy mansion. I was only able to invite one guest, and I couldn't think of anyone I'd rather have with me than my dad. He got some stories to tell his buddies back in New York, that's for sure.

—Ben Schaffer, CEO, Bulletproof Automotive/Bespoke Ventures

My father is George Naddaff, founder of Boston Market and UFood Grill. Through his business ventures, he made a connection with Mary Lou Retton, the Olympic gymnast. When dad told Mary Lou that he had a little girl—I was about six—who was into gymnastics, she sent me a special edition, signed balance beam. That was pretty much the highlight of my life. All my friends were so jealous!

—Jessica Naddaff, Master's degree candidate, Simmons College

In 2001, my wife and I took our two daughters, then 10 and 12, to visit the Hong Kong factory that makes our company's clothing. We spent a lot of time with Johnny and Lydia Chen, who own the factory, and their two children, who are approximately the same ages as our kids. The four children explored Hong Kong together and developed a friendship that stayed alive over the years. The Chens visited us in Vermont. Through them, our kids learned a lot about Chinese culture. Who knows? Maybe the four of them will carry our businesses into another generation.

—**Michael Belenky, CEO, Zutano**

My 20-year-old daughter, Leah Larson, is founder and publisher of *Yaldah* magazine, a publication for and by Jewish girls. In 2008, she entered the Wells Fargo Someday Stories Contest, which honors people with financial dreams. She won the $100,000 Grand Prize for her entry about expanding the business. The Wells Fargo team arrived at our home in a horse-drawn stagecoach and took Leah, myself, and Leah's then 10-year-old sister, Audrey, for a ride around our suburban neighborhood. Later, Leah and I were flown to San Francisco for the awards ceremony, which included a stay in a five-star hotel, a shopping spree, and another stagecoach ride— this one down Market Street, as crowds of spectators cheered us on.

—**Evelyn Krieger, Public Relations Manager, Yaldah Media**

When we launched an Internet product last year, we decided to turn it into a couple of splashy, Apple-style events in Green Bay, Wisconsin. In front of audiences totaling around 700 businesspeople, my 14-year-old son Alex skateboarded onto a fog-shrouded stage and did tricks. My 7-year-old, Alina, sang a solo.

—**Joe Kiedinger, Owner, Prophit Marketing/About Me International**

I used to travel with my mom to Los Angeles every three-to-six months to buy products for her clothing store in Arizona. I got to see all the next season's styles before anyone else and picked up ideas for my own wardrobe. As a fashion-obsessed teenager, I loved it.

—**Jennifer E. Hill, attorney, Gunderson Dettmer**

My organizational-development business worked with a foundation funded by the footwear industry. When my clients learned that my then-16-year-old daughter, Camilla, loved fashion, they invited her to come with me on a business trip to New York and gave her a pass to walk the world's finest shoe show. Back in Boston, an executive vice president of Clarks, whom I knew through the board of the foundation, gave Camilla a special tour of the company to see how shoes are designed, prototyped, made, and marketed. At the tour's end, she got coupons for free shoes.

—**Jay W. Vogt, President, Peoplesworth**

I have an advertising agency. Over the years, my daughter, Erin, has appeared in a number of ads for clients. My son, Jacob, made his acting debut in a client's commercial when he was four years old. The production company we hired started calling on Jake for other work unrelated to our clients, so he has since appeared in a number of television spots and radio commercials. He has gone on to star in a number of plays, one television drama, and several school musicals. This summer he will be attending an arts camp, and this fall he will star in Cohoes Music Hall's production of *Les Miserables*. His goal is Broadway!

—**Mark Shipley, President, Smith & Jones**

Thanks to Stonyfield, my children and I have had too many cool experiences to count. We held an event for Barack Obama at our home, and many presidential candidates have toured our plant. I often accompany Gary on business trips to Europe. My kids got to know Raffi, and have appeared on our packaging and in our ads. We've developed close friendships with many fellow entrepreneurs and their families. During the 25 years I've been hitched to Gary's business, countless dark clouds have massed and threatened. But these days, life is mostly about the silver linings.

—**Meg Cadoux Hirshberg**

Afterword: Thoughts from Gary

We entrepreneurs do not dwell much on the past. Living in the present, dashing toward the future, we cannot afford—and are not inclined—to brood about what should or could have been. But reliving through Meg's eyes the three-decade odyssey of building a business, marriage, and family has been an astonishingly revealing experience. She has exposed many hard truths: truths that, to be honest, would have been difficult to accept had I been confronted with them along the way. But if I'd faced them, and addressed them, I might have been a better husband, and maybe even a better CEO.

Meg has put into words so much of what we've both felt but never took the time to focus on and discuss. I'd like to add a few of my own reflections to the many astute insights Meg has shared.

To build an enterprise is to be obsessed and driven. If you are starting or running a business and you're *not* obsessed and driven, then don't worry about the effect of the company on your marriage. You're not going to have the company much longer. You've got to be *all in*, or your business doesn't stand a chance. Meg often describes us entrepreneurs as always being on the clock, if only subconsciously. There's no reason to feel guilty about that. That's what it takes, and that's who we are. We can't just decide not to be that way.

But it's important to admit that this makes being married to us difficult. Entrepreneurs must remember that although we and our spouses ostensibly share the same lives, we experience them very differently. What feels to entrepreneurs like a long series of sprints is often a lonely marathon for our mates. We need to regularly slow down and match their pace to join together in jogging over the rolling hills or climbing the mountains in our path.

That concept of "pace" is important. It takes longer to make connections than to make decisions. We don't judge the success of a day spent with family in terms of how much we accomplished, or how many items we checked off our To Do lists. Sometimes, the best family days are the ones when we do nothing at all. Entrepreneurial metabolisms can have trouble digesting that, but they must. Our companies demand our time, energy, and passion. Our families not only demand those same things; they also need and deserve them. And without those investments, they, like businesses, will wither and fail.

Nothing good or lasting in a business happens by accident. That is also true for families. You don't need the domestic version of a business plan, but vague promises to make more time for each other just aren't good enough. Entrepreneurs and spouses must make a real commitment and, as in business, we have to execute. Looking back, I realize that our marriage was most strained whenever we missed a few days doing something simple together: just walking or going out to dinner or a movie. When, on occasion, Meg and I were able to escape for a night away, by the following evening we felt as refreshed as if we'd been gone for a week. The amount of time we spent together didn't matter—only that we pushed everything else aside and took time for ourselves.

I agree completely with Meg that vacations have been absolute lifesavers for our whole family. They are not a luxury; they are a necessity. Find economies elsewhere. Take those trips.

And the message about unplugging came though loud and clear. I guess the smartphone doesn't need to accompany us to the beach. But I am grateful Meg acknowledges that my ability to check in with the Stonyfield team—and their ability to reach me—made many, if not most, of our trips possible. We'll keep working on that one, but I can definitely do better.

No amount of work, however, will resolve our differences over risk. I actually don't believe that entrepreneurs are genetically more comfortable with risk than others, the way some people can tolerate spicier food. I don't enjoy taking risks any more than Meg does. What's different, I think, is that entrepreneurs possess natural self-confidence. Consequently, our decisions don't seem risky to us. Like drive and obsession, we need that self-confidence to make our entrepreneurial dreams reality. I have counseled hundreds of entrepreneurs informally over the years, and I run an annual Entrepreneurship Institute—a kind of boot camp for community-minded business leaders (www.carsey-institute.unh.edu/SEI.html). Almost all those folks are attempting to do the improbable, if not the impossible. But they don't see it that way. That's why many of them go on to succeed.

When discussing our different perspectives on risk, Meg mentions that we like to use the analogy of the driver calmly negotiating a curvy road and the helpless passenger who feels sick to her stomach. I realize that the passenger seat is a very uncomfortable place to sit. But riding along in silence only makes things worse. As long as you are in that car together, you have to talk through what is happening. I don't mean the entrepreneur has to dispel the spouse's fears. I mean you must really listen to each other and seriously consider both of your opinions and feelings. In the book, Meg sometimes plays down the quantity and quality of the advice she's given me over the years. But I have benefited enormously from her perspective, and she's been right as often as I have.

When the family's security is on the line, such conversations are beyond critical. Every aspect of the plan—the timing, the expectations, the contingencies—must be carefully considered and vetted. The challenge for both entrepreneur and spouse is to know when you've said all you have to say on the subject, and to accept that the other person has heard you. Then you make the decision together. Then you both honor it. Knowing when to bid and when to fold is part of the game for both players.

*   *   *

Finally, I'd like to say something about what it's been like to live through the writing process itself. To say that the tables have been turned is an understatement. Many months ago I lost track of how many dinners I ate alone and how many evenings and weekends I played widower to the madwoman locked away in her writer's lair churning through hundreds of hours of interviews. It is no small irony that over this last year—our first with the kids out of the house—I have tasted my own medicine, forced to make room for a relentlessly demanding third player in our marriage. She calls my BlackBerry "Bond Girl"; now I need to come up with a comparable male moniker for her laptop. It followed us everywhere, even joined us in bed. More often than not, I would awaken in the morning and find the pair of them doing their tap tap tap dance beside me.

It has been truly amazing to watch Meg's extraordinary focus on this project. Readers should know that in addition to writing the book, she has kept up with her *Inc.* columns, given many speeches, spearheaded the creation of an innovative new post-treatment program for cancer patients at our local hospital, kept our house running and our dog walking, edited kids' college essays, and tended to a number of friends and family members coping with illnesses. And yes, we've managed to squeeze a few vacations in there somewhere.

In short, we have both discovered that—in terms of obsession, anyway—I am living with an entrepreneur. Believe me, it takes one to know one.

So *For Better or For Work* has been an education for me on many levels. I now know how it feels to take a backseat to THE WORK. And I believe Meg understands me better as well. Part of that comes from listening (and relating) to the stories of other driven entrepreneurs. Part comes from conversations inspired by the writing, in which we looked back on our history together, reexamining words, actions, and motivations. And part comes simply from experiencing the intense focus engendered by a passion project. Now my wife has had a taste of what the company-building phase of our lives was like for me.

In short, this book has enabled us to better understand each other and has strengthened our relationship. I admire Meg more than ever. That is saying a lot.

And this leads me to one last thought. If you just finished reading this book by yourself, I urge you to go back and share at least parts of it with your significant other. Together, pour yourselves something comforting and take turns reading chapters aloud. You may not agree on every issue. But you'll agree on what the issues are and that you're both going to do what it takes to resolve them. That will make all the difference. It sure has for us.

Gary Hirshberg

My Thanks

Most books have many parents. I owe a great debt of gratitude to *Inc.* Editor-in-Chief Jane Berentson and former *Inc.* Executive Editor Mike Hofman, who accepted my original feature article over the transom. Both my regular column in *Inc.* and this book exist because Mike and Jane said "yes." Jane had the insight to recognize an under-explored topic when she saw it—one so important and relevant to the everyday lives of entrepreneurs that she decided it deserved regular coverage and created my "Balancing Acts" column in response. Also at *Inc.* I'd like to thank Deputy Editor Dan Ferrara and Managing Editor Alexandra Brez, both of whom have been a pleasure to work with.

Most books have siblings too. They don't grow up in isolation. Friends pitch in with ideas, feedback, and support. Years before I first wrote about this topic, my close friend Lindley Shutz gently prodded me to do so. My sister-in-another-life, writer Jill Kearney, took pains to read the manuscript closely and offer thoughtful edits. A few other sisters—Janet Jacobson, Amy Vorenberg, and Marianne Jones—always said the right thing and showed up when it mattered. Michael

Lynch, Whit Symmes, and Bob Friedlander are brothers in spirit, ever generous with their time and affection. Scott and Heidi Temple provided masterful technical support and threw in bucket-loads of encouragement. My agent, Helen Rees, was contagiously enthusiastic from the start. Angela and Julio Moreira, Jen Pye, Bessy Mecham, Jane McClung, and Linda Oakes all helped in countless important ways.

I'm glad I had the good sense to choose Greenleaf Book Group to manage the book's publication. Clint Greenleaf is a true entrepreneur—smart, optimistic, and visionary. My editor at Greenleaf, Lari Bishop, awed me with her spot-on insights and edits. Neil Gonzalez did a superb job with the book's design, and Chris McRay skillfully managed the many phases of its production. Justin Branch achieved the near impossible by remaining consistently cheerful and patient as we sorted through contracts and other gnarly details. Also, a big thank-you to Linda O'Doughda, copy editor extraordinaire.

In the vernacular of any entrepreneurial business, you can make the best product in the world, but it will only gather dust unless you let customers know it exists. That was the critical role played by my publicist, Barbara Cave Henricks, and her colleague, Rusty Shelton. Calm, good-natured, and extremely savvy professionals, they were my experienced guides in the unfamiliar terrain of book publicity.

For help honing my writing skills, I thank my teacher, Mark Kramer. Mark's writing seminars, formerly at Boston University, were trials by fire. But his students understood that a phoenix just might rise from—and because of—his scorching commentary. When I occasionally write a sentence that soars, I think of Mark.

My beautiful mother, Doris Cadoux, her steadfast companion, Hal Schwartz, and my sweet brothers—Alex, Claude, and Bob—along with my wise and remarkable departed father, Alexander, form the solid loom on which I weave. My greatest good fortune in life is having been born into such an extraordinary and loving family.

My wonderful children—Alex, Ethan, and Danielle—willingly discussed with me their experiences in an entrepreneurial family, and they've kindly allowed me to use their lives as source material in the book. Both Gary and I have always relied on the unwavering support of his family—his mother, Louise, his father, Howard, and siblings Susan, Nancy, Jim, and Bill. We are also indebted to Samuel and Louisa Kaymen, our partners and friends, without whom Stonyfield would not exist. Likewise, there would be no Stonyfield without the tireless efforts of its many employees over the last 30 years, or without the faith of our original investors.

At the heart of this book are the more than 200 entrepreneurs, spouses, and other family members who gave their time and answered my many questions so thoughtfully and candidly. Each interview taught me something and brought fresh perspectives to the topic. Although not everyone I interviewed is quoted in the book, all are present here in some way. My profound thanks to each of you.

Two people were indispensable to this work. Leigh Buchanan, who edits my "Balancing Acts" column at *Inc.* magazine, graciously agreed to be my book editor as well. I now understand why many authors practically weep with gratitude when thanking their editors in the acknowledgments. To the extent that *For Better or For Work* contributes to discussions about the intersection of work and family, it is due as much to Leigh as to me. Leigh brought to this project her brilliance, her humor, her creativity, her insight, her fierce work ethic, and her high standards. She sharpened my thinking and she cracked me up. A writer could not ask for more.

My husband, Gary, has been a constant source of creative ideas, suggestions, support, and love. His optimism and strength are contagious. An unforeseen benefit of writing this book is that I learned a lot about Gary. Each new topic caused us to reflect on our own experiences, and in the process, we grew—even after 25 years of marriage—to understand each other better and empathize with each other more. As a result, I feel even greater respect for what Gary has achieved and for the strength of character required for any entrepreneur to withstand the enormous pressures of company building.

Gary, you amaze me. My love and gratitude are boundless.

About the Author

Meg Cadoux Hirshberg is a freelance nonfiction writer whose work has appeared in *Yankee*, *New Hampshire Magazine*, and *The Boston Globe Magazine*, among other publications. In 2009, she began writing a column called "Balancing Acts" for *Inc.* magazine that explores work-life balance and the intersection of family and business in an entrepreneurial setting. (For a compendium of Meg's writing, see her website, www.meghirshberg.com.)

Meg grew up outside New York City. She received a bachelor's in comparative literature from Brown University and a master's from Cornell Agriculture School. After working on an organic farm in California, running a science-education garden for elementary-school children, and managing an organic vegetable farm in New Jersey, she married Gary Hirshberg, Founder of Stonyfield Yogurt, in 1986. The couple has three children.